Third Edition

SOCIAL MEDIA

How to Engage, Share, and Connect

REGINA LUTTRELL

ROWMAN & LITTLEFIELD
Lanham • Boulder • New York • London

Executive Editor: Elizabeth Swayze
Associate Editor: Megan Manzano
Senior Marketing Manager: Kim Lyons
Marketing Manager: Kim Lyons
Interior Designer: Ilze Lemesis

Credits and acknowledgments for material borrowed from other sources, and reproduced with permission, appear on the appropriate page within the text.

Published by Rowman & Littlefield
An imprint of The Rowman & Littlefield Publishing Group, Inc.
4501 Forbes Boulevard, Suite 200, Lanham, Maryland 20706
www.rowman.com

Unit A, Whitacre Mews, 26-34 Stannary Street, London SE11 4AB, United Kingdom

British Library Cataloguing in Publication Information Available

Library of Congress Cataloging-in-Publication Data

Names: Luttrell, Regina, 1975– author.
Title: Social media : how to engage, share, and connect / Regina Luttrell.
Description: Third edition. | Lanham : Rowman & Littlefield, [2019] | Includes bibliographical
   references and index.
Identifiers: LCCN 2018008430 (print) | LCCN 2018009439 (ebook) | ISBN 9781538110805
   (electronic) | ISBN 9781538110782 (cloth : alk. paper) | ISBN 9781538110799 (pbk. : alk. paper)
Subjects: LCSH: Online social networks. | Social media. | Public relations.
Classification: LCC HM742 (ebook) | LCC HM742 .L874 2019 (print) | DDC 302.23/1—dc23
LC record available at https://lccn.loc.gov/2018008430

♾™ The paper used in this publication meets the minimum requirements of American National Standard for Information Sciences—Permanence of Paper for Printed Library Materials, ANSI/NISO Z39.48-1992.

Printed in the United States of America

Brief Contents

Contents

List of Figures

Foreword: Hello, It's Me!
Social Media in an Age of Discovery

Control

In a digital age, powered by social technologies, the operative word is "control." When literally everyone has a "voice" controlling the dialogue, discussion, and debate, the resulting advantage is incredibly powerful. Customers and employees now determine what gets made and what gets implemented, causing companies to rethink the entire business model and relationship spectrum.

The Transition to Interpreter

For public relations professionals this shift is having a profound impact on the value and efficacy of our work. Understanding the new mindset of customers and employees, who now direct the actions and reactions of organizations, being in PR is akin to asking "Who are you?" rather than stating "Here's what I want you to know." With consumers continuing to baffle marketers and communicators migrating in and out of new platforms, defying conventional methods for engagement, and choosing to listen to new voices in the purchase journey, organizations relying on traditional brand sustainability strategies find themselves in the slow lane to nowhere.

The pervasive challenge can be captured in one word: "noise."

Noise is often alluring but deadly. It causes brands to think audiences are listening or, worse, advocating on their behalf. It can cause bias inside an organization. For many marketers and communicators, the solution is to focus on exacerbating the symptoms. Produce and deploy more content. Reemphasize the brand story. Remind people who you are in new and novel ways. Invest in branded entertainment or native advertising to perpetuate the myth. But in today's attention-deficit marketplace, *less* is actually better. And by "less" I mean simple, clear, and relevant. In our work with organizations around the globe spanning multiple industries and segments, branding is about defining the *why*. Why do you exist? What makes you relevant? Why should your audiences care? Does your workforce believe? It also demands that a digital and social analysis be conducted internally and externally to discern where relevance can be found among key stakeholders.

This oftentimes can clear a path toward a new destination or white space. A place your brand can thrive anew. In a social/digital reality, brands need to be discovered, not sold. People need to experience and, yes, maybe even challenge the efficacy of your brand. Doing so creates a community of interest and an airtight affinity for your brand's essence. For PR professionals looking to discern the relevance of social in today's environment, five critical areas must be explored:

1. *Promise:* First and foremost, is your promise meaningful and purposeful to your stakeholders? How does social media planning reinforce this notion?

2. *Position:* Where do your stakeholders need to discover you? Are there specific themes, ideals, or conversations that capture your brand and place it in the proper context? What is your mindshare?

3. *Voice:* So many organizations and brands today have simply lost their voice. Many don't realize it. Voice speaks to tone, depth, courage, and perspective. Is your voice resonating properly with stakeholders? Do you actually hear you?

4. *Narrative/Platform:* Where do you live? What is your story and how do you articulate it via audiences over social and digital channels?

5. *Outreach:* How do you interact with the world? Is it where your audiences are? Can they discern you consistently?

Social Media: How to Engage, Share, and Connect is as much about comprehending what your audiences need and expect from you as vice versa. As one senior communications officer recently said, social media is about "rediscovering the romance of your promise through the conversations." To that end, organizations must solve for two things: relevance and differentiation!

As mentioned, if you are not relevant today to the people who allow you to exist—customers, employees, influencers—you aren't real. Relevance in how your sector or category is moving. Relevance in your product offering. Relevance in your message. Relevance in your value proposition. Relevance in evolution. And if you are not differentiated in your promise—the expectations people need from your brand experience—you won't command the respect (and value) necessary to sustain the business.

It is here where social media and analytics are the game changer.

Understanding your impact from a digital and social standpoint uncovers insights about how you are perceived and believed both internally and externally. Such insight then informs all of the above areas, resulting in the relevance and differentiation necessary.

We are living in a completely fluid time.

One that changes in the blink of an eye.

To be successful, organizations need to adopt the right mindset and recalibrate marketing and communications to be more agile, nimble, and confident in the vagaries of the marketplace.

Only then will brands truly survive and thrive in an "engaged economy" where customers truly "own" brands; employees truly own culture; and organizations must continually listen, connect, innovate, and involve multiple stakeholders to win.

To paraphrase the immortal David Ogilvy, we now have a chance to listen to our story versus tell it. Social media is all about stories. It's all about discovery. Both provide context, meaning, purpose, and legitimacy. Without a real understanding of what PR is about in a social and digital reality, you're truly missing its strategic import.

That is exactly what Regina Luttrell has brought out in this incredible book. Her background in leading strategic marketing and public relations for Fortune 500, government, and nonprofit organizations and her expertise in social media and digital platforms as a core component to providing customers relevance and value are captured in the pages here. As you read and assimilate its contents, be prepared to rethink your approach, your perspective, and your actions regarding social media. Social media is a bridge, a lens, and a listening tool allowing brands to build relationships, see trends and behaviors clearly, and capture insights to improve business and societal realities.

So, are you ready to pivot to the future?

Enjoy the ride.

Gary F. Grates
Principal
W2O Group

The profound effect that social media has had on the communications industry is arguably even more important to the field of public relations (PR). The emergence of social media technologies inspired the development of a new marketing model—one that promotes the user as an integral part of the conversation rather than merely an onlooker. I'm pleased that the first two editions of *Social Media* introduced thousands of students to a strategic approach for PR and social media planning. In writing this third edition, I have revised and updated major portions of the book to reflect what I heard from adopters, students, and reviewers alike. As a result, this edition captures the value that social media strategies bring to the PR industry.

One of the key factors that makes this book a favorite among faculty and students is that the tone is relaxed and pragmatic, while also succinct and useful. That hasn't changed. I have selected the best from social media management and introduced students to the newest models in PR and social media planning, allowing further insights into the process of the practice.

New in the Third Edition

"Key Learning Outcomes": Readers now have learning outcomes identified at the outset of each chapter highlighting what the learner will accomplish by the end of the chapter.

Social Media Experts: Each chapter begins with a brief introduction to an expert within social media, an SME, if you will. Profiles include those from the practice, authors, and professors.

Appendixes: New to this edition are three appendixes that provide an easy-to-follow Public Relations and Social Media Planning template outlining the Circular Model of SoMe for Social Communication (Share, optimize, Manage, engage), the ROSTIR Public Relations Planning Guide template, and the PESO model; a social media audit framework; and links to resources in PR and social media that incorporate professional organizations, tools of the trade, blogs, videos, and other instrumental sources professionals utilize daily.

Strengthened #LRNSMPR Callout Boxes: Within each of the #LRNSMPR callout boxes, readers will find discussion questions to help them review, restate, emphasize, summarize, and apply what is important from the chapter.

Updated and Expanded "Theory into Practice" Sections: Each chapter, as in past editions, includes "Theory into Practice" sections that present students with important learning scenarios applicable to the chapter and the field of PR and social media. The case studies provided within this section have been an integral component to the text, and as such, they continue to provide the reader with real-world examples of successful examples related to the topics presented within the chapter. This feature helps guide learners toward a contemporary understanding of the PR and social media profession as it stands today, as well as providing a foundation to create a comprehensive social media plan on a practical, professional basis. In this edition there are many new case studies added to the "Theory into Practice" sections. These include:

- Okay to Say
- Operation 45

- Pioneer State Mutual: Insurance Nerd Day
- 84 Lumber: "The Journey"
- Netflix Revival: *Gilmore Girls: A Year in the Life*
- Louise Delage and the Sobering Truth of Her Success on Instagram
- *Flatliners* Attempts to Create Buzz before Box Office Debut
- Creating #Cupfusion
- Woman's March: Worldwide Solidarity
- T.R.I.P. through the Multiverse
- It's a Match!
- Berkshire Museum Banking on a Quick Buck
- Pink Power: The Pussyhat Project

Stronger Focus on Small Business Illustrations: Throughout the text additional examples have been included to highlight small businesses that are using social media strategies and tactics successfully. These range from entrepreneurs to businesses with fewer than 500 employees.

Integrated International Social Media Standards: Drawing on recent examples, the book now seamlessly integrates examples of social networking platforms found around the world, social media strategies used by organizations outside the United States, and professional ethical codes used in organizations such as the Chartered Institute of Public Relations (CIPR).

Updated Statistics and Links: The most current data and statistical information has been incorporated into every chapter. Line by line, I have updated the latest figures and facts surrounding PR and social media. Each link has been modified to make it easier for readers to click on or search for important information. Bit.ly links are now customized and easy to read. For example, the Chip My Dog campaign featured in the book now has the following link: http://bit.ly/ChipMyDog.

Organization of the Text

This text is broken into three sections:

- Part I: The Advancement of an Industry
- Part II: Strategic Planning: Public Relations and Social Media
- Part III: Strategic Management: Public Relations and Social Media

Part I: The Advancement of an Industry

Chapter 1 introduces readers to the Four Quadrants of Public Relations and how social media integrates within each area. Chapter 2 provides the historical context of social media. Readers are presented with a new social media model, the Circular Model of SoMe for Social Communication (Share, optimize, Manage, engage) and the role it plays as a central function in social media planning. Finally, chapter 3 highlights how social media and public relations work together with marketing and advertising.

Part II: Strategic Planning: Public Relations and Social Media

Chapters 4 to 10 focus on social media preparation and the various social media tools available to develop creative, engaging, and meaningful social media plans. This section includes areas such as content creation and curation, "sticky" social media, and social media analytics. Each chapter is filled with nuggets of information and practical examples that every practitioner will benefit from. The ROSTIR Public Relations Planning Guide explains each step that contributes to the strategic planning of a social media plan. Comprehensive case studies are also provided as learning tools and can be analyzed, deconstructed, and applied within the framework of your own organizational social media planning.

Part III: Strategic Management: Public Relations and Social Media

The final portion of the text, chapters 11 through 14, explores social media ethics, crisis management, social media guidelines, and the future of the profession. These chapters home in on what is most relevant to managing and executing a PR and social media strategy.

To help with course preparation, ancillary materials, including an instructor's manual with sample assignments, PowerPoint presentations, templates, case studies, and infographics and illustrations included in the book, may be obtained from the publisher; email textbooks@rowman.com for details.

This latest edition aims to ensure that the foundation through which PR and social media is built continues to remain significant. I have thoroughly revamped and reorganized every chapter, considering feedback from my readers. I appreciate the insights you share, and I invite you to join me in the conversation on Twitter (@ ginaluttrell) by using #LRNSMPR to discuss the book, ask questions, or chat about any of the topics I've written about. There is an abundance of infographics to summarize chapter contents, past case studies, and videos, available at http://ginaluttrellphd.com, that further enhance the content presented within the text.

Acknowledgments

A project such as this could not be completed without a great deal of support from numerous people. To the people who always believe in me most, encourage me, and warm my heart, Todd, Emma, and Avery. And my little Coco Bean, for always being my faithful writing companion.

To Syracuse University, Dean Branham, Dr. Ford, and my very supportive team of colleagues, for your encouragement and resources that helped pull this third edition together. Particularly my research assistant and graduate student, Susie Lee (YoungYun) for your diligence in finding case studies, links, videos, and articles that have made this text so valuable.

A gracious note of appreciation to all who said yes without a moment of hesitation when I asked: Crystal DeStefano, Alison Kangas, Brandon Lazovic, Gary Grates, George Potts, Steve Radick, Adam Ritchie, Paul Roetzer, AJ Juiliani, Allison Verp, as well as Curata and the Public Relations Society of America.

Thank you once again to Rowman & Littlefield for investing in a third edition. Keeping a text such as this timely, relevant, and applicable is paramount and something you clearly understand. Much gratitude to my editor, Elizabeth Swayze, and to Carli Hansen, Alden Perkins, and Megan Manzano, for being a constant source of support.

To the students, professors, and professionals who will read this book, I thank you as well. I hope my passion for social media, public relations, marketing, and communications shines through. Feel free to connect with me on Twitter (@ginaluttrell). I can't wait to engage, share, and connect with you!

Introduction: "But I Already Know Social Media"

Consider this statistic for a moment: more than half of all human beings inhabiting this planet are currently under the age of thirty.

There's also a good chance that you, reading this book, might belong to this group.

If you find yourself in this demographic, there is a high probability that you have never known life without the Internet, never held a phone in your hand that has a cord attaching it to the wall, and most likely never gushed with excitement at a new set of bound encyclopedias on the bookshelf; and while you may be a fan of music, you probably listen to the majority of music on your laptop, iPod, or phone.

Much of your time is spent on Snapchat, Instagram, and Twitter. These social media platforms are almost a part of your DNA. Being connected has been the norm for about as long as you can remember. In fact,

- One-third of women aged eighteen to thirty-four say that they check Facebook when they first wake up in the morning—even before going to the bathroom![1]
- One in six marriages around the world now happen because of people who met using online social networks.[2]
- If all Facebook users united and formed a stand-alone country, by sheer population the new republic would be considerably larger than China. In fact, nearly two out of every seven people on the earth use Facebook each month—approximately 1.9 billion people.[3]
- Adults who actively use Twitter rank it as the timeliest source for news and events, largely surpassing "traditional" media outlets, including cable news channels.[4]

With all of this in mind, you may ask yourself, Why do I need this book? I already know social media. I live it every single day. In fact, it is safe to say, I can't live without it.

You need this book because it's different from any other textbook you've experienced. You may know how to tweet or snap an ephemeral picture message, but those experiences are personal. This book flips everything you know, or think you know, about social media around. This text examines social media through the lens of a business.

Social media has profoundly changed the way consumers engage with brands and with one another—the effects of which the public relations world has only begun to distinguish and understand in the past several years.

As brands strive to build relationships and engage in dialogue with consumers, the investment toward doing so continues to increase. In fact, according to reports from Forrester Research, in 2018 the average company will allocate 41 percent of its budget to digital methods and by 2021 brands will spend nearly $119 billion on social media endeavors.[5] Serving as facilitators for the world's content architects, these social platforms provide an unprecedented avenue for the posting and exchange of information and ideas.

As my friend Ryan Schram, chief operating officer of IZEA, so aptly put it, "Social is merely a 'teenager' in terms of how long it has been around as a concept, let alone actively in the lives of the people who participate in it."

From public relations directors to social media strategists, professionals within the industry are taking notice. Having their brands represented in the "conversations" across various social channels has become a central aspect of the planning process.

Yet so many professionals in the industry are vastly unprepared to engage.

Why? Because it is likely that they only understand social media through a personalized lens.

In this book you will learn how to interpret business objectives, understand when C-suite executives talk about the "bottom line," become intimately familiar with strategic approaches to social media planning and evaluating, and comprehend the connections between public relations and other areas of marketing. The focus uses a strategic approach to build and sustain brand relationships using coordinated efforts across the social sphere.

Social media promotes a digitally enabled, mobile environment that embraces the real-time attributes that consumers themselves not only willingly participate in but continually update. More than 2.8 billion people have access to the Internet, and 74 percent of online adults use social media. Taking part in social media provides businesses a multitude of opportunities to:

- improve brand loyalty through storytelling and content marketing
- increase conversation rates by interacting with current and prospective customers
- leverage social media to increase brand awareness and recognition
- build credibility by increasing the amount of consumer engagement and number of followers
- develop relationship capital by building strong and meaningful relationships through social channels

Practitioners will quickly realize that the strategies and concepts presented within the book can aid in the identification of many potential pitfalls that brands face and, better yet, help discover a myriad of valuable opportunities for their organizations. Readers will gain a clear understanding of how to compete and engage appropriately using social media in a competitive environment.

Social media has most certainly changed the world forever. The time is now to learn how the social sphere works.

Shall we begin?

Notes

[1] B. Parr, "The First Thing Young Women Do in the Morning: Check Facebook [STUDY]," Mashable, July 6, 2010, http://mashable.com/2010/07/06/oxygen-facebook-study.

[2] C. M. Bailey, "Match.com and Chadwick Martin Bailey 2009–2010 Studies: Recent Trends: Online Dating," Match.com, last modified March 2010, accessed January 28, 2014, http://cp.match.com/cppp/media/CMB_Study.pdf.

[3] H. Taylor, "If Social Networks Were Countries, Which Would They Be?" World Economic Forum, April 28, 2016, https://www.weforum.org/agenda/2016/04/facebook-is-bigger-than-the-worlds-largest-country?utm content=buffer68ca0&utm_medium=social&utm_source=facebook.com&utm_campaign=buffer.

[4] A. Mitchell and D. Page, "Twitter News Consumers: Young, Mobile and Educated," Pew Research Center, last modified November 2013, accessed January 28, 2014, http://www.journalism.org/files/2013/11/Twitter-IPO-release-with-cover-page.pdf.

[5] "Forrester Research." US Digital Marketing Forecast: 2016 to 2021. January 24, 2017. https://www.forrester.com/report/US Digital Marketing Forecast 2016 To 2021/-/E-RES137095.

THE ADVANCEMENT OF AN INDUSTRY

PART I

The Four Quadrants
of Public Relations

1

This chapter explores the four quadrants that public relations (PR) professionals work in—media, community, business, and government—focusing on their interrelationships and how social media plays an ever-present, integral role.

KEY LEARNING OUTCOMES

1. Identify the Four Quadrants of Public Relations.

2. Understand how media, community, business, and government play critical roles in PR planning.

3. Demonstrate how to apply the Four Quadrants of Public Relations to PR efforts.

SOCIAL MEDIA EXPERT

Safiya U. Noble, Ph.D. (@safiyanoble, website: safiyaunoble.com)

Safiya Umoja Noble is a faculty member at the University of Southern California (USC) Annenberg School of Communication, where she researches the design of digital media platforms on the Internet and their impact on society.[1] Her work is both sociological and interdisciplinary, noting the ways in which digital media impacts and intersects with issues of race, gender, culture, and technology design. She recently authored a monograph on racist and sexist algorithmic bias in commercial search engines titled *Algorithms of Oppression: How Search Engines Reinforce Racism*.[2] She currently serves as an associate editor for the *Journal of Critical Library and Information Studies* and is the coeditor of two books: *The Intersectional Internet: Race, Sex, Culture and Class Online* and *Emotions, Technology & Design*.[3]

---

[1] S. Noble, "Bio/CV - Safiya Umoja Noble, Ph.D. - Author, Teacher, Researcher," 2017, https://safiyaunoble.com/bio-cv/.

[2] S. U. Noble, *Algorithms of Oppression: How Search Engines Reinforce Racism* (New York: New York University Press, 2018).

[3] Noble, "Bio/CV - Safiya Umoja Noble, Ph.D. - Author, Teacher, Researcher."

The Four Quadrants of Public Relations Explained

In 1944 Rex Harlow wrote "Public Relations at the Crossroads," wherein he summarizes the duties of PR professionals. Harlow highlights that PR professionals contend with a myriad of relationships, including internal and external relations, personal relations, personnel relations, industrial relations, stockholder relations, board of directors' relations, customer relations, government relations, supplier-creditor relations, community relations, trade relations, opinion surveys, advertising, and publicity. Additionally, Harlow also notes that PR responsibilities of the time generally include press, radio, motion pictures, printing, public speaking, and professional writing.[1]

Even in today's rapid-paced work environment, Harlow's insights still ring true, as those of us in the PR profession understand that we must be able to do it all. In fact, it is now an expectation that we serve as experts in multiple arenas within the field to be successful in supporting the companies and organizations that we represent.

What is implied, but not directly stated, in Harlow's summary of the profession are the Four Quadrants of Public Relations. The idea is simple. Within these four quadrants all functions of PR fall. Being well versed across all quadrants, while also understanding each individual element, is critical to the development of today's PR practitioners. The Four Quadrants of Public Relations include

1. *Media*—inclusive of publicity, as well as traditional, social press, and social media
2. *Community*—inclusive of internal, external, online, employee, consumer, and personal interactions
3. *Business*—inclusive of investor relations, C-suite executive advisement, and social care (customer service)
4. *Government*—inclusive of political, lobbying, public affairs, and issues management

PR practitioners should think of each element as completely interrelated and strive to incorporate aspects of all four quadrants into their daily activities in order to develop a higher level of strategic implementation.

Success is realized when PR professionals include all four quadrants in the PR planning process. However, the supporting concepts behind the Four Quadrants of Public Relations are not new. *The novelty lies in how these quadrants are grouped and explained in an interrelated fashion.* PR practitioners have a defined responsibility to mediate between an organization and its public in order to build relationships with a variety of stakeholders by seeking, collecting, and disseminating information to the public. This information, or feedback, often provides PR practitioners and their organizations with insights into how the public perceives the organization and its operations.[2] Utilizing this open,

The Four Quadrants of Public Relations incorporates activities that promote strategic planning and implementation. *Source*: Regina Luttrell.

two-way, symmetrical communication, as exemplified by the Grunig-Hunt model, allows for a higher level of mutual understanding and offers a more balanced approach to consumer-company interactions.[3] Communication should ideally move between an organization and its publics effectively. The two-way symmetrical communication model is one of the more robust models that PR professionals practice, as it promotes a greater sense of engagement with an organization's targeted audience by listening, connecting, and facilitating through action rather than merely pushing messages out.[4] A continual, open line of communication between a PR practitioner and the publics being served is essential in our digital age of socially driven PR activities.

Historically speaking, the idea of open communication has always been at the cornerstone of defining PR.[5] Going forward, it will become increasingly important to focus on sustaining an open model of communication with the public. The theory behind the Four Quadrants of Public Relations relies heavily on this type of engagement, and since social media is also founded on the open communication concept, this communication model will take on considerable importance.

With this in mind, it is essential to understand how the four-quadrant model relies on any single segment building upon another yet maintaining its interconnectedness with all of the other segments. Let's examine how each segment works individually and then how they work together.

Spotting Trends

You hear it all the time, see it in job descriptions, and read about it in books—spotting and capitalizing on trends. Whether I'm speaking at a conference or in the classroom, I advise that to be successful in media relations a person must have the ability to spot a trend and jump on it.

One of the keys to implementing a successful media relations plan is to anticipate what journalists want to cover or need to cover before they're aware of it themselves. Since most of us cannot see into the future and do not have a crystal ball to help us, the best way to do this is to become a trend spotter.

But how exactly does anyone do that?

1. *Read:* Well, the first thing you need is to be well-read. Devour news. Read it, watch it, and listen to it. Knowing what's going on around you and around the world will help you understand what the news media are reporting on. Let's not forget about professional trade publications either. Scan various information from a variety of sources to see what's going on. Use tools like RSS feeds, newsletters, Twitter feeds, blogs, and electronic publications to keep on top of what's happening. Doing this on a regular basis will teach you which sources are valuable.

   Google Trends is an excellent tool to use as a way to follow trends in real time on the Internet as they unfold. Like so many Google tools, it's a powerful and underutilized tool. As a PR practitioner, use it to follow what's hot. If your industry falls into one of the trends, then capitalize on it, find an interesting story, and pitch a journalist. https://trends.google.com/

2. *Talk:* Talking to others is another excellent trend-spotting tactic. Get out there and get involved. Join networking associations and industry organizations, and attend events virtually and in person.

3. *Watch:* Remember that research class you took in college? You know the one . . . your professor made you watch people . . . well, put it to work. Open your eyes and see what's happening around you.

4. *Think:* Understanding and capitalizing on trends happens the more you read, talk, and watch. Making connections between what you are reading, who you are talking to, and what you are watching could result in some amazing pitches to journalists.

Your next pitch could land you or your client on the *CBS Evening News*.

Source: R. M. Luttrell, "Do You Know How to Spot a Trend and Capitalize on It?" Gina Luttrell (web log), September 3, 2013, accessed September 8, 2017, https://ginaluttrellphd.com/2013/09/03/do-you-know-how-to-spot-a-trend-and-capitalize-on-it/. Adapted and reprinted with permission from the author.

Quadrant 1: Media Relations

Peter Hilmer, principal of Flatiron Communications LLC, a New York City–based PR and digital media consulting firm, said of media relations: "One look at any PR job board will reveal that media relations remains the single-most sought-after competency by agencies of all stripes and most in-house communications departments. There's nothing like a seasoned PR pro who understands how to navigate (and have empathy for) the most sought-after reporters, bloggers and TV producers."[6]

Sharing news has deep roots in PR and will continue to play an important role. Think about this: writing and editing a newsletter, blogging about a current event, or working with the media to garner media coverage is all part of developing news.[7] In practice, PR professionals work closely with the media to distribute their messages to the public. News, specifically news sources—inclusive of traditional journalists, bloggers, analysts, editors, and producers of television, print, radio, and electronic media—have long been viewed by the public as trustworthy and highly regarded.[8] It is the job of PR professionals to build strong, mutually respectful relationships with journalists. Traditionally, PR practitioners manage their media relations responsibilities by sending press releases and pitch emails, arranging interviews, organizing press conferences, and responding to media inquiries.[9]

The outcomes of these efforts are easy to recognize in mainstream media. The messages that are communicated are carefully, tactfully, and strategically "placed" by PR practitioners across America. To the untrained eye the news is presented in a manner that appears as though a journalist researched the story, gathered the interviewees, and put the thirty-second TV news spot together. In truth, many of these news stories are the result of diligent PR practitioners. It is our job as professionals to identify a newsworthy trend and capitalize on it. "Newsworthiness is based on how, if and to what extent the story will affect a specific audience. Something isn't news just because we, as PR professionals, say that it is. As much as our clients like to think everything that their company does is newsworthy, it simply is not."[10]

The fact of the matter is that organizations utilize traditional media relations efforts regularly. For example, when the Intermountain Medical Center Heart Institute from Utah launched their 2017 My Heart Challenge: Nonprofit Edition, they developed and sent out a press release to local media. The goal of the annual hundred-day challenge is to help participants strengthen their hearts by improving their lifestyle, which, in turn, reduces their risk of developing heart disease. Their effort yielded great results. The organization landed on new outlets throughout Salt Lake City. Several newspaper placements as well as on-camera news appearances highlighted the efforts of the campaign, as the press release was written and targeted to ensure the best possible results for placement and coverage.[11] So what is the trend Intermountain Medical Center Heart Institute capitalized on? Cardiovascular disease is the number one cause of death in the United States, killing nearly 800,000 people each year. When an organization pulls together a campaign to help prevent heart disease, well, that's newsworthy.

When Chicago Lakeside Development unlocked property that had been inaccessible for nearly one hundred years, thus extending South Lake Shore Drive by two miles, the organization knew they had a hot story.[12] Zapwater Communications, the agency hired to execute the campaign, set its sights on securing national and local media coverage. The highly anticipated development of the South Lake Shore Drive extension would garner not just media interest but community, government, and business support as well. To land a national feature story in the *Wall Street Journal*, Zapwater leveraged the rich history of Lake Shore Drive, including vintage maps to round out the appeal.[13] Other press coverage included articles appearing in the *Chicago*

Tribune, Chicago Sun-Times, and *RedEye*. A press release and a community event were planned and executed, which included a ribbon-cutting ceremony, the unveiling of a steel sculpture by a local artist, and a 5K run/walk.[14] The governor of Illinois, along with a state senator, also attended the event to celebrate.

This well-planned media relations strategy secured more than 137 print and online media placements, garnering more than 20 million media impressions.[15] PR efforts were a crucial component in the announcement of the Lake Shore Drive expansion project.

Campaigns like the 2017 My Heart Challenge from Intermountain Medical Center Heart Institute and the Chicago Lakeside Development project are built on a coordinated use of varied communication techniques and tools employed by PR practitioners and the instinct to know what stories are "pitch perfect." Pitching the right story is dependent upon a practitioner's ability to spot and capitalize on newsworthy trends occurring around the world. Practitioners work with the media to place editorials in newspapers; produce video and audio news releases; arrange radio, TV, print, and social media interviews; promote websites for their organizations; and offer easy access to additional materials that complement the news stories. Through leveraging a company or organization's best assets, including subject matter experts, and seizing the news of the day, media relations can be used to strategically build a favorable image, educate the public, or engage the public.

It would be cliché to state that practitioners must be "out-of-the-box thinkers," but if we are to assess issues and trends successfully and identify the correct demographics within the public, then we must look beyond the typical confines previously presented.[16] The aforementioned examples highlight not only the importance of the relationship between the PR practitioner and the media but also the varied job duties

Public Relations In Europe

PR Across the Pond

Many global organizations consider executing public relations campaigns in Europe as they expand their business internationally. However, public relations is different in international markets. The use of public relations by companies in Europe is relatively commonplace, but how PR is practiced varies greatly from American tactics.

Get to know Europe 1

Identify which countries are important for your PR needs, and that are in line with your business objectives. Start with two or three markets, unless your budget allows for more.

2 Understand the European Media Landscape

Just like in the U.S. know the media and journalist you are pitching. In Belgium, the news agenda is feature-driven while in France journalists like exclusives and less planned editorial content. In some markets like Russia, Switzerland, and the Czech Republic you may need to pay a publication to place an article.

Localize the Story 3

Press content should not just be translated, but localized with specific European and country angles and facts for greater success.

Make Friends

4 European journalists will generally give priority to European and local stories. Get to know the journalist and their interests.

RESEARCH
Get to know other Social Media Platforms 5

Facebook, Twitter, and LinkedIn are prevalent across the European region. However many local social media channels exist, such as Xing and Viadeo.

Don't overlook the need for local social media content or targeting new channels. The company that understands how the media landscape differs by country and adapts PR tactics accordingly is the one that will succeed.

Sources: Boucetta, Yasmeen. "LEWIS 360° – The Blog of Global Communications Agency, LEWIS PR." LEWIS 360 The Blog of Global Communications Agency LEWIS PR Thinking about PR in Europe Five Considerations before You Board That Flight Comments. September 23, 2011. Accessed November 15, 2015. http://blog.lewispr.com/2011/09/european-pr.html.

Decker, Bill. "They Do Public Relations Differently in Other Countries." December 31, 2012. Accessed November 15, 2015. http://www.bizjournals.com/denver/blog/broadway_17th/2012/12/they-do-public-relations-differently.html.

By understanding the media landscape in Europe public relations practitioners can adapt their strategies and tactics accordingly.

and skills required of a practitioner within his or her daily activities, including the creation, maintenance, and cultivation of messages.

Media relations alone cannot drive a modern PR campaign. Individual news stories are too short-lived or lost altogether in the chaos of dynamic content. Today, for a story to take off, it must be amplified across multiple news and social channels, even if that means using alternative means for achieving it, such as paid or sponsored media.[17]

Quadrant 2: Community Relations

In addition to media playing a pivotal role in PR, community relations is equally important to the success of PR practitioners. The buzz surrounding corporate social responsibility (CSR) has become an integral component of community relations. With increasing frequency, companies and organizations are giving back to the communities in which they reside, requiring PR practitioners representing these organizations to further cultivate the relationships between the organization and the community. The responsibility of community relations is the second of the four quadrants that we will explore.

The term "community" no longer means just a physical community, but also includes the online community. Today's PR practitioners live with one foot in the real world and one in the virtual community. PR campaigns now require a great deal of effort from the PR practitioner to support the organization's online activities, often promoted via Facebook pages, Pinterest boards, Twitter feeds with specific hashtag identifiers, live and recorded videos, Snaps, and Instagram. Engaging the targeted audience online should now be considered a natural component of any PR campaign planning process. The most recent GAP study revealed that 17 percent of participants noted that social media pervades every aspect of their business,[18] while the most recent *State of Social Marketing* report reported that organizations are annually increasing what they spend on social media.[19] Additionally, participants of the study indicated that social media as an occupation is no longer limited to entry or mid-level employees, but has graduated into the senior-level offices, and that social media teams continue to grow as well.[20] Social media responsibilities have significantly increased and emerge as a mainstream responsibility within the industry.[21] Keep this idea in mind as we examine the second quadrant more closely.

As a rule, this role of "community liaison" helps develop crucial relationships within the community. Community relations practitioners are being asked to perform a multitude of tasks, including creation, implementation, and management of an organization's community awareness initiatives.[22] This means that these individuals promote community initiatives and programs inclusive of resource sharing, community education programs, workshops, events, and symposiums identified as key corporate areas for promotion. They are also the organizational resources who create strategic alliances with representatives of consumer, employee, and public interest groups; key provider practices; vendors; governmental agencies; and prominent community organizations.[23] Community relations practitioners may even participate in community activities surrounding corporate issues, including serving on committees, meeting with elected officials and politicians, sitting on various planning boards, attending and speaking at community board and similar meetings, creating timelines, attending various networking events, or performing other tasks.[24]

A study by NYU and Imperative found that "purpose-oriented employees" tend to remain with employers 20 percent longer than those at other companies and are about 47 percent more likely to be more engaged promoters of the companies they work for.[25] Companies are leading the way in the corporate citizenship revolution by contributing to the transformation and empowerment of the communities of which they are an integral part. This is beneficial not only for the communities but also for the corporations. It is the intention of the corporation to uphold its image and reputation within the community while also contributing in a positive way. IKEA, Starbucks, Salesforces, and Alphabet (Google) are just a few companies leading the way.

- *The IKEA Foundation* is a corporate citizenship initiative focusing on the Circle of Prosperity, a mission focusing on the betterment of everyday life for as many people as possible. The Circle of Prosperity identifies and funds home, health, education, and sustainable income programs for communities in need. One such project launched in 2017, the Brighter Lives for Refugees campaign, financed the installation of a renewable energy solar farm to Jordan's Azraq refugee camp. This investiture will ultimately realize $1.5 million in energy cost savings for the surrounding community and cut CO_2 emissions by 2,370 tons annually.[26] https://www.ikeafoundation.org/
- *Starbucks* is well-known for its execution of operational activities with social responsibility in mind. One such community-focused initiative, Conservation International's Sustainable Coffee Challenge, allowed Starbucks to commit in excess of one million coffee trees to local farmers. Additionally, the organization recently announced plans to hire more than 10,000 refugees from nearly seventy-five different countries over the next five years, as well as expand their commitment to veterans by hiring 25,000 veterans by the year 2025.[27] https://www.starbucks.com/responsibility/community/starbucks-foundation
- *Salesforce* developed and follows an integrated philanthropic approach to corporate social responsibility called the 1-1-1 model. Marc Benioff, chairman and CEO of Salesforce, noted that "the business of business is improving the state of the world."[28] The 1-1-1 model sets aside 1 percent of the company's equity for grants supporting the communities where Salesforce employees work and live, donates 1 percent of the company's products to nonprofit organizations, and allows employees to donate 1 percent of their time each year to community initiatives.[29] https://www.salesforce.com/company/salesforceorg/
- *The Jack & Mo Cooking Show*, a small business founded by a father/daughter team, offers culinary classes, meal prep kits, and birthday cooking classes in Upstate New York. This organization gives back to the community through its partnerships with charitable organizations, with a goal to educate others about food and ensure that those in need within its community have enough to eat. To that end, it has partnered with local churches, restaurants, and food banks. https://jackandmocookingshow.wordpress.com/charitable-partners/

These examples aim to highlight that a company's donations of capital or services, either within the actual community or online, become important contributions from a PR standpoint. These initiatives provide a positive impact for the populations and communities that they touch and for the organization in fostering good relationships in communities that directly impact brand and image.

Quadrant 3: Business Relations

In general, few organizations exist today that do not establish some degree of a relationship within their immediate community. Organizations must strive to interact and connect with the public in a positive manner, which, in turn, affects their external image. In today's business landscape, there is an increased level of responsibility expected of the PR practitioner to guide the CEO or other executive officials through the organization's PR plan, reputation management, and brand management.

The 2017 Edelman Trust Barometer survey revealed that trust is in crisis, both within the United States and around the world. The study revealed that two thirds of countries now fall into "distruster" territory, with trust levels below 50 percent, with the credibility of leaders also in peril: CEO credibility dropped 12 points globally to an all-time low of 37 percent, plummeting in every country studied.[30]

These perceptions can have obvious ramifications for a company's brand, image, bottom line, and ultimate ability to build trusting relationships with its consumers. By participating in a model of corporate citizenship, it is evident that one of the key responsibilities of a business is to be a good citizen. It is essential to understand that the function of the PR department is to help businesses achieve a desired level of citizenship within the community. *Therefore, PR must be a part of every department within a business.* This is an important takeaway. As a result, it is easy to see how business relations play a critical role in the daily lives of PR practitioners.

The exercise of conducting daily activities typically results in organizations performing a variety of PR activities that keep them connected with their publics. CEOs are being held accountable for the company's strategic plan, with PR departments being responsible for closely monitoring its implementation and successful execution. Strategic thinking should include, in addition to customary market and competitive obstacles, significant nation-state cultural, social, global, and political biases. To connect with consumers, organizations will commonly sign up as cosponsors of various events designed to advance human rights or address environmental opportunities.[31]

Corporate social responsibility and accountability are interwoven. PR practitioners around the globe are being called on to help both for-profit and nonprofit businesses ensure "accountability" on all levels. As large corporations expand to new geographies around the world, the ability to conduct business successfully in other countries will be judged by how well these corporations operate in their home countries.[32] The good news is that the Trust Barometer revealed that business is viewed as the only entity that can make a difference. "Three out of four respondents agree a company can take actions to both increase profits and improve economic and social conditions in the community where it operates. Moreover, among those who are uncertain about whether the system is working for them, it is business (58 percent) that they trust most."[33]

Quadrant 4: Government Relations

Government relations have long been the foundation of the PR industry, dating back to the ancient Roman and Greek civilizations.[34] While not recognized as "public relations" at the time, the activities performed could unarguably be considered PR tools and tactics. The use of persuasion within public speeches, staging of publicity events, and meeting with public officials would be interpreted as PR activities as the role is characterized today.[35]

In today's business environment, practitioners participating in government relations are also known as public affairs officers or public affairs specialists. These practitioners frequently possess the difficult job of supporting the company's public policy initiatives as well as developing legislative and regulatory proposals on behalf of the company (while simultaneously practicing effective PR strategies). It is within their job responsibilities to maintain positive relationships with the legislature since they work so closely with these elected officials. These individuals are accountable for lobbying the legislature to advocate on the behalf of legislation important to enhancing an organization in a strategic manner.

One example of note, Rock the Vote, will help clarify this concept. This PR campaign is endorsed by politicians and political groups from both major political parties. As the largest nonprofit and nonpartisan organization in the United States, Rock the Vote has been registering and turning out millions of new voters since 1990. For twenty-eight years, Rock the Vote has revolutionized the way pop culture, music, art, and technology inspire political activity. What has made this campaign so powerful is that from its conception the organization pioneered ways to make voting easier for young adults by simplifying and demystifying voter registration and elections.[36]

Prior to the 1992 and 1996 presidential elections, a nationwide PR campaign was launched focusing on the mass registration of young voters (ages eighteen to twenty-four). Resulting from the success of the inaugural 1992 Rock the Vote campaign, governmental agencies took notice and looked to achieve an even higher level of registered voter participation from this same demographic of voters in the coming election season. In 1996, Rock the Vote came to life again, and it has been a mainstay political initiative every election year since. This PR initiative ended a twenty-year cycle of declining voter participation.[37]

When Rock the Vote was initially rolled out, younger voters only had the option of signing and addressing two types of postcards pledging to vote. If we fast-forward to today, the emergence of social media has provided participants a myriad of convenient avenues allowing new voters to register.

Originally, in promoting the Rock the Vote initiative, PR practitioners utilized mass media and community events as their main avenues of distribution—specifically MTV. (Note the connection to media relations, community relations, and obviously government relations here.) Rock the Vote organizers created various public service announcements that were aired on MTV around the clock, including nationwide radio announcements, coordinated traveling bus tours to register young voters, and famous personalities hired to endorse the importance of voting.[38] In fact, Madonna wrapped herself in the American flag for the first ever Rock the Vote PSA.[39]

The campaign is keenly aware of its target audience. Countless cultural icons have lent their voice and talent to support Rock the Vote and its mission. Snoop Dogg launched the 2004 bus tour, while Lil Jon rapped the election anthem of 2014, and in 2016 they launched the #TruthToPower campaign to boost participation of Millennial voters in the 2016 general election. The Truth to Power campaign included both digital and on-the-ground voter registration drives and election turnout efforts in twelve key battleground states: Arizona, Colorado, Florida, Illinois, Iowa, Michigan, Nevada, New Hampshire, Ohio, Pennsylvania, Wisconsin, and Virginia.[40] Rock the Vote continued to partner with entertainers to develop compelling political content aimed at engaging and mobilizing Millennials throughout the general election season.[41]

Additionally, it should be noted that politicians, local and national, use PR tactics for personal benefit as they conduct their daily activities and annual campaigns. These tactics become important in instances wherein a politician desires to raise money or attract votes. When politicians are successful at

Original Rock the Vote Poster Used in the 1992 Public Relations Campaign. *Source*: Regina Luttrell.

the ballot box, they use PR to promote and defend their service in office, with an eye toward the next election. PR practitioners are responsible for leading the way in shaping these carefully worded messages as they coordinate speaking engagements; plan special events at nursing homes, churches, and day care centers; write press releases; and ensure that the politician is on message each time. This is often accomplished by providing the political speaker with carefully thought-out talking points related to the key messages of interest.

Applying an Interconnected Approach

We can see that there are many responsibilities and outcomes that rely on the skills of PR practitioners. There is not a single formula for success. Specifically, let's look at media relations. This segment of PR can be considered a stand-alone, specialized function within the world of PR, as could any of the Four Quadrants of Public Relations for that matter. However, in understanding each quadrant, the overlap between the quadrants, how to work within each quadrant, and incorporating a diverse range of essential skills, we can see a pattern for successful PR planning, process, and implementation. Aspects of each of the four quadrants rely on one another to be successful.

Within media relations, practitioners must have the ability to successfully conduct outreach to the media on behalf of an organization or company. It is essential to have the right communication skills to complete this task, along with superior writing abilities. It is also vital to understand how to reach out to the media in an acceptable way, use the appropriate channels, communicate the right message, and successfully land a newsworthy story. The skills associated with media relations should be inherent to a PR practitioner.

When working with the community, practitioners also take on the task of enhancing an organization's participation and position within the community by initiating/establishing outreach efforts. This element of a PR practitioner's role cannot be accomplished without the correct set of skills. The PR practitioner must know how to build those relationships.

The approach to business relations is executed in a similar manner to community relations. PR practitioners ultimately build and continually foster relationships within the business community. Organizations today want to make sure the actions they take are interpreted as "good citizenship." It is the job of the PR practitioner to have the appropriate skills to accomplish this aspect of developing these relationships.

Finally, PR practitioners have also assumed the role of involving their respective organizations in the development of public policy and government relations. Being able to represent an organization's interests to governing bodies and regulatory agencies with the expectation of mutual understanding is a key responsibility of a PR practitioner or, as we mentioned previously, a public affairs professional. Knowledge of public speaking, government, and effective communication are essential when working in government relations.

The profession of PR aids an organization in establishing mutually adapted relationships with external entities—be that with the media, the community, other businesses, or the government. It is the role of the PR practitioner to nurture these relationships within each quadrant of PR. Being able to interconnect and apply the required skill sets from each quadrant to gain an increased understanding of the organization's "big picture" is equally important. As evidence, PR practitioners must have a variety of expertise to accomplish their job duties, with each skill supporting one of the Four Quadrants of Public Relations: media, community, business, and government.

Okay to Say

Okay to Say (https://www.okaytosay.org/) is an example of a PR campaign that has utilized the Four Quadrants of Public Relations effectively.

Overview

Okay to Say was initiated by the Meadows Mental Health Policy Institute (MMHPI) and led by LDWWgroup, a PR agency. This PR effort is a statewide initiative in Texas aimed at ending the stigma surrounding mental health issues, as well as providing resources for those in need. The goal of the campaign is to change the conversation and perceptions around mental illness. The grass-roots movement is designed to raise mental health awareness with the knowledge that 76 percent of Texans have a close friend or family member who has experienced mental illness, and to start working to overcome the stigma.

The campaign began with the sole intent of opening a conversation around mental health in order to build common ground with affected groups and gradually influence opinions.

Media

Media efforts (https://www.okaytosay.org/news/) surrounding the campaign included partnering with twenty-three media outlets, such as the *Amarillo Globe-News*, *Austin American-Statesman*, *Dallas Morning News*, *Fort Worth Star-Telegram*, KEYE-TV Austin, KPRC-TV Houston, NBC-TV 5 Dallas, and Telemundo, among others. The Okay to Say initiative secured

- a 30-minute mental health special on NBC-TV 5 Dallas featuring Okay to Say (27,000+ viewers)
- a weeklong mental health series including Okay to Say that aired nightly during the NBC-TV 5 Dallas 10 p.m. newscast (highest-rated news program in Dallas–Fort Worth)
- approximately fifty half-page display ads in the *Dallas Morning News* valued at $500,000, which were donated to Okay to Say

Community

In addition to the media partners, LDWWgroup mobilized sixty-one-plus organizations to join the campaign, including Mental Health America of Texas, National Alliance on Mental Illness, Texas Medical Association, Texas Women's University, the University of North Texas, and the United Way. With LDWWgroup's assistance, MMHPI also partnered with children's singer/songwriter (and native Texan) Eddie Coker and the Wezmore Project, an organization that teaches children, teens, families, and educators about emotional wholeness. Together they performed 54 live concert events in 28 schools across Texas, teaching 28,000+ students and 500 teachers and administrators about the importance of learning and talking about their emotional health.

Business

LDWWgroup invited Texans to become part of the movement by engaging—actively or passively—with the Okay to Say website. Engagement flourished because participation required minimal commitment. The initial ask: learn about the topic from the supply of rich content, resources, and personal stories on the website. For visitors willing to be more involved, LDWWgroup created an "approachable" option: signing up, by name or anonymously, to show support. For people inspired to share their own experiences, visitors were invited to submit their stories to the website, which were shareable via social media. The engagement reached far beyond Texas to all 50 states and 117 countries; roughly 40 organizations plan to replicate Okay to Say in their markets across the U.S.

Government

LDWWgroup set out to create a campaign built around judgement-free online and in-person public forums where Texans were encouraged to engage and share information, resources, and stories. LDWWgroup started by building a central hub for the program—the Okay to Say website—where Texans can access information, stories, and resources surrounding mental health. Respected sports figures, celebrities, politicians, and business leaders all shared their stories through videos produced for the Okay to Say website, including former president George W. Bush; billionaire philanthropist, *Shark Tank* judge, and Dallas Mavericks owner Mark Cuban; Dallas Cowboys legendary running back Emmitt Smith; Olympic boxing medalist

Marlen Esparza; the Houston Astros' Jose Altuve; and the mayors of Austin, Dallas, and Houston.

By taking a step back to see how this example integrates each of the Four Quadrants of Public Relations, it is easier to see how each independent quadrant contributes to a fully coordinated, successful PR campaign executed by the Okay to Say initiative. Check out the infographic, videos, posters, and other initiatives on the Okay to Say website:

- "Talk Openly" infographic: https://cdn.okaytosay.org/wp-content/uploads/2016/08/6.ots_Infographic.pdf

- Senator Kirk Watson: https://youtu.be/iuqXlTr9zHs
- President George W. Bush: https://youtu.be/3OiBDpOSJWA
- Business and civic partners: https://www.okaytosay.org/partner/

Ultimately, the success of these types of initiatives are only as good as the PR practitioner's ability to see the bigger picture. While the four quadrants can be used independently, this example illustrates how effective an integrated effort between all areas can be.

#LRNSMPR

Learn Social Media and Public Relations

Apply the principles learned in this chapter to the scenarios below.

- Search the Internet and find a PR agency, investigate their case studies or read their client projects, and then examine how the company produces campaigns related to the Four Quadrants of Public Relations. Describe what types of materials they produce, for which companies, and which quadrant(s) those materials would be placed in. Is there overlap between the quadrants? Are all four quadrants used, or only a few within a campaign?
- In June 2017 the Avon Foundation for Women launched the Justice Institute on Gender-Based Violence in Santiago, Chile. This initiative calls together judges, court officers, prosecutors, law enforcement officers, representatives of

government agencies, and nongovernmental service providers with the aim of making the laws keep their promise. Read more about this endeavor and then examine how this partnership is an example of a PR campaign that has utilized the Four Quadrants of Public Relations effectively. https://www.avonfoundation.org/avon-foundation-launches-justice-institute-gender-based-violence-santiago-chile/
- You are the PR specialist for the Dollar Shave Club, and your company just partnered with No Shave November to help raise cancer awareness and funds to support cancer prevention, research, and education. Using what you have learned regarding the Four Quadrants of Public Relations, develop a PR campaign.

Notes

[1] R. Harlow, "Public Relations at the Crossroads," *Public Opinion Quarterly* (1944): 551–56.
[2] University of Florida Interactive Media Lab, "Literature Review of Public Relations Law I. Introduction," accessed December 15, 2017, http://iml.jou.ufl.edu/projects/Fall99/Westbrook/litrev.htm.
[3] D. Wilcox et al., *THINK Public Relations* (Upper Saddle River, NJ: Pearson Education, 2013).
[4] D. Moss and B. DeSanto, "What Do Communications Managers Do?" *J&MC Quarterly* (2005): 873–90; L. Wernet-Foreman and B. Devin, "Listening to Learn: 'Inactive' Publics of the Arts as Exemplar," *Communication World* (2006): 287–94.
[5] F. Seitel, *The Practice of Public Relations* (Upper Saddle River, NJ: Pearson, 2014); Wilcox et al., *THINK Public Relations.*
[6] P. Himler, "Media Relations Is Dead. Long Live Media Relations," PRsay (web log), January 15, 2014, https://prsay.prsa.org/2014/01/15/media-relations-is-dead-long-live-media-relations/.
[7] T. Kelleher, *Public Relations* (New York: Oxford University Press, 2018).
[8] Wilcox et al., *THINK Public Relations.*

⁹ Wilcox et al., *THINK Public Relations*, Seitel, *The Practice of Public Relations*.

¹⁰ R. Luttrell, "5 Questions to Ask When Writing News Releases," PRSA, February 28, 2013, http://apps.prsa.org/intelligence/Tactics/Articles/view/10097/1074/5_questions_to_ask_when_writing_news_releases.

¹¹ Intermountain Medical Center, "Intermountain Heart Institute My Heart Challenge," accessed September 8, 2017, https://intermountainhealthcare.org/locations/intermountain-medical-center/classes-events/my-heart-challenge/.

¹² Zapwater Communications, "Zapwater Chicago Lakeside Development," accessed September 8, 2017, http://www.zapwater.com/case-studies/zapwater-chicago-lakeside-development.

¹³ Zapwater Communications, "Zapwater Chicago Lakeside Development."

¹⁴ Zapwater Communications, "Zapwater Chicago Lakeside Development."

¹⁵ Zapwater Communications, "Zapwater Chicago Lakeside Development."

¹⁶ D. Anderson, "Identifying and Responding to Activist Publics: A Case Study," *Public Relations Research*, no. 1 (1992): 151–65.

¹⁷ Himler, "Media Relations Is Dead. Long Live Media Relations."

¹⁸ "GAP VIII: Eighth Communication and Public Relations Generally Accepted Practices Study (Q4 2013 Data)," University of Southern California (USC) Annenberg, Strategic Communication and Public Relations Center, 2014, ascjweb.org/gapstudy/wp-content/uploads/2014/06/GAP-VIII-Presentation-Final-6.12.2014.pdf.

¹⁹ L. Hitz and B. Blackburn, *The State of Social Marketing: 2017 Annual Report* (Seattle: Simply Measured, 2017), https://get.simplymeasured.com/rs/135-YGJ-288/images/SM_StateOfSocial-2017.pdf.

²⁰ Hitz and Blackburn, *The State of Social Marketing*.

²¹ "GAP VII: Seventh Communication and Public Relations Generally Accepted Practices Study (Q4 2011 Data)."

²² K. Keller, *Best Practice Cases in Branding* (Upper Saddle River, NJ: Pearson, 2007).

²³ Wilcox et al., *THINK Public Relations*.

²⁴ Seitel, *The Practice of Public Relations*, Keller, *Best Practice Cases in Branding*.

²⁵ J. Dickey, "Enriching the Employee Experience with Branding and Purpose," April 25, 2017, https://www.linkedin.com/pulse/enriching-employee-experience-branding-purpose-dickey-phr-shrm-cp-1/.

²⁶ N. Vilas, "Top 20 Socially Responsible Companies 2017," SmartRecruiters Blog, August 23, 2017, accessed September 8, 2017, https://www.smartrecruiters.com/blog/top-20-corporate-social-responsibility-initiatives-for-2017/.

²⁷ Vilas, "Top 20 Socially Responsible Companies 2017."

²⁸ Vilas, "Top 20 Socially Responsible Companies 2017."

²⁹ Vilas, "Top 20 Socially Responsible Companies 2017."

³⁰ Edelman, "2017 Edelman Trust Barometer," https://www.edelman.com/trust2017/.

³¹ J. Budd, "Opinion . . . Foreign Policy Acumen Needed by Global CEOs," *Public Relations Review* (2000): 123–34.

³² Keller, *Best Practice Cases in Branding*.

³³ Edelman, "2017 Edelman Trust Barometer."

³⁴ Wilcox et al., *THINK Public Relations*.

³⁵ Seitel, *The Practice of Public Relations*.

³⁶ Rock the Vote, "About Rock the Vote," accessed September 10, 2017, https://www.rockthevote.com/about-us/.

³⁷ Keller, *Best Practice Cases in Branding*.

³⁸ Keller, *Best Practice Cases in Branding*.

³⁹ Rock the Vote, "About Rock the Vote."

⁴⁰ C. Crosby, "Rock the Vote—Share with the Young Voters in Your Life," *Grand*, August 4, 2016, http://www.grandmagazine.com/2016/08/30879/.

⁴¹ Rock the Vote, "Rock the Vote Announces #TruthToPower Campaign to Boost Participation of Millennial Voters in 2016 General Election," news release, July 19, 2016, https://www.rockthevote.com/rock-the-vote-announces-truthtopower/.

The Evolution of Social Media 2

This chapter discusses the evolution of social media and situates social media within today's global environment.

KEY LEARNING OUTCOMES

1. Define social media and explain how it has contributed to the evolving role of public relations (PR).
2. Identify and recognize the stages of the evolution of social media and how the history has formed what we know today.
3. Recognize the global implications social media has had on society.

SOCIAL MEDIA EXPERT

Mary F. Cavanagh (@mfcavanagh, website: https://mfcavanagh.wordpress.com/)

Mary Cavanagh is an associate professor at the University of Ottawa's ALA-accredited School of Information Studies. She teaches courses related to the social context of information, knowledge in organizations and organizational learning, information seeking and use, program evaluation, professional practice, and research methods.[1] Her research focuses on questions surrounding social organizing, the use and value of information, and knowledge practices provided by information and cultural organizations.

---

[1] M. Cavanagh, "Mary F. Cavanagh," 2017, https://mfcavanagh.wordpress.com/.

What Is Social Media?

Why ask "What is social media?" when everybody already knows?

We're asking because organizations are failing at social media every day for numerous reasons, the most common being that they simply do not understand the premise behind social media. Another reason is that they are trying to fit marketing or advertising principles into social media since they don't understand the fundamental ideals behind social media. As a result, many organizations tend to seek outside assistance in this area and hire one of the many self-proclaimed "gurus" to manage their social strategies—but often the so-called guru isn't really an expert at all. Most organizations tend to overlook how smart their consumers really are and need to evolve beyond using the same old marketing techniques and tactics to spam consumers. Consumers know the difference between true engagements with a company or brand versus simply being sold to.

To gain a deeper level of understanding of social media, let us break down the two words separately and explore their meanings as they relate to social media.

Social: so-cial *adjective* \'sō-shəl\[1]

marked by or passed in pleasant companionship with friends or associates of or relating to human society, the interaction of the individual and the group, or the welfare of human beings as members of society tending to form cooperative and interdependent relationships with others.

As you can see, "social" relates to the need that we, as human beings, have to connect with others through companionship via relationships, either individually or in groups. Think about your own relationships. We want to be around people who make us most comfortable and have similar interests, ideas, ideals, and experiences.[2] This premise also holds true for consumers who desire to interact with companies that they relate to, connect with, and feel comfortable aligning themselves with.

Media: me-di-a *noun* \mee-dee-uh\[3]

Communication channels through which news, entertainment, education, data, or promotional messages are disseminated. Media includes every broadcasting and narrowcasting medium such as newspapers, magazines, TV, radio, billboards, direct mail, telephone, blog, and Internet. *Media* is the plural of *medium* and can take a plural or singular verb, depending on the sense intended.

The word "media" relates to the channels through which we make connections with others. The sampling provided in the definition is narrow in scope. Today, we connect through pictures, email, texting, websites, and a myriad of mobile and handheld devices.

In bringing the two words together, we can begin to understand how this book applies the term "social media" and how you should interpret the term going forward. A commonly accepted definition of the term "social media" holds that it refers to the "activities, practices, and behavior among communities of people who gather online to share information, knowledge and opinions using conversational media. Conversational media are web-based applications that make it possible to create and easily transmit content in the form of words, pictures, video, and audio."[4] Social platforms, including Facebook, Snapchat, Twitter, Instagram, Pinterest, WordPress, and LinkedIn, among others, are forms of social media. They represent conversational media since each application allows users to gather online and easily exchange photos, videos, audio files, and content while building and cultivating relationships. Social media competence should be viewed as how a company or brand effectively utilizes each of the aforementioned platforms to connect, interact, and promote trusting relationships with people.

As we begin to situate social media in a historical context, we must also understand the innate connection between social media and social networks. Social networks comprise a complex system of web-based services that allow for the self-organization of individuals to construct a public or semipublic profile with a set of users with whom they share a connection.[5] This connection is important in understanding not only the relationship between the two but also their principal differences and how they are commonly interpreted as being the same.

Social Media's Rise

We can no longer argue that social media is on the rise or that it is in the early phases of adoption. Social media is here, and it is growing by leaps and bounds. At this point in the social revolution, social media is in the refinement stage wherein best practices and case studies are being shared. People are finding new ways to engage with the brands, events, and people that matter most to them. According to the Pew Research Center[6]:

- Roughly eight in ten online Americans (79 percent) use Facebook. That means 22 percent of the world's population uses Facebook.
- Around one third of online adults (32 percent) report using Instagram.
- 24 percent of Internet users (21 percent of all U.S. adults) use Twitter.
- 29 percent of Internet users (25 percent of all U.S. adults) use LinkedIn.
- 31 percent of Internet users (26 percent of all U.S. adults) use Pinterest.
- 29 percent of smartphone owners use general-purpose messaging apps such as WhatsApp or Kik.
- 24 percent use messaging apps such as Snapchat or Wickr.
- 5 percent use apps that allow people to anonymously chat or post comments.

If we simply look at the numbers involved, now more than ever must PR practitioners understand how to create, cultivate, maintain, and grow successful social strategies by building strong social relationships.

In its current form, social media can still be considered relatively new. However, the roots of social media surprisingly began in 550 BCE with the introduction of the postal service. Historically speaking, much of what we currently define as social media occurred during the twenty-first century. To build a greater understanding of social media, it is essential to examine the early forms of social networking and how it has evolved into its current form.

Prehistory: Ancient Persia, 600–490 BCE to 1800s

The post, as it was referred to during this period, was the first form of communication between people allowing correspondence beyond the confines of their villages. It is argued that the original credible claim for the development of a true postal system has its roots in ancient Persia, attributing the invention of the postal system to King Cyrus the Great.[7] With the establishment of a postal system, people could converse with one another over larger geographical areas. However, these early forms of communication were not without problems. Letters could take hours, days, or even months to arrive at their final destinations.

It wasn't until 1792 that Claude Chappe, a French inventor, developed the first practical telecommunications system of the industrial era. He became a telecommunications mogul through what has been called the "mechanical internet."[8] The telegraph transmitted messages instantaneously, altering communication thereafter. The electronic telegraph was the first form of communication that transmitted and received messages over long distances. Rightfully so, the telegraph has earned its place in the historical landscape of social media.

1890s

The year 1890 brought the telephone, and in 1891 society was introduced to the radio.[9] The telephone and radio both brought about a sense of community. People were connected across long distances in a more intimate way. Information moved between and among people, from big cities to small, rural communities.

1960s

The 1960s were rich with introductory technologies that have since become an integral part of our daily lives. In 1966, a crude form of email first came about.

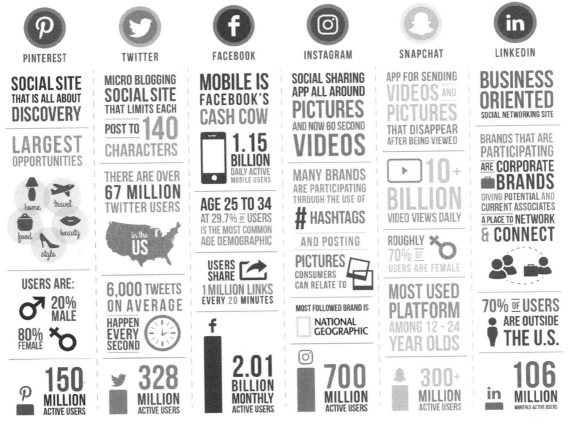

A breakdown of the most frequently used social media outlets highlighting the advantages of each platform and how they can be leveraged. *Source*: Leverage New Age Media https://leveragenewagemedia.com/blog/social-media-infographic/. Creative Commons License.

It was not the typical email as we understand it today. Early email was similar to a file directory. Users could place a message in another user's directory, where he or she would retrieve it upon logging into the system. The first email system of this type was MAILBOX, used by the Massachusetts Institute of Technology.[10] The Advanced Research Projects Agency Network (ARPANET), launched in 1969 along with CompuServe, served as the first major commercial online service in the United States.[11]

1970s

The year 1978 brought about two very important contributions to the history of social media. Multi-user Dungeon (MUD), created by Roy Trubshaw, is the first and oldest virtual community in existence.[12] Additionally, BBS, a computer system, was also introduced, allowing users to log in to a central location where they could connect with other users. Once logged in, users were able to exchange messages with others, upload or download software and data, read news, and even direct chat.[13]

1980s

In 1985, the WELL (Whole Earth 'Lectronic Link) was introduced; it is one of the oldest virtual communities that has been in continuous operation since its inception.[14] By 1988 Internet Relay Chat (IRC) was used for file sharing, link sharing, and keeping in touch.[15]

It was around this time that a real technological breakthrough was about to be introduced that would change how virtual communities formed and interacted going forward. Web 1.0 was initiated during the 1990s. This period of growth ushered in the introduction of the uniform resource locator (URL) and the basic search functions. Internet technologies became accessible to the public on a larger scale. Web 2.0 was the platform on which new, innovative applications could be built. The web became easier to navigate and offered a more dynamic user experience. The result was a generation of tech-savvy individuals who were able to navigate the ever-growing Internet. This initial foundation positioned technology where it is today.

1990s

The year 1997 marked the first introduction of what we now have come to understand as a social networking site. Coined SixDegrees, the site offered users the ability to create personal profiles, set up friend lists, and search friend lists belonging to other users within their networks. They could send messages to one another, affiliate themselves with networks, and invite family and friends to become members. This quickly became popular due to its level of interactivity.[16] In 2000, SixDegrees was purchased for $125 million. One year later it was shut down. These options may not seem impressive by today's standards; however, in 1997 no other site offered a combination of these features.[17] The concept was well ahead of its time. Additionally, LiveJournal was one of the Internet's most popular early blogging and online communities built around the use of personal journals. This community was started by Brad Fitzpatrick in April 1999.[18] During 1998 and 1999 other well-known social sites were introduced, including MoveOn, Asian Avenue, BlackPlanet, Napster, Third Voice, Epinions, and Blogger.[19]

2000s

The twenty-first century has generated many of the most popular social networking sites, many of which are still in use today. In the early 2000s some of the largest growth experienced by social networking sites occurred. In 2001 Wikipedia was first launched, 2002 brought about Friendster to the Internet, and in 2003 we were introduced to both Myspace and LinkedIn.[20] Myspace was the first social networking site to allow users to completely customize their pages and upload music and video. LinkedIn was the first social networking site dedicated to business users. Other popular social networking sites that came onto the scene in 2003 included last.fm, Photobucket, Second Life, and Delicious.[21] In 2004 Digg, a website wherein users share links and vote as to whether they "digg" the article or want to "bury" it, came into existence. Flickr popped onto the scene in 2004 as well, and now it boasts ninety-two million users who share approximately one million photos daily.[22] Ning, Orkut, mixi, Piczo, Hyves, Care2, Multiply, and Harvard Facebook were established in 2004. YouTube, the first massive video-sharing site, launched in 2005, along with high school Facebook, Bebo, Yahoo! 360, and Reddit. In 2006 Twitter and Facebook emerged and gained use and popularity quickly. Twitter's status sprang out of use at the South by Southwest (SXSW) conference.[23] Tweets increased from 20,000 per day to 60,000 per day. Today, more than 500 million tweets are sent daily. When Facebook originally launched, users signed up at an unprecedented rate. Currently Facebook is the most visited social networking site in the United States, with a user base that would independently rank as the third-largest country in the world.[24] In 2007 Tumblr and FriendFeed materialized. In 2008 we were introduced to Spotify,

Ping, Groupon, and Kontain, and in 2009 the ever-popular location-based social networking service Foursquare launched with great popularity. More recently, the photo-sharing site Instagram rose to mass appeal in 2010, along with Google Buzz and Pinterest. Continuing with this trend, in 2011 Google introduced Google+, and Pheed was unveiled in 2012, a unified platform whereby users can share photos and videos, text, create voice notes, and live broadcast. Finally, this brings us to 2013, in which Vine was launched by Twitter.[25] Vine was a mobile service that allows users to capture and share short looping videos. Similar to tweets, videos on Vine are brief, lasting six seconds or less.[26] Vine 2, or V2, is set to launch in late 2018.

Through this chronological history of the advancement of social media, encompassing both social networking sites and social media tools, we have seen brilliant developers, coders, gamers, idea generators, and early adopters. None of the technological achievements seen in the social media community would have been possible without forward-thinking pioneers who developed the principles, values, ideals, and standards behind the social media movement.

Stewart Brand, Howard Rheingold, Kevin Kelly, Esther Dyson, and John Perry Barlow were early visionaries of the Internet and the emerging digital world in which we live today.[27] Rick Levine, Christopher Locke, Doc Searls, and David Weinberger developed the first set standards for social media engagement that we have come to utilize today.

Let's meet these pioneers who made history by taking social media and making it an everyday occurrence, both personally and within a business environment.

Pioneers of Social Media

Stewart Brand
(1938–) (@longnow)

Writer Carole Cadwalladr characterized Stewart Brand as "the heart of 60s counterculture" and a widely revered "tech visionary whose book anticipated the web."[28] Brand published *The Whole Earth Catalog*, which was described by Steve Jobs as "Google only on paper" in his Stanford commencement address. The catalog contained information on everything from deerskin jackets to the latest technological advances, including ideas about cybernetics from Norbert Wiener.[29] *New York Times* writer John Markoff said the catalog was "the Internet before the Internet. It was the book of the future. It was a web in newsprint."[30]

Brand is credited with putting the two words "personal" and "computer" together, thus introducing the concept of owning your own *personal computer*

Thinking the *Whole Earth Catalog* legacy was coming to an end, Stewart Brand issued the *Last Whole Earth Catalog* in 1971. *Source*: Regina Luttrell.

to the world. He was a man before his time and "understood before almost anyone else . . . that cyberspace was some sort of fourth dimension and the possibilities were both empowering and limitless."[31] He helped shape the public's understanding of computing. This revelation led to many early Internet technologies, virtual communities, and ideals. He led the way in cofounding The WELL and later the Global Business Network, *CoEvolution Quarterly*, the Hackers Conference, and Long Now Foundation. All of these were based on the concept of a social presence among users.

Howard Rheingold (1947–) (@hrheingold)

At a time when the idea of an online community could not yet be rationalized and an emerging interest in the cultural and social implications of modern media was merely a thought, Howard Rheingold was building a foundation for these interactions. He was another pioneer who was ahead of his time. Described as a critic, writer, teacher, artist, designer, theorist, and community builder, Rheingold is "one of the driving minds behind our net-enabled, open, collaborative life-style today" and is considered a founding father of social media.[32]

Kevin Kelly (1952–) (@kevin2kelly)

For more than twenty years, innovator, writer, and technology guru Kevin Kelly has been viewed as one of the most significant information technology revolutionists of our time. As a member of Brand's original group of visionary technologists, Kelly acted as publisher and editor from 1984 to 1990 of the *Millennium Whole Earth Catalog*, where he authored articles on topics that leveraged power to individuals. He took an active role in helping to launch The WELL, and he cofounded the ongoing Hackers Conference.[33] In 1993 he launched *Wired* magazine and served as executive editor for six years, during which time the magazine was the recipient of the National Magazine Award for General Excellence twice.[34]

John Perry Barlow (October 3, 1947–February 7, 2018) (@JPBarlow)

Wired magazine contributor John Perry Barlow's manifesto, "A Declaration of the Independence of Cyberspace," could be considered his most influential early paper. In a response to the U.S. government's passing of the Telecommunications Act of 1996, Barlow wrote that the United States did not have the right to apply laws to the Internet because it was outside any country's borders. Barlow suggested that the Internet could develop its own social contracts to determine how to deal with its problems based on the Golden Rule: "Do unto others as you'd have done to you."[35] This was the first time in U.S. history that laws governing the Internet were enacted. Barlow founded the Electronic Frontier Foundation (EFF), an international nonprofit digital rights group protecting free speech, fair use, privacy, and international rights as they pertain to the Internet and addressing transparency problems that threaten digital freedoms.[36]

Esther Dyson (1951–) (@edyson)

One of the world's preeminent visionaries of the digital age, Esther Dyson has written about how the Internet affects an individual's life. She was the first individual to expand upon the notion of the "humanization" of the Internet and to introduce this concept to a wide audience. "Everything that happens on the Net will happen to human beings. . . . The Net is not going to push us into some antiseptic digital landscape."[37] Her predictions from 1998 have become today's reality. Social media allows for us to extend our emotional and intellectual selves through the use of social networking sites. We develop relationships, conduct business, share ideas, and even connect globally.[38]

The Forward-Thinking Four

Rick Levine (@ricklevine), Christopher Locke (@clockerb), Doc Searls (@dsearls), and David Weinberger (@dweinberger) teamed up to write *The Cluetrain Manifesto: The End of Business as Usual.* The book revolutionized concepts and perceptions of how business is conducted under the impact of the Internet. Through a series of ninety-five theses, they explain that businesses are fundamentally human: "Markets consist of human beings, not demographic sectors. Conversations among humans sound human. They are conducted in a human voice. Whether delivering information, opinions, perspectives, dissenting arguments or humorous asides, the human voice is typically open, natural, uncontrived."[39] The central message of the book is that the marketplace is a conversation and that the web gives people a voice. Locke, Levine, Searls, and Weinberger agree that too often conversations by individuals are ignored by large corporations because these corporations see the Internet as another vehicle to broadcast marketing messages. Consumers, employees, and stakeholders yearn for genuine dialogue on the Internet. For the first time, the ideals and basis of all interaction via social media was summarized in *Cluetrain*. The fundamentals of this new marketplace and how to converse effectively are illustrated through three simple decrees as outlined in the book:

- Be authentic to stakeholders: Talk like people and eliminate buzz words and overly technical terms.
- Have fun and laugh: People drive the Internet; they drive interactions, so be real with them and cultivate authentic conversations.
- Above all, listen: The marketplace is where conversations are happening. Without careful attention, businesses can miss out on important exchanges.

I had the opportunity to ask David Weinberger about the inspiration behind *Cluetrain*. He responded with the following:

> *Cluetrain* grew out of a set of conversations among the four of us about just how wrong the media and most businesses were about the Web. They were viewing the Web primarily as a business opportunity, whereas we thought it was obvious to the people on the Web that we were there because we finally got to talk about what mattered to us with the people we wanted to talk with, and to do so in our own voice. That is, the Web was and is social more than anything else.

Modern visionaries understand that "authenticity, honesty, and personal voice underlie much of what's successful on the Web."[40]

The forward-thinking four: Rick Levine, Christopher Locke, David "Doc" Searls, and David Weinberger. *Source*: Rick Levine, Creative Commons License.

Malcolm Gladwell (@gladwell)

Malcolm Gladwell is a researcher whose books and articles often discuss the unexpected implications of research in the social sciences. He has been a staff writer for *The New Yorker* since 1996 and has impacted social media with his books *The Tipping Point: How Little Things Can Make a Big Difference*; *Blink: The Power of Thinking Without Thinking*; *Outliers: The Story of Success*; *What the Dog Saw: And Other Adventures*, a collection of his journalism; and *David and Goliath: Underdogs, Misfits, and the Art of Battling Giants*.

Gini Dietrich (@ginidietrich)

Gini Dietrich, CEO of Arment Dietrich, reshaped PR planning through the development of the PESO model—paid media, earned media, shared media, and owned media. The PESO model combines an organization's social efforts to impact their audiences. According to Dietrich, "It's an integrated approach, so if a brand is successful in the other media types, it will be successful on social too. The PESO model creates an opportunity to become an authority on a subject, topic or industry. Social helps enhance that by providing the opportunity to network with prospects around the globe."[41] Today, practitioners employ all areas of paid, earned, shared, and owned when developing PR strategies and tactics.

Jonah Berger (@j1berger)

Jonah Berger is a marketing professor at the Wharton School at the University of Pennsylvania and author of *Contagious: Why Things Catch On* and *Invisible Influence: The Hidden Forces That Shape Behavior*. He has spent fifteen years studying how social influence works and how it drives products and ideas to catch on.

Global Perspectives

Social media can be viewed as a catalyst for global transformation. The world is changing before our eyes, day by day, minute by minute. With every change begins a metamorphosis. Philip Slater's *The Chrysalis Effect* outlines the process of change that the world is experiencing and compares these shifts to a caterpillar's metamorphosis into a butterfly.[42] Our global world, through social media, is in the midst of one of the largest transformations we have ever seen.

As a result, we are connecting with one another through social networking sites, online and virtual communities, chat rooms, instant messaging platforms, newsgroups, multiplayer games, wikis, blogs, microblogs, and video-sharing sites. People are establishing and maintaining social relationships and even organizing collective action. In recent years we have started to see a shift toward a global community that rallies the troops via social media to enact change. The Internet, cyberspace, and virtual and online communities are part of this global evolution. The "Internet has created a generation of people accustomed to finding their own answers, creating their own systems, forming their own new communities."[43] The impact that social networking sites have on society has only just begun to surface.

A year dominated by Brexit and the election of Donald Trump as President of the United States, 2016 may well be considered the year of pronounced democratic shifts occurring on both sides of the Atlantic. Not surprisingly, social media had major implications in the populist movements that supported these developments. Social media is increasingly becoming the primary source of information promoting political change both in the United States and abroad. On June 23, 2016, the

United Kingdom voted to leave the European Union. While traditional media, such as television and newspapers, were part of the information cycle, the liveliest debates happened online. By examining the hashtags #StrongerIn and #VoteLeave, both campaigns used Twitter, Facebook, and YouTube to communicate their messages. The authors of *Political Turbulence: How Social Media Shape Collective Action* stated that "there is no doubt that social media has brought change to politics. From the waves of protest and unrest in response to the 2008 financial crisis, to the Arab Spring of 2011, there has been a generalized feeling that political mobilization is on the rise, and that social media had something to do with it."[44]

When the Boko Haram organization abducted 276 schoolgirls in the northern Nigerian village of Chibok, the event not only outraged the Nigerian people but moved the world to act. While Nigerians demanded action at home, globally the social media community rallied around a call to #BringBackOurGirls. Even the First Lady of the United States, Michelle Obama, posted a photo to Facebook and Twitter of her holding a sign with the hashtag #BringBackOurGirls.[45] In less than three weeks, the hashtag was shared more than one million times by everyone from celebrities to common citizens.

During the 2016 Atlantic hurricane season, Hurricane Harvey stranded thousands of Texas residents, forcing them to seek help by posting on Facebook and Twitter. They tweeted their addresses to emergency officials, organized rescue missions through Facebook groups, and posted harrowing pictures to emphasize just how high the flood waters were.[46] A short time later, when Hurricane Irma pummeled Florida, people also turned to social media for various reasons. Some alerted worried relatives, while others found ways to volunteer, and medical providers reached those in need. Residents formed Facebook groups like Evacuees of the Keys whereby members shared school closure notices, videos of destruction, and many posts from friends and relatives searching for loved ones.[47]

These are only a few examples that illustrate just how important these new communication channels between communities have become. The acceptance of social media as a primary mode of communication is significant because it speaks to the extensive integration of social media into everyday communication. This phenomenon is even apparent from outer space—or, for you social media junkies, Google Earth—for all seven billion people who inhabit the earth share one planet. The convergence of the Internet allows us to become a single, global community by putting everyone online. Our ability to unite together universally has exploded. We work in partnership with people all over the world, from big cities to small villages, from startup companies to large corporations—everyone doing his or her part to enact change. Social media technologies offer a way to direct this massive interconnectivity of networks into real, sound solutions for a number of global concerns, including clean drinking water, improved sanitation, food production, public health, energy challenges,

The White House
Historical Place · 4,701,283 Likes · May 7, 2014 · Edited · 🌐

[f] Like Page ▾

It's time to #BringBackOurGirls.

Read about how the U.S. is helping Nigeria in the search for those who were kidnapped → http://go.wh.gov/MCNAK7

60,549 Likes · 7,473 Comments · 25,039 Shares

👍 Like   💬 Comment   ➤ Share

Former First Lady Michelle Obama tweeted a photo that shows her holding a sign reading, "#BringBackOurGirls," in reference to the missing Nigerian schoolgirls.

and nearly every other area of need. Whether we are trying to bring an end to racism, educate others on the hazards occurring to the environment, protect our children, or give selflessly amid devastation from an act of nature, the power of social media is greater than all of us. People connect, and technology facilitates these relationships.

Where Do We Go from Here?

From the humble beginning of a simple email to our robust bio-network of social platforms, social media has caused a revolution and altered modern PR. Today, organizations are beginning to understand that on the other side of the web, behind that personal computer, there are *real people*, and they can gain insights into the thoughts, views, and opinions of these people in real time simply by listening intently, engaging authentically, and having fun.

Theory into Practice

Operation 45

This chapter focused on the history of social media, the importance of understanding that humans are on the other side of the computer and a vital part of the social universe, and that when moved the social sphere will come together to mobilize. Whether mobilization takes place after hurricanes or monumental changes in the world, citizens act. Operation 45 was a result of the election of President Donald Trump.

The mission of Operation 45 (https://www.operationfortyfive.org/) is the aggressive pursuit of governmental transparency in the service of democracy. According to their website, Operation 45 is dedicated to ensuring transparency and accountability for the administration of Donald J. Trump, the 45th President of the United States.

Freedom of Information Act (FOIA) activist Ryan Shapiro and attorney Jeffrey Light head up Operation 45. Shapiro, who has been the loudest voice fighting for governmental transparency since both the Bush and Obama administrations, calls FOIA a "radical experiment in transparency," at least in theory. In practice, government agencies have become adept at deflecting or deferring FOIA requests, and it takes a special skill set to navigate these bureaucracies.[1]

Light, a specialist in FOIA litigation, and Shapiro had been doing their work part-time, but in the wake of Donald Trump's election, the duo decided that they needed to fortify their efforts. In an interview Shapiro noted that with Donald Trump's overt contempt for transparency, freedom of the press, and the Constitution itself, he and Light realized they needed to significantly expand their efforts.[2]

Thus, they founded Operation 45 to focus on these efforts full-time.

After reading and researching Operation 45, consider the following questions:

Identify how social media is being used to spread the message of Operation 45. Check out their social channels to evaluate their effectiveness:
- Twitter: @opfortyfive
- Hashtag: #whatshehiding
- Facebook: https://www.facebook.com/operationfortyfive/
- Crowdfund page: https://www.gofundme.com/operation-45

Of these social media channels, assess which are most effective and least effective; then discuss why.

In what ways is Operation 45 working for the American people?

Can Operation 45 be viewed as purely propaganda? Is it a campaign for social media reform? Justify and explain your response.

Does Operation 45 continue the same philosophy of what visionaries like John Perry Barlow, Malcolm Gladwell, Esther Dyson, or the writers of *The Cluetrain Manifesto* conceived as part of the social media revolution?

---

[1] J. Holland, "Your Guide to the Sprawling New Anti-Trump Resistance Movement," *The Nation*, March 9, 2017, accessed September 23, 2017, https://www.thenation.com/article/your-guide-to-the-sprawling-new-anti-trump-resistance-movement/.

[2] Holland, "Your Guide to the Sprawling New Anti-Trump Resistance Movement."

#LRNSMPR

Learn Social Media and Public Relations

Apply the principles learned in this chapter to the scenarios below.

- The chapter provides a history of social media and includes the Twitter handles of several key players. Find three of them on Twitter and discuss how they continue to play a role in the discussion and evolution of social media based on their tweets.

- "We are not seats or eyeballs or end users or consumers. We are human beings—and our reach exceeds your grasp. Deal with it." This passage comes from *The Cluetrain Manifesto*. What does it mean to you? Consider how it relates back to the original purpose of the social media, and where we are today. The full manifesto can be found here: http://www. cluetrain.com/passages.html.

- Beginning with President Bill Clinton, there was a broad "Hands off the net!" consensus. John Perry Barlow once said: "Governments of the Industrial World, you weary giants of flesh and steel, I come from Cyberspace, the new home of Mind. On behalf of the future, I ask you of the past to leave us alone. You are not welcome among us. You have no sovereignty where we gather." Under the Trump administration Federal Communications Commission Chairman Ajit Pai announced his plans to eliminate the clear, enforceable protections for net neutrality that the Commission had implemented in 2015. On December 14, 2017, the FCC voted to dismantle net neutrality. The following day former Attorney General Eric Schneiderman from New York State vowed to sue and stop the FCC's rollback. Consider the implications for everyday citizens and for businesses alike.

Notes

1 Merriam-Webster, *Merriam-Webster's Collegiate Dictionary,* 11th ed., 2013.

2 L. Safko, *The Social Media Bible: Tactics, Tools and Strategies for Business Success* (New York: Wiley, 2010); J. Wood, *Interpersonal Communication: Everyday Encounters,* 7th ed. (Boston: Wadsworth Cengage Learning, 2013).

3 Merriam-Webster, *Merriam-Webster's Collegiate Dictionary.*

4 Safko, *The Social Media Bible.*

5 D. Boyd and N. Ellison, "Social Network Sites: Definition, History, and Scholarship," *Journal of Computer-Mediated Communication,* no. 13 (2008): 210–30, doi:10.1111/j.1083-6101.2007.00393.x; J. Scott and P. Carrington, *The SAGE Handbook of Social Network Analysis* (Thousand Oaks, CA: Sage, 2011).

6 S. Greenwood et al., *Social Media Update 2016* (Washington: Pew Research Center, 2016), http:// www.pewinternet.org/2016/11/11/social-media-update-2016/.

7 Iran Chamber Society, "History of Iran: Cyrus the Great," accessed May 30, 2013, http://www. iranchamber.com/history/cyrus/cyrus.php; D. Mink, "The Complete History of Social Media," Avalaunch Media, April 15, 2013, accessed May 31, 2013, http://avalaunchmedia.com/infographics/ the-complete-history-of-social-media.

8 R. Beyer, *The Greatest Stories Never Told: 100 Tales from History to Astonish, Bewilder, and Stupefy* (New York: HarperCollins, 2003).

9 M. Bellis, "The Invention of Radio," About.com, last modified 2013, accessed May 30, 2013, http:// inventors.about.com/od/rstartinventions/a/radio.htm; M. Bellis, "The History of the Telephone," About.com, last modified 2013, accessed May 30, 2013, http://inventors.about.com/od/bstartin-ventors/a/telephone.htm.

10 I. Peter, "The History of Email," NetHistory, last modified 2004, accessed May 30, 2013, http:// www.nethistory.info/History of the Internet/email.html.

11 E. Qualman, "Social Media Video 2013 | Did You Know 2013," YouTube, 2012, accessed April 22, 2016, https://www.youtube.com/watch?v=PB99MjUz7YQ.

12 K. Kelly and H. Rheingold, "The Dragon Ate My Homework," *Wired* 1(3).

13 M. Sippey, "Vine: A New Way to Share Video," Official Twitter Blog, January 24, 2013, accessed May 31, 2013, https://blog.twitter.com/2013/vine-new-way-share-video.

14 H. Rheingold, "Howard Rheingold's Story," Rheingold.com, last modified 2012, accessed June 3, 2013, http://www.rheingold.com/howard.

15 M. Lucas et al., "Defining a Firewall," in *Firewall Policies and VPN Configurations,* ed. Anne Henmi (Rockland, MA: Syngress Publishing, 2006).

16 Wood, *Interpersonal Communication.*

17 Qualman, "Social Media Video 2013"; L. Prall, "Sixdegrees.com—Social Networking in Its Infancy," Afridesignad, September 15, 2010, accessed May 31, 2013, http://blog.afridesign.com/2010/09/sixdegrees-com-social-networking-in-its-infancy.

18 "Our Heritage," LiveJournal, last modified 2012, accessed May 30, 2013, http://www.livejournalinc.com/aboutus.php.

19 Qualman, "Social Media Video 2013."

20 Qualman, "Social Media Video 2013."

21 Qualman, "Social Media Video 2013."

22 D. Etherington, "Flickr at 10: 1M Photos Shared per Day, 170% Increase since Making 1TB Free," TechCrunch, 2014, http://techcrunch.com/2014/02/10/flickr-at-10-1m-photos-shared-per-day-170-increase-since-making-1tb-free.

23 Qualman, "Social Media Video 2013."

24 J. Bullas, "33 Social Media Facts and Statistics You Should Know in 2015," Jeffbullas.com, April 7, 2015, accessed October 5, 2015, http://www.jeffbullas.com/2015/04/08/33-social-media-facts-and-statistics-you-should-know-in-2015.

25 Qualman, "Social Media Video 2013."

26 Sippey, "Vine."

27 F. Turner, *From Counterculture to Cyberculture: Stewart Brand, the Whole Earth Network, and the Rise of Digital Utopianism* (Chicago: University of Chicago Press, 2006).

28 C. Cadwalladr, "Stewart Brand's Whole Earth Catalog, the Book That Changed the World," *Guardian,* last modified May 4, 2013, accessed June 4, 2013, http://www.guardian.co.uk/books/2013/may/05/stewart-brand-whole-earth-catalog.

29 Prall, "Sixdegrees.com—Social Networking in Its Infancy."

30 "Our Heritage."

31 "Our Heritage."

32 "Howard Rheingold: Digital Community Builder," TED: Ideas Worth Spreading, accessed June 3, 2013, https://www.ted.com/speakers/howard_rheingold.html.

33 K. Kelly, "Biography," KK*, accessed June 4, 2013, http://www.kk.org/biography.php.

34 Cadwalladr, "Stewart Brand's Whole Earth Catalog."

35 J. P. Barlow, "A Declaration of the Independence of Cyberspace," Electronic Frontier Foundation, last modified 1996, accessed June 4, 2013, https://projects.eff.org/~barlow/Declaration-Final.html; "Media," Business Dictionary, accessed May 23, 2013, http://www.businessdictionary.com/definition/media.html.

36 Barlow, "A Declaration of the Independence of Cyberspace."

37 "Esther Dyson," Edge, accessed June 4, 2013, http://www.edge.org/memberbio/esther_dyson; "EFF in the News," Electronic Frontier Foundation, last modified 2013, accessed June 4, 2013, https://www.eff.org/press/mentions.

38 Kelly, "Biography."

39 R. Levine et al., *The Cluetrain Manifesto: The End of Business as Usual* (New York: Basic Books, 2009).

40 R. Luttrell, "Reflections on What Technology Wants" (manuscript, California Institute of Integral Studies, 2010).

41 K. Gaab, "Social's Place in the PESO Model: Q&A With Gini Dietrich," Cision, August 8, 2017, accessed September 22, 2017, http://www.cision.com/us/2016/07/socials-place-in-the-peso-model-qa-with-gini-dietrich/.

42 P. Slater, *The Chrysalis Effect: The Metamorphosis of Global Culture* (Eastbourne, UK: Sussex Academic Press, 2009).

43 Barlow, "A Declaration of the Independence of Cyberspace."

44 H. Margetts et al., *Political Turbulence: How Social Media Shape Collective Action* (Princeton, NJ: Princeton University Press, 2016).

45 B. Reis, "Michelle Obama: It's Time to Bring Back Our Girls," Mashable, May 7, 2014.

46 B. Stelter, "How Social Media Is Helping Houston Deal with Harvey Floods," CNNMoney, August 28, 2017, accessed September 22, 2017, http://money.cnn.com/2017/08/28/media/harvey-rescues-social-media-facebook-twitter/index.html.

47 M. Mendoza, "Social Media Gets the Word Out during Irma Emergency," ABC News, September 12, 2017, accessed September 22, 2017, http://abcnews.go.com/Technology/wireStory/social-media-word-irma-emergency-49785921.

Status 3
"It's Complicated"

The relationships between public relations (PR), marketing, and advertising have changed dramatically over the past several years and have become increasingly complicated as the fields converge. This chapter examines the present-day PR industry, focusing on the relationship between PR and social media, as well as on how social media operates with advertising and marketing departments.

KEY LEARNING OUTCOMES

1. Analyze the role of PR in social media.
2. Distinguish PR and social media from marketing and advertising.
3. Determine how PR, marketing, advertising, and social media can be integrated.

SOCIAL MEDIA EXPERT

Brian Solis (@MrSolis, website: http://www.briansolis.com/)

Brian Solis, a principal partner at Altimeter and a digital analyst, anthropologist, and futurist, studies and influences the effects of emerging technology on business and society. He developed the Conversation Prism, four concentric circles representing an ongoing exploration in digital ethnography providing a unique snapshot in time of the social landscape. "Each of the concentric circles are designed to work together, to help you improve strategies and results to improve the way you work, how you build relationships with employees and customers, the ability to create and improve better products, services and experiences, and overall, the role you play and the stature you earn as a result."[1]

---

[1] B. Solis, "YOU Are at the Center of the Conversation Prism," Brian Solis, July 16, 2013, accessed September 29, 2017, http://www.briansolis.com/2013/07/you-are-at-the-center-of-the-conversation-prism/.

The Field of Public Relations Today

Over the past several years, the field of PR experienced its most dramatic paradigm shift to date. Mainstream Internet acceptance ushered in virtual communities and, with that, the vision of a global village and unprecedented expectations for PR practitioners to service a new, global audience.[1] As we now know, PR practitioners in today's digital environment possess a multitude of skills.

The mounting convergence of traditional media platforms, in conjunction with new media technologies, has created a rich mixed-media environment, promoting communication and even collaboration with an audience through the web.[2]

As professionals, we cannot deny that this emerging and evolving form of communication and promotion is advantageous for professional communicators as well as the consumers we serve.

The roles and relationships between PR, social media, advertising, and marketing are evolving.

The Courtship of Social Media

The field of PR and the idea of fostering meaningful relationships with stakeholders are synonymous. In fact, the Public Relations Society of America (PRSA) defines PR as the following: "Public relations is a strategic communication process that builds mutually beneficial relationships between organizations and their publics."[3] Social media is built upon the premise of creating authentic relationships. It is not coincidental that the two disciplines integrate so well and are harmonious in nature.

> *"We are not seats or eyeballs or end users or consumers. We are human beings—and our reach exceeds your grasp. Deal with it.*
> The Cluetrain Manifesto

We need to work to better understand why companies fail at social media. There are various reasons for this, but one major contributor to such failure focuses on when an organization attempts to mock or rush the process of developing relationships. Too often the offenders are the advertising and marketing departments. The primary function of advertising is to sell goods and services, while the goal of marketing is to achieve the organizational economic objectives using promotion, sales, and the distribution of products or services.[4] It should be clear that neither of these disciplines is independently designed to foster authentic relationships with customers.

Imagine for a minute that it is your first day at a new job. You have been shown to your office, completed the initial "walk-around," and been introduced to your coworkers. You have even attended the Monday Mojo meeting, and now it is lunchtime. One of your new coworkers, Avery, invites you to join her and others from your department to go off-site for lunch. It is close to the Fourth of July holiday, and everyone is talking about their plans for the long weekend. Avery begins to talk about the barbeque that she is hosting with family and friends at her home. Suddenly you speak up and say, "That sounds like a great time, Avery. Do you mind if my family and I come too? I'm happy to bring a side dish."

Placing etiquette aside, can you identify what is wrong with what you just said?

Everything! To begin with, you just met Avery earlier in the morning. It might even be a stretch to say that you have known Avery for more than four hours, and yet you just invited yourself to her holiday picnic. Socially speaking, this would be considered unacceptable. You have not yet had the time to develop any kind of relationship or gained enough trust with her to attend her barbeque. Additionally, Avery has not invited you (or your family, for that matter) to her family function.

This example parallels the same type of mistakes that companies make by rolling out poorly thought-out social strategies. It is easy to identify why their social media campaigns fail miserably. The organization is essentially barging in on someone's picnic and inviting its family to the table when nobody has even thought of including them.

Users of social media *invite* you into their lives once they feel they have been courted. When an organization wishes to connect with its customer base, it should consider the connection as a personal invitation into everyone's life. Remember, your customers are human beings. Their reach is greater than your grasp. Listening and conversing over time is how meaningful relationships are built and trust is earned.

It's All about "Me, Me, Me" in This Relationship

Listening does not mean talking about you all the time. Companies must abandon the "me, me, me" and "I, I, I" philosophy of chatter for a more balanced "you-we" approach. Too often a company will create an account on a social media platform to broadcast information about itself and any relevant achievements. There are countless feeds on social networking sites related to new hires, products or services, employee promotions, and long, drawn-out bios on the C-suite executives. This type of information equates to being on a date with a person who is guilty of never listening and continually boasts about his or her life and accomplishments. We would all do well to learn a lesson from Red Bull. This company consistently connects with its stakeholders in unique ways. With a networking community of more than thirty-five million followers across all of its dedicated social channels, its integrated approach makes it more than an energy drink company; it makes it one of the most comprehensive and flexible media companies in the world today.[5]

In taking steps toward becoming increasingly successful on a social level, organizations must break the habit of self-promotion. Although this sounds simple, this task can be quite difficult to correctly execute. This is due, in part, to the fact that many executives are eager to promote all the great successes happening within the company. Naturally, these same executives view the company's social networking platforms as the place to announce such content to its customer base. This is only partially the case. Company social networking sites are established to engage with consumers, not bombard them with how great the company is. If your consumers have followed your business on Twitter, shared a photo on Instagram embracing your brand, or commented on your blog, they already know how great the company is. It is your job to keep them there by contributing to meaningful conversations. It is the job of the PR professional and social strategist to understand the role that social media plays and to educate executives about how to engage with consumers using social sites. PR has traditionally been considered a function of management, with practitioners advising on strategies and coaching in tactics. This perception should also be applied to social media.

Mindful Listening in Social Media

Within the social media arena, the basic principles of interpersonal communication are a necessity. As humans, we "communicate to develop identities, establish and build relationships, coordinate efforts with others, have impact on issues that matter to us, and work out problems and possibilities."[6] Scholar Elizabeth Toth noted that interpersonal communication is the foundation for analyzing organization-public relationships.[7] This means that conversing, engaging, and developing online relationships with consumers using organizational social media channels can influence how the organization connects and build relationships with its intended audience.

Organizations should apply the Pareto Principle to the operational components of their social media campaigns. This can be achieved by posting audience relevant content at least 80 percent of the time with the remaining 20 percent specific to the company or its products. *Source:* Regina Luttrell.

The concept of listening to stakeholders has been deeply rooted within the PR industry for years.[8] By practicing mindful listening, PR practitioners build formidable relationships with external stakeholders. To be successful today, we need to continue to listen to these stakeholders for a variety of reasons, all the while mastering the many available assorted tools to collect distinct information.

Social Media Drives Engagement

Organizations cannot have social media without social listening. Companies benefit by seeing real-time insights from consumers because they establish a window into their thoughts, views, feelings, and reactions regarding a given brand. Gathering these unaltered opinions that transpire via social networking sites would have been nearly impossible prior to the mainstreaming of social media. Because consumers feel comfortable enough to praise or prosecute brands on social networking sites, their opinions can be interpreted as pure. Contributing to the conversation is how a company becomes part of its community. The moment a company embarks on a social strategy, it is no longer a logo or a tagline or a nebulous presence—it has become human. Users of social media expect genuine, authentic connections; therefore, the responsibility shifts to the brand to deliver.

Social media strategies should not be implemented in seclusion. Social media must be ingrained throughout an organization on every level and deep within every department. It makes sense that the marketing and advertising departments need to be part of the social media and PR planning process.

Can't We All Just Get Along? Integrating Public Relations, Social Media, Marketing, and Advertising

Companies are investing time, money, and energy in their social media strategies and are beginning to see the value—therefore, everyone wants to "own" the strategy. The marketing team believes it should lead the strategy, while advertising considers itself the appropriate proprietor. Neither is correct. The Chartered Institute of Marketing defines marketing as "the management process that seeks to maximize returns to shareholders by developing relationships with valued customers and creating a competitive advantage,"[9] while advertising is defined as "the action of calling something to the attention of the public especially by paid announcements."[10] Neither of these definitions incorporates people or relationships.

The underlying principle of social media is all about the participants, while the fundamental purpose of PR is to build relationships. Adam Snyder, senior vice president of digital strategy at PR and marketing agency Ketchum, said that "PR is about showing, not selling; influencing, not promoting; and earning, not buying. PR professionals have been engaged in pure social media since before the term was coined and should naturally be leading social effort."[11]

Because of the inherent connection that PR and social media share, it makes sense for PR departments to lead the social strategy. We, as PR professionals, are the ones developing the relationships with the consumer base. Years ago, I said that social media could be a department unto itself, working harmoniously with PR, marketing, *and* advertising. Progressive organizations have already begun creating social media departments. Some organizations are not quite there yet. The PR department should drive social media strategies, aligning synergies between the three.

Distinct differences between PR, social media, marketing, and advertising have also been defined. The need to integrate and send a single, clear message using various channels is evident. The 1990s gave rise to terms like "integrated marketing communications," "convergent communications," and "integrated communications."[12] More recently, we have seen integrated marketing PR, which includes social media strategies and tactics.[13] The idea of integration creates a consistent message. Success can be seen when each function recognizes that they complement one another. Each discipline has strengths, and together these strengths supplement and reinforce a comprehensive strategic plan.[14] Choosing the best attributes from each function based on its strengths and weaknesses will result in a synergy throughout the campaign. When the individual pieces work together, the whole becomes greater than the parts. Chapter 4 delves into PR and social media planning models that will tie together the ideas presented here.

Market without Selling and Still Be Profitable

By introducing integrated efforts, a brand can successfully build an online presence that can resonate with the intended consumers. However, this can be tricky to execute, since the social web is made up of people, and a very large group at that, many of whom don't want to be sold to. Companies can use social media marketing strategies or content marketing to help strike a balance between the human social networks, while also remembering that they are running businesses intended to be profitable. Social media strategic and content marketing are two successful methods being used today.

When a social media strategy is being implemented, the individual campaigns are managed directly within the social networking sites. Whether Twitter, Pinterest, Snapchat, Facebook, or another social networking site is right for a given consumer base, these sites produce content about the brand and execute the campaigns there.[15] Content marketing occurs directly on a brand website or a microsite created by the company itself.[16] These strategies can be implemented simultaneously; however, the outcomes of the campaigns can be quite different based on the specific goals and objectives. The key principle within both strategies is not to sell.

Nielsen's most recent *Social Media Report* reveals that

> thirty-nine percent of heavy social users believe that finding out about products and services is an important reason for using a social network. Companies should take heed and make it easy for potential brand advocates to find information about their products and services—preferably in the form of unbiased customer reviews. Most importantly, the findings highlighted that brands need to make it easy for potential advocates to show their support. Twenty-nine percent of heavy users actually consider supporting their favorite companies or brands somewhat to very important—so they need content that's easy to find and easy to share on Facebook and Twitter.[17]

To drive sales, businesses tend to hire spokespeople or feature their products and services on their websites or social networking sites. This type of old-school, outdated advertising-marketing mix does not resonate with the social user.[18] Products and services come secondary to sharing information, connecting with your online community, and telling your story through honest interactions with consumers. Creating content that is not about your brand but rather relates to topics your audience is interested in is the quintessential idea inherent in the clear majority of successful social media marketing and content marketing campaigns. Social media

Taco Bell's Snapchat lens garnered more than 200 million views in a single day. This campaign illustrates how successful a social strategy can be when enacted appropriately.

marketing strategies give you the opportunity to "genuinely connect with people in ways and in places where their attention is focused and impressionable, using a human voice."[19]

What do Taco Bell and Airbnb have in common? Their most recent campaigns made an impact both offline and online for marketing without selling their products. People love to feel like they are a part of something. Whatever tactics an organization decides to implement, whether it is Facebook Live, a dedicated hashtag campaign, or an experience, they should begin a conversation around the brand so that people are inspired to share within their social sphere. Jose Angelo Gallegos from Tintup runs down why these campaigns are so effective[20]:

Taco Bell Cinco de Mayo Snapchat Filter

Enabling Snapchat users to experience their own Cinco de Mayo fantasy, Taco Bell rolled out a Snapchat filter allowing fans to literally become their own taco.[21]

Incorporating Snapchat within its social sphere has never been a problem for the fast food giant. Taco Bell has successfully leveraged the channel for many years, notably introducing its Quesalupa during a Super Bowl campaign. For this campaign the company looked to a set of on-demand geofilters, enabling their vision of bringing the taco to life for its consumer base. Even though the campaign was live for one day only—Cinco de Mayo—the snapchat filter became the most viewed Snapchat lens ever. The filter produced 12.5 years' value of play in a single day.[22] Taco Bell successfully shattered a Snapchat record. Ryan Rimsnider, the senior manager of social strategy for the brand, is quoted as saying that "the foodilicious lens took six weeks to create, with his team working directly alongside Snapchat to perfect the taco-head look. In addition to some paid advertising, most of the magic happened in the app. The lens was viewed more than 224 million times in one day, with Taco Bell dishing out $750,000 for the pleasure—at a cost of just 0.3 cents per view."[23]

Commemorating the launch of Experiences to accompany a new service called Trips, Airbnb invited customers from around the globe to participate in a 24-hour Facebook Live feed dubbed We Are Here.

We Are Here—Airbnb

To create a destination of wonder, free from busy streets, overflowing inboxes, and the pressure of life, in November 2017 Airbnb launched a new app that gave access to homes, exotic places, and thrilling experiences waiting to be photographed and enjoyed.[24]

The campaign's focus centered around one question: How do you launch a product centered around the power of human connection?[25] The campaign created six separate films, across six cities, five continents, over twenty-four hours. By using Facebook Live, Airbnb streamed each film so the audience could enjoy the same experience. Each time the audience engaged through comments, those comments were incorporated into the experience.

> For example, a performance artist named Anne hosted an Airbnb Experience in Paris. She brought her guests to the square outside the Moulin Rouge, where they wrote down their hopes and fears on biodegradable paper butterflies, to be released above a metro grate and into the night sky. As Anne asked her on-screen guests what they would write down, the world naturally joined in via comments on the Live stream. Butterflies serendipitously began to appear on the on-screen table, with the comments and names from the global audience. So, when Anne and her guests released their hopes and fears into the sky, the audience at home also watched their butterflies float away over Paris in real time.[26]

In the first twenty-four hours, more than six million participants joined in on the experiences globally. This caused brand favorability to rise by 7 points, and ad recall increased by 22 points.

In these examples, none of the parent companies directly sells its products using these platforms. You do not see blatant product pitches, demonstrations, or spokespeople spewing claims. However, what you do see are brands establishing themselves as trusted, friendly resources that are available and accessible via a variety of avenues.

Why "Or"? Why Not "And"?

The lines of responsibility in the PR, marketing, and advertising departments across the country have most certainly blurred over the last decade. Social media has thrown a wrench into the neatly assembled silos that the communications industry had developed over time. Research has shown us that in addition to traditional PR activities, PR departments oversee blogging, podcast recording, video creation, social networking site management, mobile marketing, and website development, while marketing departments tend to supervise direct mail marketing, email marketing, advertising efforts, and SEO optimization.[27]

James Collins and Jerry Porras, authors of *Built to Last: Successful Habits of Visionary Companies*, proposed that rather than using an either/or philosophy, companies should adopt a both/and approach: "A truly visionary company embraces both ends of a continuum: continuity *and* change, conservatism *and* progressiveness, stability *and* revolution, predictability *and* chaos, heritage *and* renewal, fundamentals *and* craziness. *And, and, and.*"[28]

Using the logic behind Collins and Porras's philosophy, a company may ask itself, Why not have both the PR department and the marketing department blog? Each department has a great deal of knowledge to share with the social community. Why must a company choose either the PR department or the marketing department? They simply do not have to, and that is the point. Sharing resources, coordinating efforts, and offering a consistent and effective message can result in a smoother, more highly integrated effort spanning multiple departments.

I cannot claim that these departments will instantly embrace the ideas presented here, nor assert a synchronized effort all the time. But I can say that PR, social media, marketing, and advertising have begun to see the benefits of working together on a single message to achieve corporate objectives.

#InsuranceNerdDay: Pioneer State Mutual Takes on the Boring Insurance Stigma

Pioneer State Mutual, a small business out of Michigan, learned that a little bit of creativity combined with a strategic integrated campaign can yield great results.

Think about working in insurance for a moment. What word comes to mind? "Boring" is a word that Millennials in a 2016 study used to describe the industry.[1] This perception of insurance is, unfortunately, common among more than just the Millennial generation. However, insurance professionals tend to disagree with the stigma that has been attached to insurance and are proud to work in the industry.[2] This disconnect in perception creates a problem because the insurance industry is currently facing an industry-wide career crisis. By 2020 the industry will have 400,000 positions to fill because of the rapid increase of baby boomer retirements.[3] The industry is now tasked with changing the perception of insurance careers to match reality.

The industry has begun to respond to the career crisis in several ways. Some companies have chosen to beef up their internship programs, while others have started to become more involved in high school and college career fairs and speaking engagements. A movement called Insurance Careers Month was designed to call on Millennial insurance professionals to talk to their peers about the exciting opportunities in the insurance industry.[4] These measures being taken are important and are making an impact on the perpetuation of the industry, but none of them specifically addresses the boring stigma attached to insurance. This is when the social media team at Pioneer State Mutual Insurance Company (PSM) of Michigan took matters into their own hands. The PSM social media team created Insurance Nerd Day on July 18 to celebrate the passionate employees in the industry and to break the boring stigma attached to insurance.

Research/Diagnosis

The PSM social media team researched the insurance career crisis and determined that the boring stigma attached to insurance needed to be specifically addressed in a manner that spoke

directly to potential insurance employees. The PSM team saw success in its first Insurance Nerd Day on July 18, 2016, and challenged themselves to make Insurance Nerd Day 2017 even more successful.

Objectives

With the impending career crisis, the objective of Insurance Nerd Day was to double the awareness of the opportunities in the insurance industry via the Insurance Nerd Day campaign and hashtag from July 18, 2016, to July 18, 2017, from a reach of approximately 5,500 to 11,000.

Strategy

Unlike other strategies in the industry, the PSM social media team chose to focus on humor as a key component in the campaign. The name Insurance Nerd Day was selected in part because industry professionals who are passionate about the work that they do are often referred to as "insurance nerds." By using a common industry term, the PSM team was able to identify with industry professionals and increase participation. Increased participation would, in theory, lead to increased campaign popularity. The PSM team also asked participants to share why they love the insurance industry and why they would encourage others to consider a career in the industry.

Tactics

Using social media and digital marketing as the primary tool for Insurance Nerd Day, the PSM team utilized Facebook, Instagram, LinkedIn, Twitter, email, mail, and word-of-mouth advertising to promote the day.

Paid Media: The PSM team created twenty media kits to be sent out to their top social media influencers. The kit included a bow tie, nerd glasses, and a personalized note thanking them for their support and encouraging their participation in the day, along with an explanation of Insurance Nerd Day. On July 18, 2017, the PSM team posted photos and videos on social media, paying to boost the post on Facebook and Instagram. At the time PSM was not investing advertising dollars toward LinkedIn or Twitter.

Earned Media: The Insurance Nerd Day campaign earned more than 224,000 impressions across all four social media channels with participants from all over the insurance industry including much larger competitors in the industry and around the world.

Shared Media: To help spread the word about Insurance Nerd Day, the PSM social media team created the corresponding hashtag #InsuranceNerdDay and leveraged the hashtag without the use of advertising dollars on Twitter. In addition to the hashtag, the PSM team sent out emails to their network of independent insurance agents and industry partners to build up momentum before Insurance Nerd Day and encourage their participation. Several independent agencies and individuals around the industry participated by dressing up as an insurance nerd and sharing their insurance career story with their audiences. The PSM team also partnered with worldwideweirdholidays.com to create a profile explaining what an insurance nerd is and why the day was created.[5]

Owned Media: The PSM team created an album of photos of their own employees dressed as insurance nerds. The theme of the album was "mock elections," and the goal was to create a yearbook. This process involved photographing employees ahead of time, teaming up with the PSM

graphic design team, and creating the yearbook. The PSM team also worked with Human Resources to encourage employee engagement on Insurance Nerd Day by offering a free lunch for anyone who participated by dressing up. Employees were encouraged to share their stories and photos on social media to promote the industry.

Implementation—Timeline from Research to Execution

The implementation process spanned three months of planning, including brainstorming meetings, creation of promotional tools including social media posts and media kits, and emailing and sharing by word of mouth. The insurance industry was shown in a vastly different light and received positive feedback from non-industry members.

Reporting

PSM saw an immediate reach of ~850 before boosting the posts. After boosting the posts, the team saw even more results and outperformed the year before. The PSM team received positive feedback from both industry and non-industry members, across social media channels and around the world.[6] The total estimated reach for the campaign was 224,000, compared to roughly 5,500 in 2016. In 2016 Insurance Nerd Day was only promoted on Facebook and LinkedIn and was not backed by as many followers or advertising dollars. In 2017 the increase in awareness came with more preparation, money, and communication. The total amount spent for the day, including all promotional materials, advertisements, and lunch at PSM, was approximately six hundred dollars. Now that there is increased awareness of Insurance Nerd Day, the PSM team anticipates the results for 2018 to be even greater.

[1] C. Bronson, "Hiring Millennials in Insurance Shouldn't Be This Hard, New Survey Data Says," Insurance Business America, September 6, 2016, accessed August 21, 2017, http://www.insurancebusinessmag.com/us/news/breaking-news/hiring-millennials-in-insurance-shouldnt-be-this-hard-new-survey-data-says-37397.aspx.

[2] Insurance Journal, "Insurance Careers Month Asks Young Insurance Professionals to 'Spread the Word,'" February 1, 2017, accessed August 21, 2017, http://www.insurancejournal.com/news/national/2017/02/01/440547.htm.

[3] M. E. Ruquet, "Insurance Industry Crisis: 400,000 Positions to Fill by 2020," Property Casualty 360, April 17, 2013, accessed August 21, 2017, http://www.propertycasualty360.com/2013/04/17/insurance-industry-crisis-400000-positions-to-fill.

[4] Insurance Journal, "Insurance Careers Month Asks Young Insurance Professionals to 'Spread the Word.'"

[5] Worldwide Weird Holidays, "July 18 Is Insurance Nerd Day," July 17, 2017, accessed August 21, 2017, http://www.worldwideweirdholidays.com/insurance-nerd-day/.

[6] Twitter, "#InsuranceNerdDay," July 18, 2017, accessed September 25, 2017, https://twitter.com/search?q=%23insurancenerdday&src=typd.

#LRNSMPR

Learn Social Media and Public Relations

Apply the principles learned in this chapter to the scenarios below.

- In the article "Is Integrated Communications the Holy Grail or Just Cheap Talk?" Diane Schwartz likens working with colleagues from PR, marketing, and advertising departments to sharing your toys in the sandbox as a child. She laments that a common refrain among PR professionals is that "everything is integrated now"—PR and marketing go hand in hand. She questions whether or not that is really happening. Read her article; then discuss if you agree or disagree with her message. http://bit.ly/2fxRlDd
- Rhino Foods (http://www.rhinofoods.com/), a small organization with less than 140 employees out of Burlington, Vermont, is looking to develop a strategic PR and social media campaign in conjunction with their marketing and advertising efforts. Imagine that you are hired

to develop their strategic plan. Do some brainstorming and come up with a strategic plan. What ideas and activities would you suggest? How can you incorporate their company philosophy and core values into your campaign? Be creative, because they are working with a small budget.

Company History: One of Forbes's List of 28 Small Giants, the company opened its doors almost forty years ago.

In 1981, University of Vermont assistant hockey coach Ted Castle and his wife, Anne, opened a small ice cream shop, where he worked evenings and weekends. Three years later, he quit coaching and added brownies and cookies, supplying dough to fellow Vermont business Ben & Jerry's, where a staffer tried mixing Castle's raw cookie dough into ice cream. The blockbuster flavor turned Rhino Foods into a leading producer of frozen dough and other dessert products. Ice cream is a seasonal business, but instead of laying off workers in the winter, Castle developed a program to loan them to other seasonal businesses like Lake Champlain Chocolates. As Rhino grew, Castle paid above Vermont's $10-an-hour minimum wage, offered performance-based bonuses and persuaded a local credit union to make same-day loans of up to $1,000 to Rhino employees. To help the 30% of his staff that comes from Burlington's refugee community, Castle offers on-site classes in English as a second language.[1]

---

[1] B. Burlingham, "Forbes Small Giants 2017: America's Best Small Companies," *Forbes*, May 11, 2017, accessed September 29, 2017, https://www.forbes.com/sites/boburlingham/2017/05/09/forbes-small-giants-2017-americas-best-small-companies/#348508b74c32.

Notes

[1] H. Rheingold, *Smart Mobs: The Next Social Revolution* (Cambridge, MA: Basic Books, 2002); S. Fitzgerald and N. Spagnolia, "Four Predictions for PR Practitioners in the New Millennium," *Public Relations Quarterly*, no. 3 (1999): 12–14.

[2] J. Pavlik, "Mapping the Consequences of Technology on Public Relations," *Institute of Public Relations* (2009): 2–17; C. A. Platt, "Writing in Public: Pedagogical Uses of Blogging in the Communication Course," *Electronic Journal of Communication*, no. 1 (2010): 1–16.

[3] Public Relations Society of America, "What Is Public Relations? PRSA's Widely Accepted Definition," Public Relations Society of America, last modified April 11, 2012, accessed June 19, 2013, http://www.prsa.org/AboutPRSA/PublicRelationsDefined.

[4] D. Wilcox et al., *THINK Public Relations* (Upper Saddle River, NJ: Pearson Education, 2013).

[5] Red Bull Media House, "Social Media," accessed September 28, 2017, https://www.redbullmediahouse.com/products-brands/online/social-media.html.

[6] J. Wood, *Interpersonal Communication: Everyday Encounters*, 7th ed. (Boston: Wadsworth Cengage Learning, 2013).

[7] E. L. Toth, "Models for Instruction and Curriculum," *Public Relations Review* 25, no. 1 (1999): 45–53, doi:10.1016/s0363-8111(99)80126-x.

[8] Wilcox et al., *THINK Public Relations*; F. Seitel, *The Practice of Public Relations* (Upper Saddle River, NJ: Pearson Education, 2014).

[9] S. J. Paliwoda and J. K. Ryans, "Back to First Principles," in *International Marketing: Modern and Classic Papers*, 1st ed., ed. S. J. Paliwoda and J. K. Ryans (Cheltenham, UK: Edward Elgar Publishing, 2008), 25.

[10] E. Stanford, *Advertising* (San Diego: Greenhaven Press, 2007).

[11] A. Snyder, "Why Social Media Is the Perfect PR Channel," *Adweek*, June 15, 2016, accessed September 29, 2017, http://www.adweek.com/digital/adam-snyder-ketchum-guest-post-why-social-media-is-the-perfect-pr-channel/.

[12] Wilcox et al., *THINK Public Relations*.

[13] G. Giannini, *Marketing Public Relations: A Marketer's Approach to Public Relations and Social Media* (Upper Saddle River, NJ: Prentice Hall, 2009).

[14] Wilcox et al., *THINK Public Relations*.

[15] T. Murdock, "Content Marketing vs. Social Media Marketing: What's the Difference?" Content Marketing Institute, last modified February 27, 2012, accessed June 22, 2013, http://contentmarketinginstitute.com/2012/02/content-marketing-vs-social-media-marketing.

[16] Murdock, "Content Marketing vs. Social Media Marketing."

[17] Nielsen Company, *2016 Nielsen Social Media Report*, January 1, 2017, http://www.nielsen.com/us/en/insights/reports/2017/2016-nielsen-social-media-report.html.

[18] B. Solis, *Engage: The Complete Guide for Brands and Businesses to Build, Cultivate, and Measure Success in the New Web* (New York: Wiley, 2011).

[19] Solis, *Engage*.

[20] J. A. Gallegos, "The Best Social Media Marketing Campaigns of 2017 (So Far)," TINT Blog, July 14, 2017, accessed September 29, 2017, https://www.tintup.com/blog/best-social-media-marketing-campaigns-of-2017/.

[21] Gallegos, "The Best Social Media Marketing Campaigns of 2017 (So Far)."

22 L. Johnson, "Taco Bell's Cinco de Mayo Snapchat Lens Was Viewed 224 Million Times," *Adweek*, May 11, 2016, accessed September 29, 2017, http://www.adweek.com/digital/taco-bells-cinco-de-mayo-snapchat-lens-was-viewed-224-million-times-171390/.

23 Gallegos, "The Best Social Media Marketing Campaigns of 2017 (So Far)."

24 Airbnb, "We Are Here," accessed September 29, 2017, https://www.airbnbwearehere.com/.

25 Airbnb, "We Are Here."

26 Airbnb, "We Are Here."

27 D. Guth and C. Marsh, *Public Relations: A Values Driven Approach*, 5th ed. (Boston: Pearson Education, 2012).

28 J. Collins and J. Porras, *Built to Last: Successful Habits of Visionary Companies* (New York: HarperCollins, 2004).

STRATEGIC PLANNING: PUBLIC RELATIONS AND SOCIAL MEDIA

PART

The Road Map to Success 4
Developing a Social Media Plan

The development of a social media plan helps create a road map for companies to follow in achieving their social media–related goals. This chapter introduces readers to three models that play a critical role in the planning process—the Circular Model of SoMe for Social Communication, the PESO model, and the ROSTIR Public Relations Planning Guide—and introduces readers to a step-by-step social media plan that can be easily implemented within any organization.

KEY LEARNING OUTCOMES

1. Describe how the Circular Model of SoMe for Social Communication and the PESO model play a critical role in researching and developing a social media plan.

2. Through research and planning, discover the best channels to reach intended key publics with creative tactics.

3. Devise a strategic public relations (PR) and social media plan using the ROSTIR Public Relations Planning Guide.

SOCIAL MEDIA EXPERT

danah boyd (@zephoria, website: http://www.danah.org/)

In addition to being a visiting professor at New York University's Interactive Telecommunications Program, danah boyd is a principal researcher at Microsoft Research and the founder of Data & Society. Within the academy and as a researcher, her scholarly work examines the connection between technology and society.[1] She was an integral part of a three-year ethnographic project funded by the MacArthur Foundation and led by fellow researcher Mimi Ito. The project examined youths' use of technologies through interviews, focus groups, observations, and document analysis.[2] She authored an article in the *MacArthur Foundation Series on Digital Learning, Identity Volume* called "Why Youth (Heart) Social Network Sites: The Role of Networked Publics in Teenage Social Life."[3]

---

[1] d. boyd, "danah boyd," 2017, http://www.danah.org/.

[2] M. Ito et al., *Living and Learning with New Media: Summary of Findings from the Digital Youth Project* (Chicago: MacArthur Foundation, 2008).

[3] d. boyd, "Why Youth (Heart) Social Network Sites: The Role of Networked Publics in Teenage Social Life," in *MacArthur Foundation Series on Digital Learning—Youth, Identity, and Digital Media Volume*, ed. D. Buckingham, (Cambridge, MA: MIT Press, 2007).

The Significance of Research and Planning

Successful campaigns begin with the acknowledgement that every situation and organization have challenges and opportunities.

Conducting Research

Conducting research helps a practitioner diagnose precisely what is needed to develop a strategic plan. In fact, research is widely accepted as the first step in the development process. A skill set comprising multiple research techniques, including primary and secondary, as well as a toolbox of analytical tools, provides a practitioner with the appropriate perspective that can aid in the "diagnosis" of communication challenges that an organization may face. Leveraging these formal research techniques can also help in identification of an appropriate audience, strategy and tactical refinement, and evaluation of success.[1]

The Public Relations Society of America (PRSA) defines research as "the systematic gathering of information to describe and understand a situation, check assumptions about publics and perceptions, and check the public relations consequences."[2] Research helps define the problem and publics. Doug Cannon suggests practitioners should answer the following questions[3]:

- Whom do we want to reach?
- What do we want them to do?
- What messages do we want to communicate to each public that could:
  - Increase knowledge?
  - Change opinions?
  - Encourage desired behavior?

Some key research terms are defined below.

- *Primary:* Primary research is any type of research that an organization independently collects. Examples include surveys, interviews, observations, and ethnographic research.[4]
- *Secondary:* Secondary research includes the gathering of insights from research conducted by others, often involving the collection and analysis of a significant amount of existing reports, studies, or other primary research sources.[5]

The process of gathering information generally begins by analyzing a variety of relevant secondary sources. In some cases, this may be the only option that is available due to human or financial resource constraints. Practitioners will need to understand the needs of the organization and how the appropriate research will be used to best define the scope of research.[6] Secondary research may be the appropriate method of research for many situations; however, primary research will also be necessary to establish benchmarks for desired outcomes. Good research incorporates both primary and secondary research approaches to better inform a decision.

- *Formal Research:* A systematic collection of information that can be replicated and subjected to an analysis of its reliability and validity.[7]
- *Informal Research:* The ability to gather information through conversations and a general assessment of important issues and trends. Informal research does not enjoy a high degree of reliability and validity, often because of its use of nonprobability sampling.[8]
- *Qualitative:* A research method that uses flexible and open-ended questioning, often with a small number of participants/respondents, and that cannot be extrapolated to large populations.[9] Examples include in-depth interviews, case studies, and focus groups.

- *Quantitative:* A research method that uses standardized and closed-ended questions, often with many participants/respondents, and that generally can be extrapolated to large populations.[10] Examples include surveys, content analyses, and experiments.

Preparing to Plan

Planning can take various forms; however, a good campaign should include an effective strategy to support an organization's business, marketing, sales, and communications objectives. In their text *Using Research in Public Relations*, Glen Broom and David Dozier state that "strategic planning is deciding where you want to be in the future (goal) and how to get there (the strategies). It sets the organization's direction proactively, avoiding 'drift' and routine repetition of activities."[11] The best planning is systematic, meaning that practitioners set out to gather information, analyze it, and creatively execute what they have discovered.

This chapter introduces ROSTIR (research/diagnosis, objectives, strategies, tactics, implementation, reporting/evaluation) as the overarching framework, along with two additional complementary models that fit within an overall social media campaign. Much like a puzzle, each portion is a step toward developing and launching a comprehensive social media plan. Within this planning model we use Circular Model of SoMe for Social Communication and PESO: paid media, earned media, shared media, and owned media.

Preplanning Phase: Circular Model of SoMe for Social Communication
ROSTIR:
- Research/Diagnosis
- Objectives
- Strategies
- Tactics
  - PESO: paid media, earned media, shared media, owned media
- Implementation
- Reporting/Evaluation
Trifecta to Success: ROSTIR + SoMe + PESO

When correctly implemented and properly maintained, a social media plan becomes a tangible driver for new leads and provides a platform for customers to participate in important conversations related to the brands that they resonate most closely with.

Social media plans are a series of proposed actions that produce specific results. They are akin to a PR, marketing, or communications plan but specific to a social media strategy. Companies that plan their social media efforts prevent execution of haphazard, meaningless actions that add little value to their organizational goals. Social media plans can outline a specific campaign over a week, a month, a quarter, or for the entire year.

Within this text you will learn how to develop, write, and use the next evolution of the strategic planning process using the ROSTIR (research/diagnosis, objectives, strategies, tactics, implementation, and reporting/evaluation) model developed by myself and fellow researcher and writer Luke Capizzo.[12] This model underscores critical steps in the development of successful campaigns by incorporating an array of interrelated tactical elements.[13]

Circular Model of SoMe for Social Communication

The landscape of social media is a complex bio-network of overlapping platforms that vary in use and support communication through networking sites, publishing applications, discussion boards, and mobile applications. The social sphere presents organizations with a vast array of tools, communities, and social sites that they can use to interact with consumers. The Circular Model of SoMe for Social Communication (*Share*, *optimize*, *Manage*, *engage*) is a primary component of the social media research and planning phase. In keeping with a more simplistic approach to understanding the application of social media planning, this model is based on the fundamentals supporting *The Cluetrain Manifesto* and James Grunig's two-way symmetrical model of communication.

The authors of *The Cluetrain Manifesto* sought to share their belief that authenticity to stakeholders through listening is the backbone of the social sphere. The marketplace is where conversations are happening. Without careful attention, businesses can miss out on important exchanges. Similarly, Grunig and Todd Hunt's two-way symmetrical model of communication uses communication to negotiate with the public, resolve conflict, and promote mutual understanding and respect between the organization and its stakeholders. The model ensures that decisions made by an organization are mutually beneficial between itself and its audiences.[14]

Social media is immensely complex and rapidly evolving. Social media through social networks allows people to connect with others who share similar interests,

The Circular Model of SoMe for Social Communication (Share, optimize, Manage, engage) is meant to be the first step in planning a full social media campaign. *Source*: Regina Luttrell.

passions, and beliefs. From one month to the next, new platforms arise, apps are developed, and techniques are reimagined. The Circular Model of SoMe for Social Communication is intended to aid an organization's implementation of the strategies that are associated with individual campaigns. The structure provided is meant to be part of the brainstorming, preplanning, and initial research phase that leads into the strategic planning framework ROSTIR.

Share: Where is my audience? What types of networks are they engaging on? Where should we be sharing content? It is vital that social media strategists understand how and where their consumers interact. This is a company's opportunity to connect, build trust, and identify channels that allow for true interactions.

- Publish useful content—this means brands should abide by the 80/20 rule.
- Spread the company message via targeted platforms.
- Develop relationships while building trust.
- Stay abreast of the latest trends.

With 53 percent of Twitter users recommending companies or products in their tweets and 48 percent of people delivering on their intention to buy the product, sharing appropriate information within the correct category of the social web is extremely important.[15] Astonishingly, 90 percent of online consumers trust recommendations from people they know, and a whopping 70 percent trust the opinions of unknown users.[16] Why would a company *not* want to get to know its consumers and influencers? Create and publish content that resonates with your audience. Use the power of storytelling to share messages, build stronger relationships, and discover trends. Storytelling is the most effective way to communicate. Through stories, companies can better connect with their audience by stimulating feelings, ideas, and attitudes. When developing content to share, focus on the audience and what's most important to them. Anyone can sell a widget. What you want to do is get inside the hearts and minds of your customers.[17]

Optimize: What type of content should be shared? Do we have brand influencers and advocates? To optimize any conversation, listening is paramount. A strong communication plan that optimizes your content results in maximum impact of messaging, brand, and value.

- Enhance efforts through the organization's other initiatives including marketing, advertising, PR, and communications (PESO: paid media, earned media, shared media, owned media).
- Utilize influencers, subject matter experts (SMEs), and internal/external audiences.
- Augment with curated content.
- Play to the strengths of converged media efforts.

As a company evolves and the needs for a more sophisticated content strategy arise, it becomes important to utilize a multitude of media types for your outreach efforts. The days of an organization simply telling a story are gone and have shifted to discovering and leveraging the right platforms that allow you to communicate your message. For this purpose, developing a sound content strategy can help in project prioritization, needs identification, and resource allocation (including human, financial, and time) in a most efficient manner.

Keep in mind that the best content strategies don't simply emphasize blogs and social media. Rather, great content strategies recognize each type of media as an opportunity to merge the benefits of all contributing media channels. Content plans that assimilate owned, earned, and paid media will assist your business in achieving its goals and position your organization as a leader in the industry. The following can help you achieve this for an organization.

Manage: What relevant messaging should we manage, monitor, and measure? Metrics are integral in managing a social strategy.

- Identify appropriate social media monitoring tools—Hootsuite, Zignal Labs, IZEAx, Meltwater, Cyfe.
- Learn how you can best use the tools.
- Through these tools, listen and discover what is being said about you and your brand.
- Find applicable communities and conversations.
- Uncover and discover key influencers.

An organization must listen to what is being said and learn from the conversations being shared. Your stakeholders will talk about your brand with or without you. However, the conversations that they have will be much richer if, as a practitioner, you are part of them. PR practitioners operate in a new world where people have come to expect transparent communication. It is our job to give them that. Meaningful exchanges filled with substance lead to mutual fulfillment. Social listening tools allow organizations to track and measure in real time the conversations that are being had about you, your company, the products that you offer, and just about any topic being discussed across the web's social media landscape. Sprout Social, Meltwater, Hootsuite, Cyfe, Zignal Labs, and Social Mention are a few examples. By simply being informed about what is being said about your organization and on what social networks the conversations are taking place, it will be easier to participate in authentic exchanges between your consumers and your business.

Engage: Whom should we engage with, when, how, and how often? Cultivating an engagement strategy can be difficult, but once a company realizes the benefits of authentic engagement, true relationships will form.

- Enter the conversation.
- Add value to communities.
- Engage with your audience.
- Respond quickly and with authenticity.

Engaging in conversations with your consumers and influencers is the most critical component of a social strategy. The more challenging question to answer might be "Where to engage?"

I equate social strategies to the rush of website creation in the late 1990s. During this period of advancement, nearly every manager approached his or her PR practitioner and laid down the decree "Build us a website!" Naturally, our response as PR practitioners was to ask, "What is the purpose of the website? Whom are we targeting? What is our message?" Not surprisingly, without a blink of an eye, this nebulous manager would spout back, "I don't know! But everyone else is building one, so we need one too!" As advanced as social media has become, this still happens. In today's workplace, PR practitioners hear "Everyone has a Snapchat account; we should too!" This response is not the answer. An organization needs to be where its consumers are. If your consumers are not on Snapchat, then don't waste precious resources targeting an area that will yield very little. With that in mind, it should be obvious that no two social strategies will look the same. Social strategies are unique to each company and each brand.

Coca-Cola, for example, does not employ the same strategies and tactics for Coke that it uses for Sprite. The social strategies that work for Panera Bread will not necessarily work for Gerber.

Conversations occurring on social sites happen quickly, sometimes in a matter of seconds. Consumers have come to expect quick responses from PR practitioners and social media strategists who manage an online presence. Surprisingly, many companies are not prepared for the quick response that consumers have become accustomed to. Responses are often limited by availability of time on any given day, other job responsibilities, and simply the ability to manage the volume of interactions that emanate from a company's various social streams. In 2008 we saw for the first time the term "attention dashboard." This is described as a tool that pulls content from various sources across multiple networks into one place to monitor, manage, and engage in what is being shared on the social web. Today these are better known as "social media dashboards." HootSuite and Cyfe are among the most popular and widely used social media monitoring systems on the market, both offering comprehensive free options. By incorporating these tools within its communications arsenal, a company can listen to what is being said about the brand, stay current with conversations, respond to consumers in real time, send private messages, share links to company news and recently published blog posts, and monitor trending conversations.

Social Media Plan in Six Steps

Step 1: Research and Diagnosis[18]

Both research and diagnosis occur in the first step. Practitioners conduct primary and secondary research to better understand the organization and its environment. Once research is completed, it is time to diagnose the challenges and opportunities by defining the problems or possibilities for the organization. Here the target audience(s) and stakeholders are pinpointed and prioritized. Whether the company has cornered a niche area or your products or services target the general public, social media efforts should be directed toward a specific audience. For example, Axe body spray, a brand of Unilever Global, targets males eighteen to twenty-four years old; the wildly popular television series *This Is Us* hits a wider-ranging demographic of adults eighteen to forty-nine years old; the craft beer industry centers on upper-class American males ages thirty to thirty-four years old; and the jewelry brand Alex and Ani targets Millennial women ages twenty to thirty years old. Some campaigns have multiple audiences depending on the objectives set forth in the campaign. Take the time to properly understand the demographics that you are interested in connecting with.

Strategic plans usually include an introductory statement that outlines what the company wants to achieve and why. Valid objectives cannot be set without a clear understanding of the situation that led to developing a social media plan.[19] Some questions to ask when writing the situation statement include: Why is a plan necessary? Are we trying to overcome an issue or challenge? Is this a one-time product launch? Are we introducing new services? Are we looking to engage more genuinely on our social platforms? Is this long-term planning? The following is an example from a PRSA Silver Anvil Award–winning case study. Sanofi Genzyme, a global life sciences company, launched a global campaign to shed light on the impact of multiple sclerosis (MS).

Twenty years ago, with no treatments on the market to treat multiple sclerosis (MS), the only option for people living with the progressive and often

6 steps of the ROSTIR Public Relations Planning Model

Developing a social media plan helps create a road-map for companies to follow in achieving their social media–related goals. The process has been deconstructed into concise steps that allow for proper planning and effective implementation.

Research #1

Start with research so that you can diagnose why a strategic plan may be necessary.

Keep your audience in mind. Listen and design your strategy around their needs.

Objectives #2

Objectives are stated in terms of program outcomes rather than inputs and must be measurable.

Objectives should target: the audience or public, specific outcomes, measurement or magnitude of the change required to reach this outcome, and the target date.

Strategy #3

The overarching strategy should focus on how each objective will be achieved.

Tactics #4

Tactics are the tangible aspects of the strategy.

Tactics include annual meetings, open houses, events, blogs, case studies, infographics, mobile apps, and traditional PR efforts.

Implementation #5

Timing plays a critical role in the implementation of the overall plan.

Develop a calendar and budget with milestones and deadlines to help guide the implementation process.

Reporting #6

Practitioners must put metrics in place to track the results of each campaign. Reporting and evaluation can take place throughout the entire process.

Developing a social media plan helps create a road map for companies to follow in achieving their social media goals. The ROSTIR (research, objectives, strategies, tactics, implementation, reporting) model includes six concise steps that allow for proper planning and effective implementation.

debilitating disease was to hope for the best. By 2016 the MS treatment landscape was crowded, and Sanofi Genzyme (SG) was one of many pharmaceutical companies who offered treatments to help delay disease progression. While MS therapies had advanced, MS awareness programs still focused on encouraging patients to have a rosy outlook—masking the realities of the disease and encouraging the MS Community to accept burdens rather than take action to address them head on. But the truth is, if left untreated, MS may impact all aspects of patients' lives, well beyond what's commonly discussed. To help Sanofi Genzyme rise to the top of the crowded MS landscape, Cohn & Wolfe (C&W) launched vs.MS, a global initiative to shed light on and address the true impact of the disease. vs.MS is the first industry-led effort that gets real about disability from MS— what it looks like, what it feels like and what can be done about it.[20]

Organizations perform a SWOT (strengths, weaknesses, opportunities, and threats) analysis during the research and diagnosis phase. This is "a study undertaken by an organization to identify its internal strengths and weaknesses, as well as its external opportunities and threats."[21] This type of analysis can be performed for an organization, product, place, industry, brand, or person. According to MindTools, "what makes SWOT particularly powerful is that it can help you uncover opportunities that you are well-placed to exploit. And by understanding the weaknesses of your business, you can manage and eliminate threats that would otherwise catch you unaware."[22]

Step 2: Objectives

Once you have a clear situation statement, setting objectives is the next logical step. Describe your organization's objectives for your social media plan using SMART objectives: *s*pecific, *m*easurable, *a*ttainable, *r*elevant, and *t*imely.[23] Describe how these objectives support your organization's mission. The program outcomes will define the objectives. The objectives here are overarching in nature, not to be confused or intermingled with the specific objectives located in the tactics section of the social media plan. When the Virginia Lottery launched its eight-week intensive campaign *Honoring Virginia's Teachers, One Thank-You Note at a Time*, it set the following SMART objectives[24]:

1. Increase adult Virginians' awareness that Lottery profits support public education by 2 percent, as measured by the Lottery's annual benchmark study.
2. Spur the submission of at least 23,000 thank you notes to Virginia teachers; encourage at least 1 percent of teachers to redeem their notes and participate in a prize drawing.
3. Generate at least 1 million earned impressions between media and social media coverage for the campaign.

Step 3: Strategy

Strategies are the big-picture decisions made to utilize specific channels. The strategy focuses on achieving the objectives. Describe how and why various campaign components will accomplish the overall goals. Guidelines and key messages are often included in this section. The aim in this section is to leverage organizational strengths. Strategies should reflect the unique internal and external organizational environment to tell the right story and connect with the intended audience.

Niagara Conservation used a playful campaign, #WhatTheFlush, to tout the water-conserving advantages of the Stealth® Toilet. Their strategy was four-tiered:

1. "Leverage celebrities and influencers as brand ambassadors to create the kind of endorsements that could reach millions of consumers.
2. Drive purchase intent by creating disruptive and memorable advertising/digital content that fosters an emotional connection with consumers.
3. Secure earned media awareness of Niagara's Stealth® Toilet to keep its benefits at the top of consumers' minds.
4. Use social media to expand campaign reach by recruiting more consumers to connect with Niagara online."[25]

Up to this point, the format that we have followed mirrors that of a traditional PR plan. This is where the social media plan begins to diverge from the PR plan. In general, most of the platforms used within the social sphere are included in this plan. However, as we have previously read, not all social media channels are appropriate for every business. Tactics can be unique for each business and consumer. Companies must decide which social platforms are right for their audiences. It is okay if Instagram is not part of your plan. If a company's audience is not engaged on Instagram, then it might not be a smart use of resources to maintain an Instagram account.

When AARP (American Association of Retired Persons) decided to become actively involved on social media platforms, the organization gathered as much statistical information as possible about its constituency, particularly about their social media habits. This research revealed that their target audience spent the most time on Facebook. Jen Lee Reeves, AARP's manager of digital strategy, noted, "Your organizational voice depends on the social media platform, and the research shows that people 50 and up are on Facebook. Most of our members are female, and while they might be on Twitter, they're not engaging there; they are just reading. We want them to

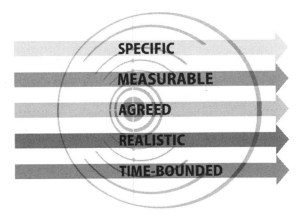

Smart objectives allow practitioners to develop specific, measurable, agreed/achievable, realistic, and time-bound goals. The more granular your objectives are defined, the easier it is to demonstrate results.

engage, so we put our emphasis on the platform where they are engaging—where they are liking, sharing and connecting. And with our people, it's on Facebook."[26]

Knowing your audience and its members' social habits is essential to successful implementation of a social media plan.

Step 4: Tactics

Tactics are the tangible aspects used when implementing the plan. Tactics include all areas found within the PESO model—paid media, earned media, shared media, and owned media. Near each tactic you will see that I have included the associated category from the PESO model that the tactic would fall into. Keep in mind that paid, earned, shared, and owned overlap, and crossover does occur. For example, when you are developing content on behalf of your organization for the company-owned Pinterest account, your actions would fall into the "owned media" area of the model. However, when a consumer pins and shares that content, it then becomes "shared media." Step 4 tasks practitioners with developing creative and effective messaging supported by research.

Social Press: Just as PR professionals pitch traditional journalists, PR professionals and social media strategists must pitch bloggers and other online influencers. (Earned Media)

Time Spent: Consider how many hours per day, week, and month will be devoted to this tactic.

Objectives:

Regularly update bloggers about products and services. Conduct interviews, conferences, and networking events.

Metrics:

Posts and referrals from the social press

Engagement and conversation

Influence

Opinion and advocacy

Impact and value

Blogs: Blogs are a simple way to connect with and share timely, relevant information with customers. They are a direct communication channel with your target audience. (Owned Media)

Time Spent: Consider how many hours per day, week, and month will be devoted to this tactic.

Remember, a good rule of thumb is to post once a day (if possible), or at a minimum, three times per week.

Create an editorial calendar for your blog to stay motivated and to provide a guideline for content.

Objectives:

Increase recognition: for example, x number of posts.

Increase engagement: for example, encourage comments; add social sharing buttons.

Metrics:

Engagement and conversation

Influence

Opinion and advocacy

Impact and value

Number of posts

Number of social shares—Digg, Twitter, Facebook, etc.

Audience growth—unique and return visits

New subscribers

Inbound links clicked

Social Networks: Various social networking platforms may be part of a social media strategy. This section includes some of the most frequently used sites. (Owned Media, Shared Media)

Time Spent: For each social network, consider how many hours per day, week, and month will be devoted to each social networking site.

Establish a goal for the number of posts per day.

Share engaging content, videos, links, images, charts, and data.

Make sure to promote upcoming events, show behind the scenes, and give sneak peeks.

Create special event pages.

Use converged media tactics whenever possible to cross-promote messages across all social media.

Facebook:

Develop a business presence through fan pages.

Build trust with ratings and reviews.

Maintain a robust brand presence.

Join Facebook groups.

Create your own group.

List events.

Demonstrate creative ways to use your products.

Create incentives for referrals and shares.

Target prospects with Facebook ads. (Paid Media)

LinkedIn:

Establish a set goal for the number of posts daily.

Form a group.

Identify other groups to follow and participate.

Encourage employees to participate.

Listen and participate in question-and-answer posts.

Pinterest:

Establish goals for the number of pins per day.

Create boards to leverage content, company culture, and a behind-the-scenes atmosphere.

Promote consumer boards that illustrate a passion for the brand.

Find boards from thought leaders, customers, partners, other businesses, and influencers.

Twitter:

Establish how frequently the company Twitter account will tweet daily.

Compile a list of employees, vendors, customers, and users; follow them, retweet when appropriate, and engage frequently.

Use links and images to enhance your tweets.

Host Twitter chats to engage with customers and expand reach and authority.

Instagram:

Encourage employees to share any interesting PR- or marketing-related photos from social marketing or company events.

Take pictures at relevant company-sponsored events like trade shows, product launches, and community happenings.

Invite influencers to take photos and share them with their followers.

Develop an Instagram contest. (Paid Media)

Metrics: Metrics for each social networking site follow AMEC (Association of Measurement and Evaluation of Communication) measurement standards. In the measurement and analytics chapter of the text, we will take a deeper dive into how to measure social media efforts.

Exposure

Engagement

Influence

Advocacy

Impact

Social Apps, Voting, and Crowdsourcing:

Time Spent: Consider how many hours per day, week, and month will be devoted to social apps, voting, and crowdsourcing. (Owned Media, Shared Media)

Objectives:

Add social elements to every strategic campaign to expand company reach and increase engagement.

Run promotional campaigns and contests to spread the message.

Promote content when applicable via social crowdsourcing and voting sites.

Let consumers have a say through crowdsourced events or interactive voting.

Metrics:

Engagement and conversation

Influence

Opinion and advocacy

Impact and value

Trends over time

Video: Social video, live or recorded, that is designed to be seen and shared through social networks. Video can include traditional advertising such as a commercial, or something as open as a live stream on Snapchat or Periscope. (Paid Media, Shared Media, Owned Media)

Live Video:

Time Spent: Consider how many hours per day, week, and month will be devoted to creating, posting, and managing live-streaming apps like Periscope, Facebook Live, Twitter Live, or Instagram Stories. (Owned Media, Shared Media)

Objectives:

Create content that can easily be streamed.

Engage with audiences through live Q&A sessions.

Metrics:

Engagement and conversation

Influence

Opinion and advocacy

Impact and value

Online Video:

Time Spent: Consider how many hours per day, week, and month will be devoted to creating, posting, and managing online videos. (Owned Media)

Objectives:

Create a video series.

Upload videos to the company website, YouTube, Facebook, Vine, Instagram, and other video platforms.

Metrics:

Engagement and conversation

Influence

Opinion and advocacy

Impact and value

Podcasting:

Time Spent: Consider how many hours per day, week, and month will be devoted to the development of podcasts. (Owned Media)

Objectives:

Create a podcast directory.

Use past webinars in the resource section on your website.

Promote content through podcast directories and iTunes.

Interview and record company thought leaders; share their insights with your community.

Metrics:

Engagement and conversation

Influence

Opinion and advocacy

Impact and value

Presentation Sharing:

Time Spent: Consider how many hours per day, week, and month will be devoted to developing content to share on sites (such as SlideShare). (Owned Media, Shared Media)

Objectives:

Highlight organizational thought leaders—if someone from your company is presenting at a conference, post the presentation to SlideShare.

Determine the number of SlideShare presentations that need to be created on a monthly or quarterly basis.

Post company webinars, slide decks from conferences, and infographics with important data.

Use specific keywords for SEO optimization.

Metrics:

Engagement and conversation

Influence

Opinion and advocacy

Impact and value

Step 5: Implementation, Budget, and Timeline

The objectives, complexity, and timing of the campaign will ultimately dictate the timelines. Some campaigns last six weeks, while others can last six months. Campaigns can be seasonal or targeted to a specific product or event. For example, the Lay's® Do Us a Flavor™ Choose Your Chip Contest accepted entries for four months in an effort to develop new potato chip flavors. As entries were submitted, members of the public were allowed to vote on their favorite chip for an additional three months. Additionally, it is important to remember that every social media plan requires a budget. Organizations are interested in understanding the scope of expenses related to the campaigns. Budgets should take into consideration both the human resource and out-of-pocket expense components. Allocate at least 10 percent of a budget to unexpected costs.

Step 6: Reporting and Evaluation

Reporting, also known as evaluation, directly correlates to the stated objectives. Practitioners must put in place metrics to track the results of each campaign. Reporting and evaluation do not have to take place at the end of a campaign, and honestly can occur at any point. Savvy practitioners evaluate the metrics throughout the process. In doing so, a practitioner will know whether or not the stated objectives, strategies, and tactics are resonating with the intended audiences. It is appropriate to measure objectives at any point during the implementation phase through the conclusion of the PR campaign.

After completing these six steps, an organization has developed a complete social media plan. This plan can be incorporated into an existing PR plan or used as a stand-alone depending on how the plan was developed.

As you read each "Theory into Practice" case study, think about the six steps described in this chapter, along with elements from the Circular Model of SoMe for Social Communication, the strategic planning framework ROSTIR (research/diagnosis, objectives, strategies, tactics, implementation, and reporting), along with the tactical elements of PESO (paid, earned, shared, and owned media). Try to identify which section the information would likely fall into within the framework of the social media plan. This will provide you with the opportunity to practice populating a plan, which can then be used as a resource for quick reference.

Theory into Practice

84 Lumber: "The Journey"

For 84 Lumber and its competitors within the building materials industry, sales are often driven by the relationships with their professional customers. To promote sales and position 84 Lumber for national growth, the company needed people. However, despite having more than 250 stores across the U.S., brand awareness outside of southwestern Pennsylvania, where the company was founded and is headquartered, was near zero. Recruiting top talent is somewhat difficult if no one knows who you are. So 84 Lumber president and owner Maggie Hardy Magerko threw down the gauntlet in December 2016: "I want everyone in the country to know the 84 Lumber name!"

Traditional recruiting tactics—ads in the classified sections of local papers, posting on job boards, and word of mouth—had been used for years, but if 84 Lumber wanted to attract more top talent to its locations across the country, the company had to do something different, drastically different. Not only did 84 Lumber need to attract more candidates; it had to attract different candidates.

Ideally, if you want everyone in the country to know your name, what better way to do it than by getting on the country's biggest stage? A ninety-second Super Bowl commercial and companion digital campaign focused on a journey of sacrifice and commitment . . . through the lens of an issue that was being talked about at every dining room table and boardroom in America: immigration. The narrative would drive dialogue and deliver on 84 Lumber's two goals for this campaign—generate national brand awareness and act as a launch pad for the company's 2017 national recruitment campaign. To watch the entire commercial, visit http://bit.ly/84lumbercommercial.

Research/Diagnosis

84 Lumber and its agency partner Brunner conducted a brand tracking study, inclusive of social media listening, in January 2017 to determine company and competitor awareness and perception and purchase behavior among builders, remodelers, and homeowners. This data was then used to create target audiences and to provide recommendations on how to best allocate the budget to drive the greatest impact with consumers.

This research highlighted a spate of mergers and acquisitions that left the building materials category highly fragmented. Building materials suppliers like 84 Lumber had the lowest national awareness in comparison to big box retailers (examples of which are Lowe's and Home Depot) and local lumberyards. Not only was overall awareness low, competitive parity among building materials suppliers was high. There was virtually no difference in the perception of staff quality, the ability to stock the most sought-after products, or the capacity to customize orders.

Additionally, 84 Lumber discovered that home builders and remodelers perceived local lumberyards more favorably than 84 Lumber or its similarly sized competitors. Local lumberyards were perceived to have higher-quality customer service, knowledgeable employees, and more reliable delivery. The data suggested that local lumberyards were benefiting from a halo effect—the favorable bias that builders and construction pros have toward these outlets had been formed and nurtured over many years.

With all of this in mind, it was clear that the building materials industry was ripe for disruption. If 84 Lumber or anyone else in the space wanted to differentiate themselves, they had to be bold. They had to act differently. They had to do something that would drastically alter the perception of 84 Lumber and the entire building materials category.

This research led directly to the development of *Adweek*'s number one Super Bowl commercial, "The Journey," not to mention the kickoff of a national conversation around the skilled labor shortage.

Objectives

* In just eight weeks, deliver a legendary Super Bowl commercial as defined by industry pundits, pop culture editorialists, and the general population.
* In the two to three weeks prior to the Super Bowl, create interest and intrigue among industry pundits, pop culture editorialists, and the general population in the commercial prior to the spot airing at halftime and measured by social media conversations and press coverage.
* Upon completion of the spot airing at halftime and for the next forty-eight hours, maximize reach and engagement with the commercial's online conclusion measured by video views, strength of topic on social media platforms, overall online impressions, engagement by high-profile social media handles, press coverage, and direct brand engagement in social media conversations.

Strategy

84 Lumber and Brunner used the findings of the brand tracking study to create an integrated marketing plan to launch "The Journey." With just forty-four

Messaging Communications Hierarchy

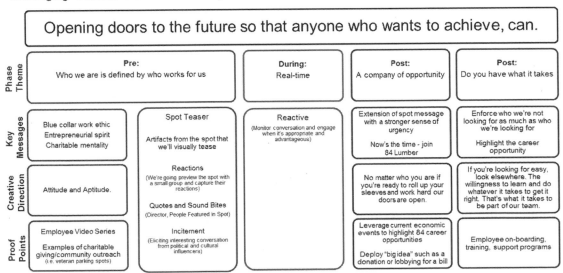

Messaging Communications Hierarchy. *Source:* Brunner and 84 Lumber. This and all following images in this chapter are reprinted with the permission of Steve Radick and George Potts of Brunner.

Role of Social Media: Actively engage the intended audience while managing the space and conversation.

Pre-Super Bowl	During Super Bowl	Post-Super Bowl
Build Anticipation / Demonstrate Reality	**Monitor and Engage**	**Manage and Activate**
• Owned Social Properties – Present theme/message. Create engagement.	• Owned Social Properties – Monitor the space, execute planned responses and remain nimble to respond in real-time	• Owned Social Properties – Continue pre-theme and introduce post-theme. Continue monitor and engage.
• Paid advertising – Increase brand awareness and reach the target audience (males 20-29)	• Paid advertising – Continue to increase brand awareness and reach the target audience (males 20-29)	• Paid advertising – Drive career page visits through paid recruitment efforts
	• Earned – Monitor (off presence) and engage	• Earned – Monitor and engage with influencers who are referencing the spot

KPIs: Engagement, Reach Rate, Impressions, Click-thru Rates, Response Rate, Completed Views, Volume of Mentions

Role of Social Media.

days from concept to finalization, the strategy had to be focused, agile, and efficient. Using a pre-, real-time, and post–Super Bowl construct, Brunner developed a messaging communications hierarchy and detailed roles for each integrated facet as well.

In the lead-up to Super Bowl Sunday, the focus was on building anticipation for the commercial, as the company deliberately chose not to release it early. Instead, the story focused on a lumber company leading the rebound of the housing industry. However, once FOX rejected the original story, the strategy underwent a 180-degree shift. Instead of running only a ninety-second commercial, 84 Lumber would also have a five-minute film that would be teased throughout the game, with the conclusion housed online, where restraints were lifted and the company could still tell the story that the will to succeed was always welcome at 84 Lumber.

However, 84 Lumber had a very limited paid media budget to spend pre–Super Bowl. That meant that, together with Brunner, the company had to use social/shared and earned media to

Role of Digital Media: Building brand visibility and relevance while capturing qualified leads (target audience).

Pre-Super Bowl	During Super Bowl	Post-Super Bowl
Present and Relevant	**Monitor, Optimize and Engage**	**Reach Target & Capture Leads**
• Paid Search & Digital Media – Brand presence in Pre-Super Bowl related search terms and content. The space will be competitive. Assets noted in pre content will be leveraged here.	• Paid Search & Digital Media – Brand presence in Super Bowl related search terms and content.	• Paid Search & Digital Media – Brand presence in Post-Super Bowl related search terms and content.
• Pre-theme Content – Purchase key terms associated with pre-theme to support Social and Web efforts	• Customized Messaging – Remain nimble and respond to audience behavior	• Post-theme Content - Purchase key terms associated with post-theme to support recruitment efforts

KPIs: Impressions, Video Views, Click-thru Rates, Conversions

Role of Digital Media.

Role of Public Relations: Make sure the world knows about the opportunities that await you at 84 Lumber.

Pre-Super Bowl	During Super Bowl	Post-Super Bowl
Build Anticipation	**Lead the Conversation**	**Attack and React**
• Mainstream Media – Get ready for what's coming	• Mainstream Media - NYT Exclusive Interview w/ Maggie or Maggie Op/Ed	• Mainstream Media – this is who we are. Join us.
• Building Industry Trades – It's time we make a splash	• Building Industry – we are the leading voice of the industry	• Building Industry – We need top talent.
• Marketing Trades - here's why we're doing a SB Spot	• Marketing Trades – let's win the creative conversation	• Marketing Trade – The Super Bowl was just the start
• Local Media – Local Pride	• Local Media – Local Pride	• Political Media – get on their agenda
• Internal Communications – build excitement	• Internal Communications – Increase morale	• Local Media – Local Pride
		• Internal Communications – create brand advocates

KPIs: Media sentiment, Media Placement, Media Mentions, Media Impressions, Video Views, Quality Media Coverage

Role of Public Relations.

tease the controversial elements of the commercial to ensure that people knew they had to go online to watch the full film. This gave 84 Lumber the ability to lead conversations about not only building materials but also politics, immigration, recruiting, and advertising. From the *New York Times* to the *Wall Street Journal* and *Good Morning America*, as well as major social media platforms such as Facebook and Twitter, the company turned what could have been a catastrophic event—FOX's rejection of the spot three weeks before the game—into a media relations jackpot.

With three weeks before the game, Brunner had to make sure 84 Lumber was the most talked about brand, and then use the reveal of the full film to ensure that the conversation continued after the game too.

Tactics

A Super Bowl commercial isn't just a commercial. It's an integrated marketing campaign. And in 84

Role of Website: Create a central "hub" for engagement, information, and routing to other properties

Pre-Super Bowl	During Super Bowl	Post-Super Bowl
Set the Foundation	**Engagement Support**	**Continued Support**

• Update website to support content recs:
  o About
  o Careers
  o Contact
  o Footer
	• Launch microsite
	• Ongoing Super Bowl content updates to 84lumber.com
	  o Home page
	  o About
	  o Careers
	  o Create connections between microsite and 84lumber.com
		• Ongoing content edits
		• Continued monitoring of digital properties

• Update imagery where needed		
• Align to content pillars for messaging needs; prepare assets (video, imagery, content) for Super Bowl	• Continued monitoring of website hosting infrastructure to ensure uptime	
• Analytics tagging for measurement		
• Ensure hosting infrastructure updated in preparation for traffic		
• Begin building microsite for launch		

KPIs: Traffic, Sessions, Content Engagement, Form Submits, Job Applications

Role of Website.

Lumber's case, it began just six weeks before the Super Bowl. As the only ninety-second commercial airing during the 2017 Super Bowl, "The Journey" had to be more than a commercial. It had to be the start of a movement.

With the announcement of 84 Lumber's Super Bowl commercial on January 10, the company broke building materials convention and began speaking directly to the general public instead of focusing solely on customers.

While "The Journey" was the campaign anchor, it was only ninety seconds of a campaign that made 84 Lumber the most talked about brand of Super Bowl LI. In addition to a comprehensive SEO and SEM campaign to catch search traffic from media coverage and social media chatter, Brunner utilized all facets of the PESO model:

Paid Media:
- Full sponsorship of the Super Bowl Green Room including onsite integration
- Broadcast partnerships with ESPN, FOX, and FOX Deportes

Earned Media:
- Multifaceted PR efforts including:
  - Media relations
  - Key messaging and fact sheet development
  - Issues management
  - Reputation management

Owned Media: A dedicated microsite and digital display ads

Shared/Social Media:
- Compelling content coupled with strategically targeted paid social media and lightning-fast real-time conversation engagement via a war room
- Social media facets including original post content, community management, and proactive engagement in online conversation beyond the 84 Lumber social presence and targeted paid ads (see slide 3 in the Social Media Case Study PowerPoint presentation for relevant images)

Implementation

In the three weeks prior to the Super Bowl, Brunner leveraged social media and the news to keep 84 Lumber on the national agenda. After *Campaign* magazine broke the story that FOX had rejected the

commercial, 84 Lumber became the linchpin for a national conversation around advertising in the era of President Trump. Articles in the *New York Times* and the *Wall Street Journal* led to coverage in *Variety*, Mashable, *USA Today*, *Rolling Stone*, and, ultimately, *Good Morning America*. By focusing on publications that would drive hundreds of other articles, Brunner saturated the media landscape before the commercial even aired.

In addition, Brunner created a natural feedback loop leveraging the news media buzz to drive attention to vague posts on 84 Lumber's social media presence. Posts teased elements of the spot, which created more news stories, which then trafficked more people to the presence.

The full ninety-second commercial was then leaked to *Adweek* days before the game, creating yet another news burst.

Fortune Favors the Brave.

84 Lumber Super Bowl Commercial - The Entire Journey
10,310,250 views • 3 days ago

84 Lumber Super Bowl Commercial – Complete The
1,128,626 views • 3 days ago

84 Lumber Super Bowl Commercial - The Journey
3,132,072 views • 6 days ago

Video Views   1,952,578

Video Views   683,513

Facbook and Youtube – 84 Lumber.

Reporting

The goal of 84 Lumber's Super Bowl commercial wasn't to sell more lumber—it was to make sure the world knew who 84 Lumber was. And it certainly did that.

Key results "The Journey" drove:

- *Adweek* rated it the number one Super Bowl LI ad (http://www.adweek.com/brand-marketing/the-5-best-ads-of-super-bowl-li/).
- Within one minute of the commercial's airing, the microsite that housed the conclusion, www.journey84.com, received more than 300,000 hits (after one hour this rose to six million).
- Net tonality score increased 28%
- 14,000+ media placements that were shared more than 147,000 times
- 5.5 billion earned media impressions
- More than 4.5 billion potential social media impressions
- Number two share of voice among all Super Bowl advertisers
- Seventeen million–plus cumulative video views

The Journey Begins – Debuts at #20; top 50 through Sunday

The Entire Journey
- #1 Late Sunday through all day Monday
- Stayed in top 20 all day Tuesday

Top trending topic Sunday night and all day Monday.

Worldwide Trends

Country Trends

United States

#SuperBowl
Julio Jones
#weaccept
84 Lumber
Luke Bryan
Cam Newton
Alfa Romeo
Blount
Transformers
America the Beautiful

Trending all day Monday and Tuesday regionally throughout the United States.

TRENDING

84 Lumber
180K people talking about this

Jane the Virgin
4.6K people talking about this

Nicki Minaj
1K people talking about this

Hebrew University of Jerusalem
7.9K people talking about this

Tesla Model S
31K people talking about this

Curt Schilling
3.4K people talking about this

Orange Is the New Black
38K people talking about this

Tara Palmer-Tomkinson
39K people talking about this

Patagonia
200K people talking about this

New Orleans, Louisiana
30K people talking about this

Twitter – 84 Lumber.

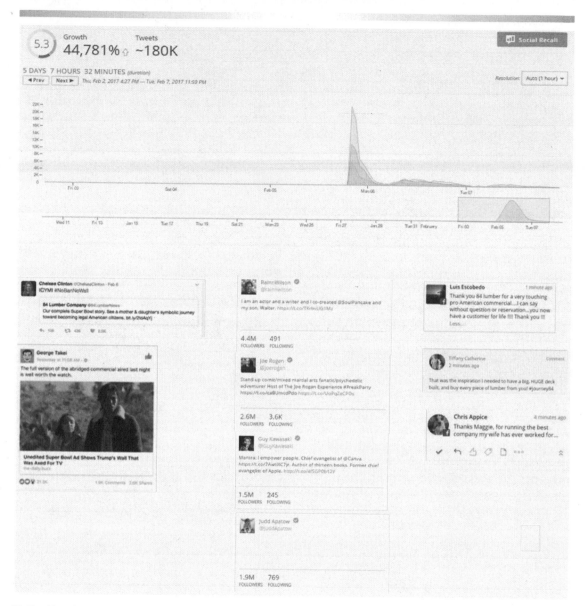

Twitter Trends – 84 Lumber.

- Top trending topic on three major social media platforms
  - Number one trending video on YouTube during the Super Bowl
  - Number four trending topic on Twitter during the Super Bowl
- More than 1,200 real-time, personalized social media brand responses in just twenty-four hours
- 44,000+% increase in Twitter activity
- High-profile social media influencer attention and praise4.12

- The 84 Lumber website received ninety million–plus impressions and more than 337,000 clicks.

Since the Super Bowl, brand awareness spiked more than 25% and advertising awareness more than doubled. The business impacts are even more impressive. Since February 6, 2017, 84 Lumber has received more than 92,000 applications and more than 135,000 people have opted into the 84 Lumber talent network. There has also been a noticeable difference in the quality of these candidates. Management trainee candidates are consistently more experienced and educated. Recruiters say they no longer have to explain who 84 Lumber is when they're at job fairs. Prospective employees seek them out, not only to apply for a job, but to explain exactly why they're looking for a career at 84 Lumber.

"The Journey" has also won numerous film awards, including:

* Bronze Lion at the Cannes International Festival of Creativity

* D&AD Wood Pencils for Cinematography for Film Advertising and Editing for Film Advertising
* Bronze Pencil Award in Long Form, Single Branded Entertainment
* Bronze Award at the A-List Hollywood Awards in the Online Video category

To see the 84 Lumber case study video, visit http://bit.ly/84LumberCaseStudy.

#LRNSMPR

Learn Social Media and Public Relations

Apply the principles learned in this chapter to the scenarios below.

* Discuss the value of a social media plan. Is it essential? Why or why not? Use what you have learned to support your responses.
* How does the Circular Model of SoMe for Social Communication work in conjunction with the ROSTIR (research/diagnosis, objectives, strategies, tactics, implementation, and reporting/evaluation) model? Where does PESO (paid, earned, shared, and owned media) fit within the larger social media plan?
* Conduct research on your favorite organization or brand. Visit their website; read the history of the organization; peruse their products; identify their mission, goals, and target audiences;

and become familiar with all aspects of the business. Visit their social media pages. How do they implement the Circular Model of SoMe for Social Communication? Share: Do they abide by the 80/20 rule? Optimize: Do you see cohesive messaging across all channels—paid, earned, shared, and owned? Are they using subject matter experts? Manage: Can you identify key influencers? Engage: Does the brand enter the conversation? If they do, is it quickly and with authority? Finally, based on your research, work backward to pull together what you believe to be their social media plan. Use the strategic planning framework ROSTIR to create the plan. Identify the tactics used within the campaign.

Notes

[1] R. Luttrell and L. W. Capizzo, *Public Relations Campaigns: An Integrated Approach*, 1st ed. (Thousand Oaks, CA: SAGE Publications, 2018).

[2] D. Cannon, ed., *Study Guide for the Examination in Accreditation in Public Relations* (New York: Public Relations Society of America, 2017),https://www.prsa.org/wp-content/uploads/2016/07/apr-study-guide.pdf.

[3] Cannon, ed., *Study Guide for the Examination in Accreditation in Public Relations*.

[4] Purdue OWL, "What Is Primary Research and How Do I Get Started?" accessed September 30, 2017, https://owl.english.purdue.edu/owl/resource/559/01/.

[5] Luttrell and Capizzo, *Public Relations Campaigns*.

[6] Cannon, ed., *Study Guide for the Examination in Accreditation of Public Relations*.

[7] R. Smith, "Research Methods," accessed September 30, 2017, http://faculty.buffalostate.edu/smithrd/PR/researchmethods.htm.

[8] Smith, "Research Methods."

[9] Smith, "Research Methods."

[10] Smith, "Research Methods."

11 G. M. Broom and D. M. Dozier, *Using Research in Public Relations: Applications to Program Management* (Englewood Cliffs, NJ: Prentice Hall, 1990).

12 Luttrell and Capizzo, *Public Relations Campaigns.*

13 Luttrell and Capizzo, *Public Relations Campaigns.*

14 J. E. Grunig and T. Hunt, *Managing Public Relations* (Belmont, CA: Thompson Wadworth, 1984).

15 "Twitter Statistics."

16 "Twitter Statistics."

17 R. Luttrell, "Once Upon a Time . . .," October 13, 2017, https://ginaluttrellphd.com/2017/10/13/once-upon-a-time/.

18 Luttrell, "Once Upon a Time . . ."

19 G. T. Cameron and D. L. Wilcox, *Public Relations: Strategies and Tactics* (Boston: Pearson/Allyn and Bacon, 2009).

20 Sanofi Genzyme and Cohn & Wolfe, "Vs. MS, a Global Sanofi Genzyme Initiative," PRSA Silver Anvil Award, Public Relations Society of America, http://apps.prsa.org/SearchResults/Download/6BW-170417121/0/vs_MS_a_Global_Sanofi_Genzyme_Initiative.

21 "SWOT Analysis," https://www.google.com/search?q=Dictionary.

22 MindTools, "SWOT Analysis: Discover New Opportunities, Manage and Eliminate Threats," https://www.mindtools.com/pages/article/newTMC_05.htm.

23 J. Kyrnin, "SMART Goals," About.com, 2012, http://webdesign.about.com/od/strategy/qt/smart_goals.htm.

24 Virginia Lottery and Padilla, "Honoring Virginia's Teachers, One Thank-You Note at a Time," 2017 Silver Anvil Award Winner, Public Relations Society of America, http://apps.prsa.org/SearchResults/Download/6BW-1701C17347/0/Honoring_Virginia_s_Teachers_One_Thank_You_Note_at.

25 Niagara Conservation and Padilla, "#WhatTheFlush: Disrupting the Water Conservation Conversation," PRSA Silver Anvil Award, Public Relations Society of America, 2017, http://apps.prsa.org/SearchResults/Download/6BE-1705CB17059/0/WhatTheFlush_Disrupting_the_Water_Conservation_Con.

26 A. Crawford, "How AARP Found Its Social Media Voice," Public Affairs Council, July 22, 2014, https://pac.org/news/comm/how-aarp-found-its-social-media-voice.

Contemporary Media Relations 5

Today's practitioner moves in a fast-paced, real-time environment. Now, more than ever, it is vital to gain the attention of journalists between all of the media-rich messages they receive daily. This chapter explores how to break through the clutter and get your message heard by today's journalists, bloggers, and online influencers.

KEY LEARNING OUTCOMES

1. Understand the differences between traditional media relations and media relations on the social sphere and how the two overlap and connect.

2. Understand and distinguish the role of the public relations practitioner versus the journalist.

3. Learn the elements of a pitch email, digital press release, and online media center.

SOCIAL MEDIA EXPERT

Sarah Atkinson (@Comms_Sarah)

Sarah Atkinson is vice president of communications for Europe, Middle East & Africa (EMEA) at CA Technologies. In her role she oversees the strategic management of the company's internal and external communication across the region. She leads the organization's Create Tomorrow corporate social responsibility program, which promotes STEM careers to secondary school and university students, particularly women and girls.[1] Among her many duties Atkinson focuses on media relations, social media, employee communications, executive communications, and corporate social responsibility (CSR).[2]

---

[1] CA Technologies, "CA Technologies VP of EMEA Communications Joins techUK Board," news release, October 21, 2015, https://www.ca.com/gb/company/newsroom/press-releases/2015/ca-technologies-vp-of-emea-communications-joins-techuk-board.html.

[2] 30% Club, "Women for Media," accessed October 21, 2017, http://womenformedia.30percentclub.org/.

Ushering in a Wave of New(s) Consumers

Gone are the days when the paperboy diligently delivered the morning newspaper before sunup and subscribers eagerly read it page by page. No longer do we gather at five in the evening to watch the day's top news stories or turn on the radio to catch a noteworthy broadcast. In today's media-rich environment, a multitude of outlets exist for Americans to obtain their daily news fix. Online platforms play a pivotal role in how we consume news.

According to the Pew Research Center, 38 percent of adults often acquire news online, either from news websites/apps (28 percent), on social media (18 percent), or both.[1] Of those surveyed, two thirds (66 percent) get news on both mobile and laptop/desktop devices, while 13 percent obtain news using a desktop/laptop and 5% do so on a mobile device.[2] However, of those who receive news on both, the majority prefer mobile—56 percent to 42 percent—over a desktop computer.[3] The popularity of traditional media platforms, including television, radio, and print, has been edging downward over the past decade.[4] Today, Americans are integrating technology into how they consume news, using both digital and traditional sources at a much faster pace than first imagined.[5]

The methods by which Americans interact with news have also changed. A large number of Internet users are continually available to engage in conversations or discuss events that are happening around us. A two-minute advertisement posted by *The Guardian*,[6] a British newspaper, illustrates just how much of an active role viewers and periodical readers play in responding to news coverage or, as some may argue, even contribute to the news. The video ad "reimagines the Three Little Pigs as a modern news story, beginning with the Big Bad Wolf's death in a boiling pot and a SWAT team descending on the home of the porcine suspects. Throughout the video, reporters follow every twist and turn with help from readers across social media."[7] The commercial brilliantly illustrates the intimate relationship consumers have with news and with those who report the news.

Practitioners should also learn to recognize that anyone can be a publisher or editor. When blogs initially began popping up on the Internet, they signaled a substantial paradigm shift. Anyone with access to the Internet could have a voice—and today, millions of people effectively leverage this platform. Readers regularly publish comments on journalists' articles, tweet views and opinions, and debate one another (and journalists alike) about the coverage, facts, and details of a story. Social media essentially utilize word-of-mouth strategies at broadband speeds with instantaneous diffusion.

Today's reporters must have the capacity to write, be an on-air personality, and shoot/edit video while interacting and maintaining an online presence. The new reporter, along with consumer-generated news and online influencers, has altered the landscape of media relations. There was a time when public relations (PR) practitioners knew—and I mean *really knew*—the reporter who covered their beat; they knew they could count on a truth-seeking editor and understood that an honest, unbiased story would run.[8] Americans could rely on three television networks and a handful of dependable, honorable newspapers to deliver the top stories.[9] Today, conglomerates, fragmented media, breaking news in a twenty-four/seven cycle, and the ever-present online platforms dominate media relations protocol.

The practice of PR in other countries is changing as well. Researcher Angelina Tu notes that PR in Asia is influenced by large corporations interested in promoting their products or services. However, this standard is beginning to experience a shift. The key for PR practitioners in Asia is to adjust their approach. Tu proposes that organizations move beyond media relations and look for other ways of influence. In today's marketplace an organization or brand must focus on always being available to broaden its influence within a specific consumer base. To do so successfully, businesses need to leverage their own branded content, strategically incorporate social components, and strive for third-party validation. Tu states: "It is imperative that we don't increasingly see traditional media relations as shrinking or increasingly as the elephant in the room. Rather we see that it still matters in a media landscape that is continuously broadening itself and making its presence felt more than ever before. PR does not equal media relations. Media relations is but a subset of PR."[10]

This unparalleled shift in news reporting, including how news is obtained, has had a direct impact on media relations and given rise to what has come to be known as "social press." Traditional media relations and social press have become standard job duties for today's PR practitioner. To penetrate news outlets and reach our audiences, we must now build relationships with traditional journalists as well as bloggers, online reporters, administrators, citizen journalists, and new influencers.

Community of New Influencers

In today's modernized societies, PR practitioners are engaging with a different type of media professional. In addition to traditional journalists, practitioners are building formidable and fruitful relationships online at the same time. Not that long ago PR pros asked journalists for a "desk-side" meeting or networked at an after-hours gathering. Today, professionals can instantly engage with a wealth of online influencers using media like Twitter, Facebook, LinkedIn, and other powerful blogs and forums. Social networking sites are a way to complement traditional media relations by bringing the relationship between PR professionals and their contacts to life online.

Influencer Relations

PR professionals have been criticized over the years for attempting to apply traditional media relations tactics to online relations. Simply put, these tactics are different. A new set of tools is required in an online world above and beyond the previously accepted conventional tactics and press releases. When we build relationships online, we are opening the door to building a successful relationship in the social press world.

Blogger Relations

A predominant opinion in the online community is that the blogosphere is fueled by *people*—people who are part of the human network of connections that we make on a regular basis.[11] These individuals can be journalists, analysts, experts, or simply writers who are passionate about sharing their views. And they should be taken seriously. As with pitching traditional journalists, it is critical to get to know bloggers as well. It is essential to understand the blogger's focus and point of view, writing style, blogging experience, audience, and preferred method of contact. These questions are not unlike the ones that you might already utilize when getting to know a journalist. To send a press release to everyone in the newsroom is inappropriate. The same rule of logic is implied in blogger relations: don't spam bloggers with irrelevant information that has little or nothing to do with their area of expertise.

In 2007, Chris Anderson, editor of *Wired Blog Network* and *The Long Tail*, wrote a blog post that sent shock waves throughout the PR profession, so much so that it still resonates today.[12] He published hundreds of PR professionals' email addresses after one too many "lazy flacks" bombarded his inbox with irrelevant news. You read that correctly: *he published their email addresses for the world to read*. His post came out of frustration. Bloggers want PR professionals to tell a story that is engaging and relevant to their readers, just like journalists. Engaging genuinely and effectively takes a good deal of practice. Effective blogger relations can be boiled down to two simple rules. Rule No. 1: Follow, listen, and interact. Rule No. 2: Be a good storyteller.

Rule No. 1: Follow, Listen, and Interact

According to Nielsen, bloggers are active across many social media platforms. These individuals are two times more likely to post and comment on consumer-generated video sites like YouTube and nearly three times more likely to post on message boards and in forums.[13] Finding the right blogger will become critical to a company's overall plan to gain social press, earned media, and awareness. As a rule, big does not always mean better in the blogosphere. Search for blogs that are relevant to your company or area of expertise. Find out where your customers are on the web, whom they read, and who influences them. If you do not know where to begin searching for this information, consider using tools like Technorati, Alltop, or Gorkana and search their databases.[14] Messe Frankfurt says, "Blog posts enjoy a high-level credibility among their readership, because they are usually very personal and honest while also remaining entirely independent. In addition to this, blog posts often link to videos or product websites, and are therefore highly relevant providers of traffic."[15]

Once you identify a list of bloggers who are influential within your company's sector, become knowledgeable, transparent, and trustworthy to them. Begin establishing a relationship with them. This is done through careful exploration of their blogrolls.[16] PR practitioners should read the blog frequently and comment regularly. The only way to form a solid relationship with a blogger is by understanding him or her. Make sure you link to the blog, even tag the blog in your own company blog, tweet important articles that the blogger writes, Pin a good article to your company Pinterest board, and participate in the blogger's community without the anticipation of being covered.[17] Ultimately, you want to immerse yourself within their blog world. This takes time and patience, but the rewards are bountiful.

Rule No. 2: Be a Good Storyteller

You must first establish a solid relationship with a blogger before you can tell your story.[18] PR professionals have always been storytellers. To effectively tell your story to a blogger, you need to make sure that it is interesting and compelling. Creating videos and offering ebooks, interviews, podcasts, images, or a Pinterest board can help tell your story and grab the blogger's attention.[19] Your content should be genuinely useful and exciting. A "one-size-fits-all" approach will not work with bloggers.

The Perfect Pitch

Once you have established yourself and your company as part of the blogger's community, pitching your news to him or her will become easier and easier. Keep in mind, just as in traditional media relations, there are rules. In fact, the rules are similar.

Personalization: When pitching to bloggers, address them by name and demonstrate that you've read their blog by injecting a reference to it in your opening sentence.[20] This illustrates that you are interested in what they are writing about and take part in their community because you know them, understand them, value their likes and dislikes, and have a keen appreciation for what types of articles their readers want to hear more about.

Creating an Impact—Softly and with Value: Bloggers aren't into press releases that include quotes from CEOs; nor are they inclined to respond when asked to write a blog post or for a retweet of a recently published article.[21] What a blogger wants is a compelling story that is truly interesting and connects back to the purpose of the blog.[22] *A story is not worth covering simply because the company we work for thinks it is.*

Brevity: There are 440 million blogs worldwide.[23] On average, bloggers write between three and five blog posts each week. The 4th Annual Blogger survey revealed that the "average blog post takes 3 hours and 20 minutes to write. In 2017 bloggers spent 39 percent more time on a typical blog post than in 2014. What's more, 49 percent of bloggers spend 6 or more hours writing each post."[24] A blogger's time is precious, so the better written and honed your pitch is, the better your chances for a response.

Online influencers permeate the Internet. Twitter, Facebook, and niche forums have become havens of influence within the media world—both online and behind the desk.

Twitter Relations

PR professionals should get in the habit of using Twitter to engage with online influencers rather than simply using it as a network to connect with peers.[25] According to a survey from Muck Rack, 70 percent of journalists see Twitter as a valuable social media tool.[26] Poynter research revealed that journalists are the largest and most active verified group on Twitter, making up 24.6 percent of the service's authenticated users.[27] Twitter has come to play a vital role in how journalists gather and break news, as well as how they locate credible sources that become critical contacts as they are putting a story together. Prior to the social media revolution, journalists relied on wire services to gather important information. With the creation and availability of Google Alerts, HootSuite, and other similar platforms, journalists can essentially create their own newswire services.[28]

As PR practitioners, we need to better understand how to leverage services like Twitter in shaping our news sources and information channels. Identifying influencers can become much more straightforward and simplified than first thought. Here are three simple ways to do just that:

1. Locate new influencers, by using tools like Social Mention or Twitter Search to find influencers who are relevant to you.
2. Become active on the social sphere with journalists, bloggers, online influencers, and editors.
3. Look through your media lists, contacts, and stacks of business cards. Then take those names and find those professionals on Twitter and other social networking platforms. Once you have identified influencers who are pertinent to you or your business, build your relationship with them. Refer to their blogs, newspapers, or the media that they work for and take part in discussion forums, offer up items you see that may be of interest to them, and connect them with sources. Just because you follow them does not mean they will follow you, so you need to put in twice the effort to make them notice you and become a trusted resource.

Developing a strong online presence with influencers will carry over into traditional media relations. The two are a bridge to one another and are not mutually exclusive. Media relations are still considered a top skill that all PR practitioners must possess, hone, and cultivate.[29]

Progressive Media Relations

The role of PR practitioners is to regularly manage the relationship between their organization and the media, regardless of the medium.[30] The evolution of media communicated through the Internet has led to a compression in publication timing and a greater focus on breaking news, neither of which diminishes the job of

What Do Journalists Want?

Meeting Reporters' Needs
Understanding the challenges and goals of today's reporters is paramount!

Breaking News
77%
Linking company news to the breaking news of the day is likely to elevate the success of your pitch. By integrating your PR campaign with timely, relevant information, you can differentiate your brand's story from other pitches and press releases that reporters receive.

Photos
73%
Reporters indicate that photos are their most favorite asset that PR professionals provide. Attention grabbing photos, graphics, infographics, and videos not only help the media outlet, but also tell a brand's story in their own voice.

Interesting
60%
The next press release you write should not only focus on the breaking news that you are sharing, but include facts, angles, quotes and other assets to increase the value to reporters.

Facts
70%
Journalists often describe the essence of their work as finding and presenting "the facts." Give them what they want. Include quotes, statistics, and numbers that help tell the story.

0 10 20 30 40 50 60 70 80 90 100

Company Website 92%
Company's Online Newsroom 77%
Social Media 42%   Spokespeople 42%
Trade Publications 41%   Blogs 34%
Wikipedia 32%

Where Do Reporters Conduct Their Research?

Daily Dose of SM
67% of journalists spend up to two hours a day on social.

Email Rules
83% of reporters prefer being pitched via email.

You Had Me at Hello
79% of journalists said the subject line impacts their interest in reading a press release.

Sources:
Business Wire http://bit.ly/21L7ir6
Cision: bit.ly/1VJyVuW

More than half of journalists surveyed in a recent Social Journalism Study believe that they would not be able to carry out their work without turning to their social media accounts for help. Yet, when being pitched a story idea by PR practitioners, 83 percent prefer an email over a tweet. *Source:* Infographic design: Regina Luttrell; source content: Cisison (http://bit.ly/1VJyVuW).

the reporter or the PR professional. Each profession still has distinct roles and responsibilities.

Reporters' Job

Reporters are tasked with a relatively short list of duties compared with those of PR professionals. They *must*

- generate reader interest
- objectively tell *all* sides of the story, *not just your company's*
- gather information from multiple sources: customers, competitors, analysts
- obtain timely, useful information
- work under deadline pressure (twenty-four/seven news cycle and second-to-second tweets)
- report on a variety of news, which may or may not include your area of expertise, industry, or company

PR Practitioners' Job

The responsibility of a PR practitioner is a bit more complex, but the fruits of building a healthy relationship with journalists, bloggers, and online influencers are most often realized through news coverage, fair reporting, and an enhanced receptivity to pitched stories. You are the middleman, the connector between an organization and the public. Once you establish yourself and your area of expertise, you can become a valuable resource for journalists.

Try to keep the following principles in mind when working with traditional media or hybrid media (indicative of media in their original medium—newspaper, radio, TV), as well as online media formats, including websites, blogs, and social networking sites:

- Establish credibility.
  - Get as much information as possible prior to meeting or pitching to journalists.
  - Understand the journalist's interests and, yes, even biases.
  - Become familiar with the journalist's knowledge of the industry. So often, journalists have multiple beats to report on. Your industry may be one of three or four that the journalist covers, and so understanding the depth to which he or she is familiar with your topic will be important as you build up your relationship with this person.
- Distinguish the media outlet and its audience.
  - Tailor your message to the audience and the journalist. This means you need to do your homework and know the readership and the reporting style of the person you are pitching.
  - Time your message to publication or the journalist's deadlines.
  - Initiate contact if and when appropriate.
- Distinguish pitches between online influencers and traditional media.
- Know and respect the journalist's deadline.
- Determine your agenda.
  - Analyze your audience.
  - Identify your objectives.
  - Identify the key points or messages that you want to promote.
- Do not wing it!
  - Set time aside prior to meeting any reporter or taking part in an interview to relax and collect your thoughts.
  - Rehearse your key messages. Be sure to support your points with colorful anecdotes and compelling statistics. Keep your responses as jargon free as

THE JOB OF A REPORTER

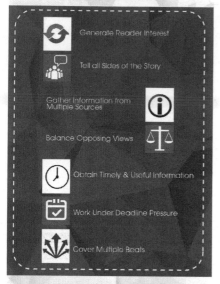

- Generate Reader Interest
- Tell all Sides of the Story
- Gather Information from Multiple Sources
- Balance Opposing Views
- Obtain Timely & Useful Information
- Work Under Deadline Pressure
- Cover Multiple Beats

THE JOB OF A PR PRACTITIONER

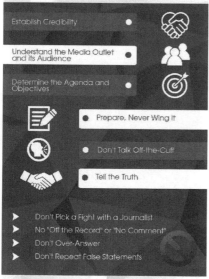

- Establish Credibility
- Understand the Media Outlet and its Audience
- Determine the Agenda and Objectives
- Prepare, Never Wing It
- Don't Talk Off-the-Cuff
- Tell the Truth

- Don't Pick a Fight with a Journalist
- No "Off the Record" or "No Comment"
- Don't Over-Answer
- Don't Repeat False Statements

Never Miss Critical Deadlines
Give Facts, Not Opinions
Devour News
Say Thank You

Public relations practitioners and journalists have a symbiotic relationship. Each has their own focus, but both come together to facilitate story ideas and media opportunities. *Source*: Regina Luttrell.

possible. Your company may have an acronym for every day of the week, but it does not mean that anyone outside your company understands the meaning. For example, in the telecommunications industry a frequent acronym used is "COW." To the average person this is an animal, but to a well-versed telecomm person it is a "cell-site on wheels." See how easily one could misinterpret the meaning?

- Do not forget to provide the most important information first!
- Tell the truth: Do not lie, because the truth will eventually reveal itself.[31] You risk ruining the credibility and relationship that you have worked so hard to foster. PR practitioners should never withhold bad or negative-leaning information, because it can turn into a damaging, negative story quite easily.
- Do not pick a fight: Journalists are neither friends nor enemies; they are professional colleagues. They never forget how to work with PR professionals, but if you make an interview difficult, they will remember you and may opt not to call on your expertise.[32] You need them just as much as they need you.
- Fatal flaws—do not succumb!
  - *Commenting "off the record":* There is no such thing! PR practitioners and journalists develop healthy, professional relationships over time, but make no mistake—regardless of how friendly you become with the journalist, anything that you say is fair game and can be reported in a story. Take it from Barbara Morgan, the communications director for New York City mayoral candidate Anthony Weiner. Her comments to a reporter landed her in hot water all over the news and social sphere when she called intern Olivia Nuzzi a myriad of less than flattering adjectives. (Read the full article: http://bit.ly/WeinerSpokeswoman.)
  - *Answering "no comment":* This makes it look as if the company has something to hide.
  - *Speaking "off the cuff":* When you speak from the hip, you risk committing an outrageous verbal faux pas. People who work with the media must remember that they "are" the company. Regardless of personal feelings, such a person represents the company at all times. Speaking "off the cuff" can get your media representative in quite a bit of trouble and possibly damage the organization's image and brand. It is a good idea to develop a media relations policy for working with the media to ensure that all representatives understand the company's etiquette.[33]
  - *Repeating false statements:* Don't do it. Each spoken word during an interview is a sound bite or quote.

If the reporter phrases a question negatively or uses undesirable language, and you then repeat the negative wording when responding, your overall message could be interpreted adversely.

- *Not sticking to the facts:* It is okay if you don't have an answer, but get back to the journalist as soon as possible with the information. It is quite common to respond with something like "I don't have those numbers in front of me, but let me find out and I'll get back to you."
- *Over-answering:* Once you have made your point, stop talking. Too often we are afraid of silence. Avoid filling the silence. Over-answering can lead to "off the cuff" responses, and we all know where those can lead!
- *Missing deadlines:* The news cycle moves quickly. It is our job to help journalists meet their deadlines. Your company can easily be overlooked when a journalist is on deadline and cannot reach you for a comment. More often than not, this is becoming common practice in our digital-driven news cycle.
- Devour news! Whether you get your information online, in print, over the airwaves, or on the run via mobile devices, you must always be informed as to what is going on in the world, what stories are trending, and which stories journalists in your industry are reporting on.[34]
- Say thank you! Too often PR professionals neglect to send a quick note of appreciation for the reporter's time and the ensuing article.

New Tools of the Trade
Online Media Centers
Make a Good First Impression

Research indicates that reporters continue to take on more work with fewer resources. PR professionals can make the job of any media representative easier by creating online media centers allowing journalists a quick and efficient way to find key information necessary to pull together a story. If a reporter must dig too deep to find information on a company to determine whether the story has any merit, he or she will simply leave the website. An online media center helps tell a company's story. It is our job as PR professionals to make it easy for journalists. Developing a compelling online media center, with relevant information, is fairly straightforward. The content should be accessible, easy to share, and easy to find.

Accessible

Flashy is not necessarily better. Too often companies choose appearance over content. Grandiose images, varied logos, flash technology, video intros, and just about every social media technology out there lack true value if journalists cannot find the information they need to complete a story. The phrase "Content is king" applies to online media centers. Content is the driving force behind long-standing, trusting relationships between PR professionals and journalists. Content such as social media–generated press releases, executive bios, white papers, company logos, and photographs are all essential elements within a company's media center.

An important aspect of accessibility to a journalist is the ability to be "found." Make sure to take the appropriate steps to maximize the company's SEO and SEM strategy and confirm that the online media center is easily located using major search engines. If this is done properly, web searches using Google, Bing, and Yahoo! should locate the company media center at the top of the results. Journalists should find a prominently featured tab dedicated to the online media center on the website's main home page. Allow journalists to subscribe to categorized RSS feeds or receive email updates when new content becomes available. RSS feeds, email updates, and e-newsletters will draw journalists to the website over and over. Journalists who subscribe to the company's content are demonstrating that they are interested in the company and that the content the company is generating is relevant to them. Moreover, they see the company as a resource for future stories.

Easy to Share

Make content easy to share and bookmark—assign each page a unique URL for easy linking, and add social media tags to allow your audience to spread the content for you. You can also embed supplemental video and photos within the media center to make your site more compelling.

Easy to Find

Frequently journalists complain that they are unable to find necessary information. This might include a photo, an old press release, or the contact information of the media relations department for the company. In general, company websites are designed for customers looking for products, services, or information about a company. This makes it critically important to prominently feature the online media center on the home page of the website to make it easier for journalists to contact a company representative. Companies may also refer to the online media center as a "press center" or "newsroom." Regardless of the name, the focus and purpose remain the same: companies can present themselves to an expansive audience with the intent to motivate more significant participation and openness while potentially boosting organic website SEO.[35]

"Reporters need specific content and look to online newsrooms to find it. When they research a company, the first place they look is the company's own websites (92 percent), online newsroom (77 percent), and social media channels (42 percent). Reporters prefer websites with a range of usable content, in easy-to-find, easy-to-use formats."

Business Wire Media Survey

Components of an Ideal Online Media Center

Online media centers should be viewed as a press kit in digital format.[36] They contain similar elements to those found within a physical press kit but are clickable and shareable—both of which are essential elements of media relations in our connected world.

> *Press Releases:* The ideal media center incorporates the most recent press releases and features them prominently. The media center home page should list three to five of the company's most recent press releases and link to a separate archive section. Press releases should be listed in reverse chronological order, with the most recent press release listed first. For press releases that garner media coverage, include links to the articles near the press release. McDonald's separates its press releases into corporate news and financial news and makes it easy for journalists to quickly and efficiently locate the information that they need.[37]
>
> *Contact Information:* Media contacts are one of the most important elements in an online media center. Journalists often complain that they cannot quickly locate the PR contact information on a media center webpage without clicking at least five times.[38] This can potentially lead to missing out on media coverage for the company. The contact information for the PR person should be prominently displayed. For the benefit of journalists who are working on tight deadlines and need to reach someone immediately, list the

Social Media Newsroom Template

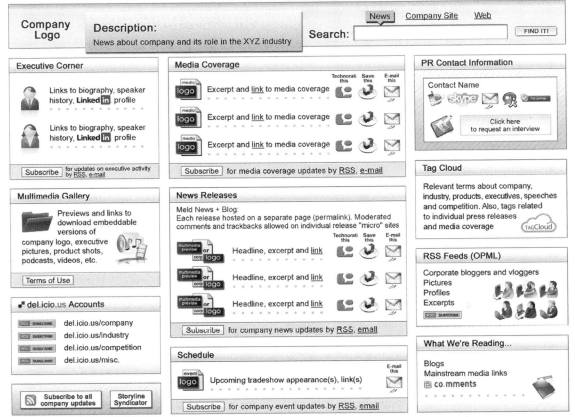

SHIFT Communications developed the first template that companies could use as a guide to evolve their online newsrooms for the "social media" age. *Source*: SHIFT Communications.

best telephone number, email address, and any social media channels that they can quickly utilize. If a company representative is not directly available to the reporter, or if the reporter cannot easily find a phone number, the journalist will move on to another source. Including a tab titled "Media Inquiries" with the phone numbers and email addresses of the persons responsible for responding to journalists is simple and effective. Southwest Airlines, Lands' End, and Dick's Sporting Goods have all adopted this strategy.[39]

With online publishing moving faster than ever, journalists rely heavily on press releases to meet reporting deadlines. Eighty-nine percent of journalists who responded to the Media Survey from Business Wire said they used press releases.

Business Wire Media Survey

Company Background/Statements: Include information that explains the history of the company or product(s). Starbucks, for example, includes a tab titled "Views."[40] Within the Starbucks "Views" tab, consumers can read about the company's stance on topics like fostering a culture of responsible self-government, comprehensive health care, the earth's changing climate, and more.

Leadership Team: Within this tab, integrate short biographies of the company owners or founders as well as the top leadership team. Often the name of the individual, the individual's professional title, and a photograph are included. Make the images clickable so that a journalist can select the person they wish to learn more about. The Campbell's Soup Company provides a list of its executive team members,[41] while Hewlett-Packard uses a yearbook-style format (http://bit.ly/HPExecutiveTeam) that provides the journalists with the option of immediately downloading a high-resolution image of the individuals comprising the executive team, since their photos are provided as part of the biographies. Again, this tactic makes reporters' work easier because they now have an image to include in their article.

Multimedia: The multimedia tab should include photographs of essential personnel, special events, products, and logos, as well as infographics and video snippets. White papers, reports, webcasts, presentations, and b-roll round out a well-apportioned multimedia area. Some companies create separate tabs or provide a drop-down menu related to multimedia. One of the most comprehensive multimedia centers can be found on the Coca-Cola Company's website (http://bit.ly/CocaColaPressRoom).

Data: In today's data-driven, artificial intelligence, world a section dedicated to the data is key. News outlets have been using AI driven content for years.

Products: Include a list of products or services, with a brief description of each. Include copy that illustrates why the products or services are significant in the marketplace.[42]

FAQs/Fact Sheets: Many companies have a list comprising the FAQs from media representatives. Use this portion of the online media center to answer those questions. It is also a best practice to include a fact sheet or sheets depending on the business. Starbucks provides a general company fact sheet, company timeline, and a series of fact sheets on its products (http://bit.ly/StarbucksFactSheet).

Speakers or Interview Topics: Perform the legwork for a journalist by providing a list of topics that company spokespeople can speak to. Consider this tab the company's "expert's directory," an online resource typically developed by the PR department for use by members of local, regional, and national media who are seeking sources for interviews, inquiries, news, and feature stories. In providing an avenue for a company's experts to converse with members of the media, the company not only gains media exposure but also enhances its public image and illustrates the wealth of expertise that the company possesses.

Additional items to consider for the company media center include an AddThis or ShareThis solution that allows the media to share content more easily.[43] It is also a good idea to incorporate a calendar of events, highlighting upcoming events or trade shows, speaking engagements, and community appearances. Providing links to the company newsletter can also be beneficial and provides journalists with insights not available through press releases, fact sheets, white papers, images, or b-roll footage.

Navigating the Online Media Center

The design of the online media center is almost as important as the content itself. A website designer can help develop the best layout, navigation, and features based on specific requirements. However, the online media center should have its own navigation tab featured on the home page of the company website. Information presented within the online media center should be partitioned into separate tabs. This will make it easy for a journalist to navigate from one tab to the next without ever having to leave the online media center. For example, an organization may want to include separate tabs that indicate newsroom, historical press releases, a calendar of events, financial press releases, media contact information, and the latest featured story.

As technology and communication channels continue to evolve, the development of online media resources is now a business essential. Online media centers are vital for the modern journalist—equally as important as a traditional or social media press release. As a result of this trend toward companies providing more online content, the required elements within a press release have also changed. Not only do audiences desire substantial content that communicates an overarching story, but they also expect to see video, pictures, infographics, stats, and quotes. The public in general now yearns to experience the news, not just read about it. With this in mind, it is essential that practitioners understand how an online (social) press release differs from a traditional press release with respect to content and format.

> **"**Text-only press releases are slowly being phased out. While an overwhelming majority of journalists want press releases to include photos (73 percent), a significant number also prefer graphics (43 percent), infographics (32 percent), logos (29 percent), and videos (27 percent) to round out their reporting. **"**
>
> *Business Wire Media Survey*

Modern Press Releases

One of the most noteworthy events in the history of PR occurred on October 28, 1906. A tragic accident led to the advent of the first press release. PR expert Ivy Lee was working with the Pennsylvania Railroad when the tragic accident occurred. The lives of fifty passengers were taken when a three-car train of the Pennsylvania Railroad's new electric service jumped a trestle in Atlantic City, New Jersey, and plummeted into the Thoroughfare Creek.[44]

It is reported that Ivy Lee convinced the railroad company to release a statement about what had occurred. In doing so, Lee set in motion what is now considered the first press release. Ivy Lee created a public statement and presented it to journalists at the location of the train accident.[45] The *New York Times* was said to have been so utterly impressed with Lee's information that the newspaper printed the press release word for word on October 30, 1906.[46] Although it is rare for media outlets to use them verbatim these days, press releases still act as a starting point for journalists, bloggers, and content creators to compose a story.

A press release that is newsworthy, specifically targeted, and well written is always appreciated by media professionals. In printed form, the structure of the traditional press release has not evolved considerably in format. However, press releases communicated via social media are vastly different.

In the broadest terms, a social media press release, also referred to as a social media news release, can be defined as "a single page of web content designed to enable the content to be removed and used on blogs, wikis and other social channels."[47] SHIFT Communications developed the world's first social media press release template in 2006. The format of the social media press release has gone through many iterations and revisions over the years; however, there are some elements that have remained constant.[48]

SHIFT Communications Social Media Press Release Live Example

How to Make a Social Media Press Release [tweet this]

Making a social media press release is relatively straightforward. It's nothing more than a variable width table with the shareable social content in it. Remember that the goal of a social media press release is to make every piece of it shareable.

Everything you see on this page has a sharing mechanism of some kind, from the title itself to the story to the individual pieces of content. This way, everything is separable and divisible. If a media influencer just wants to use the video on their site, they can. If a podcaster just wants to grab the audio for inclusion in their show, they can. There's no requirement that you ship the entire thing lock, stock, and barrel.

The SMPR was created entirely in a plain vanilla HTML editor like Adobe Dreamweaver or BlueGriffon, using various social networks and content networks to provide the individual pieces.

There's a third hidden piece that's not immediately obvious. This social media press release is being hosted not on our corporate web site, but by our marketing automation system. As a result, it can detect when people who are already in our marketing database are looking at it, clicking on things, and sharing stuff, so we know if it resonates or not.

Like this? Let us know in the comments:

Nancy Griffin

Video

Audio

SHIFT Communications pioneered the first social medial press release. *Source*: SHIFT Communications.

> *Contact Information:* Prominently feature the media relations personnel contact information at the top. In addition to traditional details like an email address and office and mobile telephone numbers, include other pertinent contact information, such as other social media platforms that the company uses. Keep in mind that you should only list the outlets that you would want a media representative to use to contact you. It's OK if you want bloggers and journalists to simply call or email you, but do not list a Twitter handle if you do not intend to respond via Twitter.
>
> *The Headline:* A good headline has always been integral to entice a journalist to read your press release. You want the headline to immediately gain readers' attention so that they will continue to read further. Write captivating copy and include specific keywords that are likely to be picked up by search engines.
>
>> *Length:* Headlines should fall between 60 and 120 characters in length. Shorter headlines are easier to share on social networking sites like Twitter and Facebook and are more easily read via subject lines in an email inbox. Additionally, many of the top search engines have specific headline character limits. Google displays headlines that are 60 characters in length, Bing allows for 71 characters, and Yahoo! displays 120 characters.
>>
>> *Format:* Bold the headline and capitalize each word except for prepositions and words three characters or less. For example, "Consumers Find Social Media Increasingly Trustworthy."[49]

The Blog Post Heard around the World[1]

Influential Silicon Valley journalist and blogger Tom Foremski's now famous blog post, "Die! Press Release! Die! Die! Die!" sparked a revolution in the PR industry. The way PR professionals announced news to the media had not changed since 1906. Our tactics were stale.

When Formeski wrote this post, the year was 2006, and the PR industry was experiencing vast changes. Blogs, bloggers, citizen journalists, and social networking sites began to flood the scene. The long-standing rules between journalists and PR professionals were in a state of flux. Bloggers were "rogue" and played by different rules. For the first time bloggers like Chris Anderson were "outing" bad PR professionals,[2] and the industry began its transformation. Journalists needed more from PR professionals, and Foremski's blog post announced what was necessary—loud and clear!

To Foremski's credit, he did not just condemn and criticize the press release; he deconstructed what the problem was and suggested alternatives. Essentially, he put the framework together for what we now know as the social media press release. He suggested that PR professionals should deconstruct the press release into specific sections and tag the information so that media personnel could compile and connect useful information to aspects of the story. It was also suggested to include a larger number of links within the press release body and other relevant links to news articles and references. Foremski also proposed that a specific section of the social media press release include a brief description of the announcement, various quotes from C-suite executives, and financial information in varied formats.

Today's press releases need to adhere to the requirements of a modern-day audience in response to the way that information is obtained. Press releases that are interesting, informative, and entertaining need to be nimble and fit into multiple formats in order to resonate.[3] Captivating visuals, tweetable headlines, interesting factoids, keyword-friendly text, and easy-to-share pages provide the user with an enhanced experience over a traditional press release. Take the time to examine the overall outcomes and the actions that you want to inspire with a press release hosted within the social sphere.

---

[1] T. Foremski, "Die! Press Release! Die! Die! Die!," *Silicon Valley Watcher*, February 27, 2006, http://www.silicon-valleywatcher.com/mt/archives/2006/02/die_press_relea.php.

[2] C. Anderson, "Sorry PR People: You're Blocked," *The Long Tail*, October 29, 2007, http://bit.ly/1bRpBRy.

[3] M. Georgieva, "3 Characteristics of Successful Modern-Day Press Releases," HubSpot, October 21, 2011, http://blog.hubspot.com/blog/tabid/6307/bid/27623/3-Characteristics-of-Successful-Modern-Day-Press-Releases.aspx.

The Introductory Paragraph: Using the standard inverted pyramid—who, why, what, when, and where—tell the whole story. Provide a synopsis of the information contained within the press release. A succinct introductory paragraph is critical since many distribution channels only display the headline, a short summary, and a link to the news release.

Length: One to four sentences.

Format: Sentence case—capitalize only the first word as well as any proper nouns.

Supporting Paragraphs/Details: Develop a well-written message that resonates with your audience by capitalizing on traditional PR writing styles and incorporating bulleted points. The information provided within this section should tell your story. Stay away from advertising or marketing speak. Integrate details that support the main points, add interest, or reinforce a message. In traditional press releases the use of multiple quotes can be frowned upon, but multiple quotes from staff, customers, or experts in the field can help round out the story in social media press releases. Bloggers and journalists like to have many quotes to choose from. Statistics and charts can provide additional research and numbers often appreciated by journalists. Be sure to include links throughout the body copy.

Length: 300 to 800 words.

Format: Sentence case—capitalize only the first word as well as any proper nouns.

Example: The following release was written and released by Prudential and is an excellent example of the elements used in social media press releases: http://bit.ly/PrudentialPramerica.

Anchor Text Links: Social media press releases incorporate many anchor text links. Anchor text links are keyword-rich phrases that are linked to a relevant page on the Internet, which then provides additional details related to the phrase.

Data: Create a space where bloggers and journalists can find links to the data, stats, research, and statements highlighted within the press release.

Multimedia: Provide a variety of videos, photos, and sound bites that can be used to write the story. For example, if a new partnership is being announced, include a video interview with the CEO. If a new product is being launched, give bloggers and journalists an inside peek at the product by sharing multiple images or even a short video of the product.

Mobile-Friendly Audio: When including audio sound bites, use a service such as SoundCloud. This service is mobile compatible and allows readers to see and hear all aspects of your social media press release even when they are on the go.

Video: Videos can be created on any platform, but recent research has shown that YouTube is one of the best video options.[50] YouTube is fully mobile and provides one of the largest audiences available. Videos can play on a variety of devices, allowing journalists, bloggers, and content creators to view your video no matter where they are. It is also important to note that nearly all social networks recognize YouTube URLs and allow videos coming from the site to be played instantly.

Infographics: Infographics have exploded in popularity across social media and mainstream media outlets. They are an excellent way to highlight research, focus group results, survey outcomes, or insights from the company's latest white paper.

Sharing Tools: Incorporate buttons allowing readers to share and save webpages of interest. Social media is all about sharing information, and so it is important for readers to have the option to pin it, tweet it, like it on Facebook, share it on LinkedIn, and email it to friends. Many of these sharing buttons can be set up to share specific content or are text enabled so that your message is disseminated in the way that you intend.[51]

Social Commenting: Conversations are paramount on social media. Encourage conversations by integrating common plug-ins that foster discussions.

Creative Commons License: Dissemination of news in a connected world requires new policies. Too often bloggers and other content creators will see warnings like "Media use only" when visiting online media centers. This type of messaging can often dissuade these reporters from covering a company. A Creative Commons license is an online copyright release that clearly articulates how the content can be used and shared and should be considered as part of any media center's content-related policies. Removing any barriers or concerns about copyright that may cause your audience to hesitate is a best practice.[52]

The takeaway here is that a company should want its social media press releases to be shareable. Unlike traditional press releases that were deliberately sent specifically to journalists, social media press releases can be found, shared, and circulated through the social sphere. Prezly (http://www.prezly.com), MarketWired (http://www.marketwired.com), CNW (http://www.newswire.ca/en/index), and Pitch Engine (http://new.pitchengine.com) offer services to help with creating social media press releases and online media centers, as well as with distributing the finalized content.

HARO: Help a Reporter Out

Connecting with reporters has never been easier. In addition to social networking sites, there are online tools that PR professionals have available to help connect them directly with journalists, bloggers, and online influencers. As an example, HARO (Help a Reporter Out)[53] is a free service that connects reporters looking for sources on articles they are developing. Individuals who sign up for the service receive three emails a day that include queries from independent writers, freelancers, bloggers, and big media outlets, including the *New York Times*, *HuffPost*, ABC News, *Chicago Tribune*, Mashable, the *Wall Street Journal*, and *Good Morning, America*, among others. In addition to simply responding to inquiries, the emails can also be used to observe and jump on stories that are currently trending.

The Email Pitch

Responding to a HARO query is fairly straightforward. Since you already know what the journalist is looking for, it is easy to pull together a response. Here is an example of a HARO query, followed by the response this author provided:

Education

27) Summary: Seeking communications/social media expert to discuss origins of viral trends

Name: Mark Kosin FashionBeans

Category: Education

Email: query-7gfd@helpareporter.net

Media Outlet: FashionBeans

Deadline: 10:00 AM CST – 1 December

Query:

Preparing an article on the origin of current social media trends with a look at modern and historical origins. For example, who posted the first "selfie" online? What about the first self-portrait photograph ever? Can we see connective tissue between them?

Requirements:

Professors of communication who can speak to modern and ancient cultural communication would be ideal to speak with. Also interested in the insight of social media and internet historians.

Response:

Subject Line: HARO - Origins of Viral Trends

Good morning, Mark,

You can trace the origins of social media back to Ancient Persia with the advent of the first postal system which opened communication and brought about a larger sense of community. Of course, there is connective tissue between where we've been and where we're going. I'd be happy to answer some specific questions if you'd like. I'm a professor of PR and Social Media at Syracuse University and am the author of Social Media: How to Engage, Share, and Connect.

Kind Regards,

Gina

By the way, the first person to ever post a selfie was instagrammer @jennlee. She debuted the selfie along with the first use of the hashtag.

This HARO response resulted in the following article: http://bit.ly/memeshashtags.

Crystal DeStefano, president and director of public relations for Strategic Communications, states that in addition to responding to queries from sources such as HARO or direct emails from reporters, PR professionals must be proactive. She offers an example here:

Hi [reporter name],

For National Alzheimer's Awareness Month, [organization name] is hosting an informational speaker series on "Understanding Memory & Aging" with industry experts on [dates] at [location].

According to Alzheimer's International the disease

- Affects nearly 44 million people worldwide
- In 2017, Alzheimer's cost the United States $259 billion

- By 2050, costs associated with dementia could be as much as $1.1 trillion
- The global cost of Alzheimer's and dementia is estimated to be $605 billion, which is equivalent to 1% of the entire world's gross domestic product.

This is an important topic your readers need to know more about. If you are interested in speaking with our experts before the public, these professionals are available for media preview interviews on November 1 between Noon-2:00 p.m.

These interviews will only happen if we pre-schedule them. I will follow up tomorrow; however, if you have questions or would like to schedule directly, please call me at the phone number below.

[Signature]

[Contact information]

Where Do We Go from Here? Online Media Centers and Social Media Press Releases

In today's fast-moving business environment, wherein breaking news is often tweeted before major news outlets can even broadcast the story, many of the key conversations that we participate in happen in our online communities. It is here that our media influencers reside and where their messages carry an elevated level of importance. For this reason, PR practitioners must make every effort to ensure they have identified and cultivated a relationship with the correct media influencers in support of their organizational business strategies and objectives.

Knowing how to communicate and with the right tools is critical. Social media news releases achieve three times as much coverage as traditional news releases.[54] Today's PR practitioners need to understand that company media centers and social media–based press releases are only effective if they incorporate the right content using the right platform. The advent of new "modernized" media relations requires practitioners to embrace new methodologies and technologies and learn how to best communicate and interact with journalists, bloggers, and content creators. Incorporating interactive and multimedia content is now considered the norm and should be done to enhance a story in ways that traditional media could not.

Those PR professionals who follow the influencer relations guidelines and develop content ready for the social sphere will become instrumental in today's media relations field.

Netflix Revival: *Gilmore Girls: A Year in the Life*

This Stars Hollow Website was constructed specifically for the Gilmore Girls revival.

Our obsession with traveling back in time and reinvigorating our favorite TV classics has reached an all-time feverish high. *Fuller House*, *Will & Grace*, *Girl Meets World*, and *Raven's Home* are just a few of the most popular shows brought back to life.

"Reboots," as they are called, "are television shows that span multiple decades, some dating back to the 1960s and some that went off the air less than a decade ago. Many of the reboots feature members of the original casts, though in some cases, the sad fact of human mortality has made that impossible."[1] *Gilmore Girls* was probably the most elaborately planned revival to date.

On November 25, 2016, the highly anticipated premiere of *Gilmore Girls: A Year in the Life* aired on Netflix. According to *AdAge*, Netflix's *Gilmore Girls* revival ranked as the number three most-watched original series on the platform.[2]

Research/Diagnosis

A Nielsen study highlighted a 25 percent increase in utilization of smartphones, tablets, streaming boxes, and game consoles among eighteen-to-thirty-four-year-olds in the one year spanning 2014 and 2015. In contrast, and within the same demographic, viewership using the standard television fell by 10 percent over the same period.[3] This trend has continued to accelerate and diverge even more widely in today's technologically advanced landscape.

Recognizing this pattern, platforms like Netflix, Hulu, and Amazon Video are creating content that resonates, some being original programming, while others, like *Gilmore Girls*, are revivals.

According to Daniel Buckzpan, "from 2000 to 2007, *Gilmore Girls* was one of the WB network's most popular shows. The story of a single mother and her daughter became famous for its fast-paced dialogue, which the characters deployed at roughly the same speed as a livestock auction-eer. It went off the air in 2007, just as *Time* had named it one of its 'All-Time 100 TV Shows.'"[4]

It made sense to bring back this all-time fan favorite show.

Objectives

In the months leading up to the launch, Netflix developed a sophisticated social media and PR campaign to heighten the anticipation for the premiere of the four-part series and drive views.[5] By increasing anticipation for the revival through the campaign's strategies and tactics, Netflix could increase the number of viewers.

Strategies

The campaign had three main strategies[6]:

1. Appeal to the original fan base. Posting series throwbacks and being active on social media enticed original *Gilmore Girls* fans excited about a possible reboot prior to the official announcement of the revival.
2. Netflix was eager to entice younger generations who were not original fans to watch the reboot.
3. Through sophisticated content creation, Netflix created content that set out to generate global buzz by using earned and owned media tactics.

Tactics

Netflix's PR and social media campaign included a variety of tactics to increase buzz surrounding the revival prior to the premiere date. The key to Netflix's strategy was to engage the public through a variety of tactics that encouraged the public to share and engage with Netflix, the characters of *Gilmore Girls*, and each other.

The revival's social sharing was fueled by the interaction of the cast on social networking sites including Twitter, Facebook, and Snapchat. Netflix connected with the audience by sharing snippets like who would be joining the cast, behind-the-scenes videos of what it was like being back on set in Stars Hollow, and character interaction.[7] The importance of the "share-ability" of the reboot could not be understated and ultimately led to its success.

Paid Media: With Luke's Diner pop-ups, fans were presented with a unique opportunity to enjoy a cup of coffee at diners just like Luke's. In concert with their social media efforts, Netflix paid to host these one-day events, leveraging "experimental marketing" methodologies. Each event not only unveiled a pop-up coffee house but also successfully supported numerous promotional goals including establishing a substantial amount of social buzz and landing media coverage, ultimately translating into media leads.[8]

Earned Media: Media outlets dashed to cover the buzz resulting from the pop-up coffee shops, landing in both local and national news outlets including *Us Weekly*, *Entertainment Weekly*, and Buzzfeed.[9] Netflix enhanced the reach of the promotion, both socially and digitally, by encouraging media coverage, which was ultimately shared judiciously throughout the social sphere.[10]

Shared Media: A multipronged approach was used to connect with fans.

Instagram: The pop-up shops included cups with Luke's iconic logo, the infamous "No Cell Phones" sign was added for a touch of nostalgia, and some shops even had a cardboard cutout of actor Scott Patterson.[11]

Snapchat: *Adweek* reported that more than 500,000 people used the specially developed Snapchat filter, resulting in over 880,000 impressions.[12]

Twitter: Every actor, and even some characters such as Kirk, tweeted to help drive engagement.

Facebook: Announcements, behind-the-scenes photos and videos, and commentary were created to engage fans.

Hashtags: Netflix used a few hashtags throughout the campaign; however, #GilmoreGirls, #LukesDiner, and #festival-offourseason were the most widely used.

Owned Media: The Festival of Four Seasons was another innovative and creative tactic. For two days fans could experience their favorite and most memorable pieces of *Gilmore Girls* thanks to the successful partnership of UCLA and Netflix in preparation for *Gilmore Girls: A Year in The Life*. UCLA utilized its Dickson Court and transformed it into a real-life Stars Hollow with fan favorites including Luke's Coffee, Kim's Antiques, a seasonal photo booth, twinkle lights, Taylor's Olde Fashioned Soda Shoppe, the gazebo, Miss Patty's Founder's Day punch, and Kirk's Button Emporium.[13] As if the sheer volume of excitement from Stars Hollow locations wasn't enough, the Festival of Four Seasons decided to include citizens from Stars Hollow as the icing on the cake. Event organizers anticipated huge crowds and advised visitors to secure their spot in line early and plan on spending forty-five minutes to an hour inside the festival.[14] Some coffee cups from the Luke's Diner event held a promo code for a free three-month trial of Netflix. Finally, the Stars Hollow website (https://townofstarshollow.org/) offered fans multiple ways to engage with the show: free downloads; tweeting congratulatory messages to the bride and groom; and a "Dear Kirk" advice column on Facebook, Twitter, and through email.

Implementation

The campaign ran from the official announcement of the reboot on January 29, 2016, to the premiere of the four-part series on November 25, 2016. *Gilmore Girls: A Year in the Life* illustrates a well-crafted campaign to bring back the beloved TV show.[15] Netflix combined paid, earned, shared, and owned to launch a sophisticated PR and social media campaign.

Reporting

The success of the campaign hinged on the willingness of fans to engage and share the content using social media. "*Entertainment Weekly* reported that Symphony, a streaming tracking company, claims that *Gilmore Girls: A Year in the Life* brought in 5 million viewers (18-49 viewers) within the first 3 days of release."[16] Following the premiere on Netflix on November 25, 2016, an estimated 1.6 million media impressions were reported in the first thirteen hours, and 1.4 million *Gilmore Girls* mentions on Twitter in the same time frame. According to *AdAge*, the revival ranked as the number three most-watched original series on Netflix, following the season 4 premiere of *Orange is the New Black* at number two and the season 1 premiere of *Fuller House* at number one.[17]

I thank Josie Bobeck, Nicole Raymond, Hope Sayler, and Courtney Schultz for inspiring and contributing to parts of this case study through their research which was used to write this case study.

1 D. Buckszpan, "'Full House' and 7 Other Long-Forgotten TV Shows Coming Back," *Fortune*, February 26, 2016, http://fortune.com/2016/02/26/fuller-house-tv-reboots/.
2 *AdAge*, "'Gilmore Girls' Early Ratings: Revival Ranks as One of Most-Watched Netflix Originals," December 1, 2016, http://adage.com/article/media/gilmore-girls-ratings-revival-ranks-watched-netflix-originals/306977/.
3 Buckszpan, "'Full House' and 7 Other Long-Forgotten TV Shows Coming Back."
4 Buckszpan, "'Full House' and 7 Other Long-Forgotten TV Shows Coming Back."
5 Bobeck, Josie, Nicole Raymond, Hope Sayler, and Courtney Schultz. "Gilmore Girls: A Year in the Life." December 2016. Written for the class "Integrated Campaigns" at Eastern Michigan University, https://docs.wixstatic.com/ugd/49c25e_af73a52723fe4ffcadc41274bbb84426.pdf.
6 Bobeck et al., "Gilmore Girls: A Year in the Life."
7 L. McClelland, "Gilmore Girls Revival: A Case Study in Millennial Marketing," Medium, November 30, 2016, https://medium.com/the-mvp/gilmore-girls-revival-a-case-study-in-millennial-marketing-b99af1df2cb2.
8 Buckszpan, "'Full House' and 7 Other Long-Forgotten TV Shows Coming Back."
9 T. Hardes, "How to Create a Social Media Campaign like Netflix," Echo (web log), October 28, 2016, http://www.echostories.com/social-media-campaign-gilmore-girls/.
10 Hardes, "How to Create a Social Media Campaign like Netflix."
11 Hardes, "How to Create a Social Media Campaign like Netflix."
12 Hardes, "How to Create a Social Media Campaign like Netflix."
13 Bobeck et al., "Gilmore Girls: A Year in the Life."
14 "Town of Stars Hollow," accessed November 28, 2016, https://townofstarshollow.org/.
15 Bobeck et al., "Gilmore Girls: A Year in the Life."
16 A. Mourad, "Data, Data, Data: How Gilmore Girls Made a Comeback in 2016." E-Nor Analytics Consulting and Training, March 14, 2017, https://www.e-nor.com/blog/data-visualization/data-data-data-how-gilmore-girls-made-a-comeback-in-2016.
17 *AdAge*, "'Gilmore Girls' Early Ratings: Revival Ranks as One of Most-Watched Netflix Originals."

#LRNSMPR

Learn Social Media and Public Relations

Apply the principles learned in this chapter to the scenarios below.

- This chapter discussed the importance of working with journalists. Choose a local nonprofit organization or your favorite brand. Imagine you are their media relations manager. Find a story that you feel is newsworthy. Research at least three reporters who would want to cover the story, explain how you would pitch them and why, and then write a pitch email, a pitch Tweet, and a pitch via LinkedIn.
- John Hall, cofounder and CEO of Influence & Co., said,

  The age of the standard press release is no more. Unless you're Apple—or you have some truly ground-breaking product—you're wasting your resources if you're continuing to write and distribute traditional press releases to journalists and outlets to get them to cover your news. Rather than trying to gain media coverage through ineffective press releases of a time gone by, it's critical for PR professionals and marketers to embrace new and different ways of getting news about our offerings and accomplishments to our audience members. Take advantage of social media, develop relationships with industry leaders and influencers, and incorporate quality visuals in your messages to get the attention of journalists and outlets that can help you spread your message.[1]

Ponder this statement; then discuss the implications of this quote on today's media relations activities.

- Planning is the key to designing an effective online media center and developing a social media press release. Company webpages can be great resources and highlight many of the aspects that are mentioned in this chapter. Visit an online newsroom from the list provided:

United Nations: http://www.un.org/press/en
Global Down Syndrome Foundation: https://www.globaldownsyndrome.org/2017-press-releases/
The newsroom of your university or college

After exploring the media centers, provide answers to the following questions:

1. How easy is it to find the online media center from the home page of the website?
2. Once in the online media center:
   a. Is the contact information prominently displayed?
   b. Are there clearly marked tabs devoted to specific information?
   c. Are there links to rich content like infographics, webcasts, podcasts, and audio files?
3. Does the company provide contact info, names of press contacts (including contact info), RSS links, and social media platforms?
4. Is the information accessible on a mobile device?
5. Is a Creative Commons license in place, or is the information strictly for journalists?

---

[1] J. Hall, "7 PR Trends You Need to Know in 2016," *Forbes*, December 14, 2015, https://www.forbes.com/sites/johnhall/2015/12/13/7-pr-trends-you-need-to-know-in-2016/#1e3da5d5235c.

Notes

[1] A. Mitchell et al., "The Modern News Consumer," Pew Research Center, July 7, 2016, http://www.journalism.org/2016/07/07/pathways-to-news/.

[2] Mitchell et al., "The Modern News Consumer."

[3] Mitchell et al., "The Modern News Consumer."

[4] T. Rosenstiel, ed., "Ideological News Sources: Who Watches and Why. Americans Spending More Time Following the News," Pew Research Center, 2010, accessed July 22, 2013, http://www.people-press.org/files/legacy-pdf/652.pdf; K. Hampton et al., ed., "Social Networking Sites and Our Lives: How People's Trust, Personal Relationships, and Civic and Political Involvement Are Connected to Their Use of Social Networking Sites and Other Technologies," Pew Research Center, 2012, accessed July 22, 2013, http://www.pewinternet.org/files/old-media/Files/Reports/2011/PIP%20-%20Social%20networking%20sites%20and%20our%20lives.pdf.

[5] Rosenstiel, ed., "Ideological News Sources"; Hampton et al., ed., "Social Networking Sites and Our Lives."

[6] "Cannes Lion Award-Winning 'Three Little Pigs Advert,'" *The Guardian*, February 29, 2012, https://www.youtube.com/watch?v=vDGrfhJH1P4.

[7] T. Nudd, "The 10 Best Commercials of 2012," *Adweek*, November 26, 2012, accessed July 14, 2013, http://www.adweek.com/news/advertising-branding/10-best-commercials-2012-145324?page=1.

[8] F. Seitel, *The Practice of Public Relations* (Upper Saddle River, NJ: Pearson Education, 2014).

[9] Seitel, The Practice of Public Relations.

[10] A. Tu, "In Asia, PR Must Move beyond Media Relations and Look for Other Ways of Influence," *Asia Pacific Public Relations Journal* 17, no. 2 (2016): 4–8, http://novaojs.newcastle.edu.au/apprj/index.php/apprj/article/view/88/64.

[11] B. Solis, *Engage: The Complete Guide for Brands and Businesses to Build, Cultivate, and Measure Success in the New Web* (New York: Wiley, 2011).

[12] C. Anderson, "Sorry PR People: You're Blocked."

[13] Nielsen Company, "Buzz in the Blogosphere: Millions More Bloggers and Blog Readers," last modified March 8, 2010, accessed July 26, 2013, http://bit.ly/16i9ZC1.

[14] J. Romo, *Share This: The Social Media Handbook for PR Professionals* (West Sussex, UK: Wiley, 2012).

[15] Messe Frankfurt, "PR 2.0: Blogger Relations," Connected (web log), November 11, 2014, https://connected.messefrankfurt.com/2014/11/11/blogger-relations-pr/.

[16] Solis, *Engage*.

[17] Solis, *Engage*.

[18] A. Parker, *Share This: The Social Media Handbook for PR Professionals* (West Sussex: Wiley, 2012), chap. 15.

[19] Solis, *Engage*.

[20] R. Johnson, "Pitching the Perfect Pitch to Bloggers," Hoosier PRSA Blog, July 12, 2010, http://bit.ly/1bgXi1i.

[21] G. Livingston, "Anatomy of a Great PR Pitch," Geoff Livingston, September 9, 2010, http://bit.ly/1aDVpYM.

22 Livingston, "Anatomy of a Great PR Pitch"; Johnson, "Pitching the Perfect Pitch to Bloggers"; H. Whaling, "Effective Blogger Relations," prTini, September 15, 2010, http://bit.ly/13YJhlZ.

23 Mediakix Team, "How Many Blogs Are There in the World?" Kix (web log), September 14, 2017, http://mediakix.com/2017/09/how-many-blogs-are-there-in-the-world/#gs.sWiwOc4.

24 A. Crestodina, "Blogging Statistics and Trends: The 2017 Survey of 1000 Bloggers," Orbit Media Studios, October 25, 2017, https://www.orbitmedia.com/blog/blogging-statistics/.

25 Parker, *Share This*.

26 R. Lerner, "Twitter Tops Snapchat—Among Journalists, at Least," *Forbes*, May 26, 2017, https://www.forbes.com/sites/rebeccalerner/2017/05/26/twitter-tops-snapchat-among-journalists-at-least/#738693677b79.

27 B. Mullin, "Report: Journalists Are Largest, Most Active Verified Group on Twitter." Poynter, March 2, 2017, https://www.poynter.org/news/report-journalists-are-largest-most-active-verified-group-twitter.

28 H. Hahn, ed., "What Is Good Twitter? The Value of Social Media to Public Service Journalism," Eurovision, 2013, accessed July 26, 2013, http://bit.ly/15kr5An.

29 Seitel, *The Practice of Public Relations*; D. Wilcox et al., *THINK Public Relations* (Upper Saddle River, NJ: Pearson Education, 2013).

30 Seitel, *The Practice of Public Relations*.

31 Seitel, *The Practice of Public Relations*.

32 Seitel, *The Practice of Public Relations*.

33 Seitel, *The Practice of Public Relations*.

34 Seitel, *The Practice of Public Relations*.

35 C. Penn, "Social Media Press Release 2.0," SHIFT Communications, December 2013, http://www.shiftcomm.com/2012/12/social-media-press-release-2-0.

36 E. Verlee, "How to Create a Good Online Media Center," PR in Your Pajamas, http://prinyourpajamas.com/online-media-center.

37 For the McDonald's Newsroom's press releases, visit http://news.mcdonalds.com/Corporate/Press-Releases.

38 "Online Newsroom Best Practices," PR Newswire, last modified 2013, accessed November 26, 2013, http://www.prnewswire.com/knowledge-center/online-public-relations/Online-Newsroom-Best-Practices.html.

39 For Southwest Airlines' "Media Inquiries" page, see http://www.swamedia.com/pages/contacts; for the Lands' End media contacts, see http://www.landsend.com/newsroom/media_contacts; for the Dick's Sporting Goods "Press Room" page, visit http://www.dickssportinggoods.com/corp/index.jsp?page=pressRoom&ab=Footer_Know_PressRoom.

40 For the Starbucks Newsroom "Views" page, visit http://news.starbucks.com/views.

41 Campbell's Soup Company, "Leadership Team," http://www.campbellsoupcompany.com/about-campbell/executive-team.

42 Verlee, "How to Create a Good Online Media Center."

43 J. Kessel, "The Online Media Room: Why It Needs to Be Part of Our Communications Strategy," Kessel Communications, http://kesselcommunications.com/the-online-media-room-why-it-needs-to-be-part-of-our-communications-strategy.

44 M. Belles, "How to Write a Press Release—Invention of the First Press Release," About.com, last modified 2013, accessed December 7, 2013, http://inventors.about.com/od/pstartinventions/a/press_release.htm.

45 Belles, "How to Write a Press Release."

46 M. Kennedy, "The History of the Press Release," eReleases, March 29, 2010, http://www.ereleases.com/prfuel/history-of-the-press-release.

47 I. Capstick, "Social Media Release Must Evolve to Replace Press Release," Media Shift, April 23, 2010, http://www.pbs.org/mediashift/2010/04/social-media-release-must-evolve-to- replace-press-release113.

48 Penn, "Social Media Press Release 2.0"; "Writing Great Online News Releases," PRWeb, last modified December 2013, accessed December 8, 2013, http://lp.prweb.com/Global/FileLib/Guides/PR-WEB_-_Writing_Great_Online_News_Releases.pdf; S. Bruce, *Share This: The Social Media Handbook for PR Professionals* (West Sussex, UK: Wiley, 2012), chap. 16.

49 "Writing Great Online News Releases."

50 Capstick, "Social Media Release Must Evolve to Replace Press Release."

51 Capstick, "Social Media Release Must Evolve to Replace Press Release."

52 Georgieva, "3 Characteristics of Successful Modern-Day Press Releases."

53 See the Help a Reporter Out website at http://www.helpareporter.com.

54 A. Parker, "Social Media News Releases Achieve Three Times the Pickup," ShowMeNumb3R5, March 22, 2011, http://www.showmenumbers.com/news-release-distribution/social-media-news-releases-achieve-three-times-the-pickup.

Content Creation and Curation 6

Corporations create and curate their own content using multiple media platforms. Completing this takes time; doing it effectively takes knowledge, skill, and the right tools. In this chapter you will learn how to successfully use self-publishing tools to connect with consumers and disseminate your company's message, while concurrently selecting and organizing content.

KEY LEARNING OUTCOMES

1. Distinguish between content creation and content curation.

2. Grasp the essential components of corporate blogging.

3. Understand how organizations can use podcasting as part of their public relations (PR) and social media strategies.

SOCIAL MEDIA EXPERT

Daniel Burrus (@DanielBurrus, website: https://www.burrus.com/blog/)

With more than 104,000 Twitter followers and a blogging fan base that spans the globe, it's no wonder that Daniel Burrus arguably writes one of the most influential blogs around. He is considered a world-leading futurist regarding global trends and innovation.[1] The *New York Times* has referred to him as one of the top three business gurus in the highest demand as a speaker. Burrus has authored seven books, including *Flash Foresight*, *Technotrends*, and *The Anticipatory Organization: Turn Disruption and Change into Opportunity and Advantage*.

---

[1] D. Burrus, "About Daniel Burrus: Keynote Speaker, Business Strategist, and Global Futurist," Burrus Research, https://www.burrus.com/about/about-daniel-burrus/.

Content Reigns Supreme

Journal articles, trade magazines, conferences, and blogs all repeatedly preach the mantra "Content is king, content is king, and content is king." Bill Gates was the first to introduce this premise to readers in his aptly titled article "Content Is King." In this piece Gates discussed the impact that the Internet would have on the creation and curation of content by noting, "One of the exciting things about the Internet is that anyone with a PC and a modem can publish whatever content they can create."[1] This statement foreshadowed the world that we live in today. The Internet ushered in a revolution of self-publishing tools and leveled the playing field.

On a similar note, a good tool is only considered valuable when it appropriately supports a set of desired tactics. Social media strategies have become integral to social development because they provide channels that connect audiences with similar interests, thus enabling dialogue where meaningful relationships can be forged. Information is the key to holding any customer's attention. By developing a solid social strategy and focusing efforts on superior content creation, a business can

- build long-lasting relationships
- increase a company's social influence
- improve SEO efforts

Content Curation versus Content Creation

Creating Curated Content

Content curation is the process of gathering existing information from blogs, social media posts, or other platforms relevant to a particular topic and sharing it with your brand's followers. Practitioners who are leading content strategy tend to follow the loose rule of approximately 70 percent/30 percent created to curated content when pulling together copy.[2] Third-party information such as articles, tweets, photos, video, music, and more make up curated content. PR practitioners use this material to bundle ideas and contextualize information in what can be seen as a "news-like" format.[3]

The art of content curation illustrated in five simple steps: title, image, copy, quote, and a call to action. *Source:* Curata (curata.com).

Mitchell Hall, content marketing director for Curata (www.curata.com), developed a list of five elements to include when curating content.

1. *New Title:* Always craft a new headline to avoid competing with the original article in search engine results. A good headline can be the difference between someone clicking on your article or ignoring it. Five sites worth bookmarking when curating content:
   - Upworthy.com: Although many of these titles can be outrageous, simply browsing this site will help in brainstorming catchier titles.
   - UpworthyGenerator.com: This website provides a new Upworthy-style title every time you click "Generate." Again, while these titles can be outrageous—and in this case, fake—it's a good jumping-off point to start pushing the boundaries with headlines.
   - TitleCapitalization.com: This tool comes in handy any time you are wondering which words are capitalized in a title. Simply paste your title into the field on the home page and it automatically corrects capitalization errors.
   - UberSuggest.org: This website helps find popular keywords surrounding various topics to help your article rank higher in search engine results.
   - Thesaurus.com: Never underestimate the power of a synonym. Often, simply inserting one word in place of another can take your title to the next level.
2. *New Image:* To avoid copyright issues and add originality, use an entirely new image. Useful image sites include
   - Stock photo libraries such as Shutterstock, iStock, and RGBStock

- The Creative Commons for free "Copyleft" images in a range of licenses
- Image creation tools such as Canva
- Basic design tools such as PowerPoint, and more sophisticated tools such as Adobe Creative Suite and the free, open-source GiMP

3. *Body Text:* Original body text should take up the majority of the post. Include the following elements:
   - *Attribution* of the original article and author (with a link to the article)
   - *Commentary* and/or annotation. Frame the original article in a useful way to your readers by citing the content's relevance to them and provide your own analysis on the topic or issue at hand.
   - *Links to created content.* You've no doubt spent time creating unique and interesting blog posts, ebooks, and other resources. Now is the time to link back to these assets—when they relate to the topic—and give your audience additional value/further reading.

4. *Quote:* Draw in a quote from the original article, or even several quotes. The exact format can vary depending on the length of the original article and its topic. Be sure to pick a quote or stat that will surprise, educate, and/or entertain your readers. This is your opportunity to bring in intelligent outside voices—one of the main advantages of content curation.

5. *Call to Action:* A call to action (CTA) is necessary for every blog post, but it's especially important for curated content. Don't leave readers hanging. Link to a piece of your content that helps expand their knowledge on the subject at hand.

   Offer readers a piece of gated content such as an ebook or a webinar to help generate new leads and nurture existing leads. Keeping leads engaged reinforces how you are catering to their needs and bringing them value on a consistent basis.

Creating Original Content

Content creation is the process of creating your own content and sharing it with followers or subscribers. There is nothing better than writing your own content. Most organizations develop a content strategy to follow as a blueprint, incorporating various platforms such as blogs, podcasts, infographics, case studies, images, and more. According to Justin McGill from Hubspot, to develop a content strategy an organization must first audit the content it currently has. The best way to accomplish this is to review the organization's content marketing initiatives spanning the past year and identify any new projects that will complement the upcoming goals and objectives of the company.[4] Next, he suggests figuring out who the audience persona is. This is important because organizations can then focus on creating specific content that will be inherently more valuable to the target audience.[5] When this is executed correctly, an organization can look to target a new type of consumer or continue to grow the market within the current demographic. Understanding and reviewing the target audience parameters on a continual basis is critical to expanding an organization's audience reach. Finally, determine the types of content the organization wants to produce. Infographics, videos, ebooks, blogs, and podcasts are some of the most popular. This chapter will cover how a company can create original content using blogs and podcasts.

Blogging

News Blogs

You probably read more blogs than you think. According to Elise Moreau, blogging is one of the most popular ways to report on newsworthy topics. *HuffPost,*

BuzzFeed, Mashable, *The Daily Beast*, and TechCrunch are some of the most widely read and popular blogs.

HuffPost[6]: Founded in 2005 by Arianna Huffington, Jonah Peretti, and Kenneth Lerer, *HuffPost* (formerly *The Huffington Post*) specializes in reporting news stories and events including world news, entertainment, politics, business, and style, among others. *HuffPost* has millions of bloggers who contribute content daily.

BuzzFeed[7]: BuzzFeed is a trendy news blog that targets Millennials. In addition to offering social news and entertainment articles, in recent years BuzzFeed has begun publishing serious news and long-form journalism on topics like technology, business, and politics.[8] BuzzFeed is so popular that Syracuse University offers a class that specializes in developing content for the platform.

Mashable[9]: Pete Cashmore started Mashable in 2005. The blog reports within several areas including entertainment, technology, business, culture, and science. With hubs in the UK, Asia, France, India, and Australia, Mashable is one of the largest and most reputable go-to sources for all things in digital culture, according to writer Elise Moreau. The blog has 28 million social media followers, boasting 45 million monthly unique visitors and 7.5 million social shares a month.[10]

TechCrunch[11]: Michael Arrington started TechCrunch in 2005 with the purpose of developing content surrounding the culture of the Internet, technology, computers, social media, websites, and fledgling companies. What started out as a blog by Arrington is today a network of its own, creating content for related websites such as CrunchNotes, MobileCrunch, and CrunchGear.

The Daily Beast[12]: Tina Brown, former editor of *Vanity Fair* and *The New Yorker*, launched *The Daily Beast* in October 2008. *The Daily Beast* delivers its readers news and opinion pieces on topics such as entertainment, books, fashion, technology, politics, financial news, world news, arts and culture, drink and food, and style.

Corporate Blogs

The general population uses blogs more frequently than any other self-publishing tool. Around the globe more than two million blog posts are published daily on the Internet. It is estimated that by 2020 there will be 31.7 million bloggers in the United States.[13] WordPress and Tumblr are the most popular blogging platforms because they have easy-to-use, easy-to-understand interfaces that facilitate growth from novice blogger to pro blogger.[14] Blogs tend to focus on a single area of interest, an industry, or a particular topic. The blogosphere contains everything from "foodie" blogs to "techie" blogs and everything in between. Maintenance of a blog is generally the responsibility of an individual, group of individuals, or corporation. The intent of a blog is to encourage communication by establishing conversations within a community of like-minded people. Interactive in nature, blogs incorporate text with photos, links, and videos, allowing the author to paint a complete picture of the topic of interest.[15] PR professionals can utilize blogs as a platform to create branded content, a form of owned content, which should be shared across multiple social platforms.

Not surprisingly, corporate blogs can be a blessing and a curse.[16] As with other forms of communication via the social web, corporate blogs provide information about a company using open, two-way communication. They establish a channel that can demonstrate expertise; communicate insights; listen, engage, and respond to customers; and promote meaningful conversations about the company and its principles, values, and vision.[17] Oftentimes corporate bloggers become industry experts on the subjects that they support regarding a company's services and products. By positioning the blog content properly, corporate bloggers can provide valuable information to all interested parties on a consistent basis. Companies that maintain blogs or participate in blogging communities effectively deal with a myriad of issues, including crisis situations, often in the very medium where these topics are first discussed. By participating in these conversations, corporate blogs allow a company to react quickly. If properly executed, blogs are a platform where a company can determine the direction of content.

When 81 percent of American online consumers trust information and advice from blogs and 61 percent of U.S. online consumers make purchases based on recommendations from a blog, a comprehensive strategy should be considered.[18] Generally speaking, corporate blogs that resonate stick to the 80/20 rule.[19] That is, they contain content that is relevant to their audience at least 80 percent of the time to increase engagement. The remaining 20 percent is dedicated to content about the company or company products. Blogs that establish a purpose and encompass the larger online community make sense.[20] With that in mind, some disadvantages of corporate blogs do exist and pertain directly to the messenger, messages, and content. Many discussions focus on who, within the organization, should hold the responsibility for blogging.[21] Initially, corporate blogs acted as personal journals. This, in theory, would empower executives to become effective bloggers by allowing their voices to benefit from personalization.[22] If a company chooses a poor corporate blogger, it could have a negative effect on the blog. That is why there are few examples of good corporate blogs. Notwithstanding, Southwest Airlines and Dell are two companies that consistently maintain excellent corporate blogs.[23]

Nuts about Southwest, the corporate blog maintained by Southwest Airlines, is successful because it has everything to do with its customers and nothing to do with the marketing of the company.[24] The blog is separate from the company website and is maintained by a myriad of bloggers—thirty in all—including employees, customers, and partners. This variety is exactly what makes it unique and effective. The blog embraces the "FunLUVing" attitude of the company and connects Southwest employees with its community of flyers in a fun, engaging way.[25] Nuts about Southwest provides information ranging from blog posts to videos, social updates, photos, Pinterest boards, and podcasts—all with the user in mind. This simple-to-use platform also incorporates the use of tags that allow users to quickly find the content they want to read or see.

Direct2Dell, the official Dell corporate blog, was launched in 2006 and is one of the oldest business blogs that thrives in its market segment.[26] The intent of the blog is to open the lines of communication between the customers and the company—*to participate in the conversation.* With regular updates, the blog provides a balance of commentary on new products, product releases, consumer services, customer tips, and issues that are relevant to customers. If we apply the 80/20 rule to this blog, it is easy to see why the Direct2Dell blog is effective in promoting conversations with the company's customer base.

There are many attributes, features, and elements that contribute to the success of corporate blogs. Because blogs provide an opportunity for organizations to talk directly to more than 180 million people at any given moment, ensuring proper maintenance of a company blog is paramount.[27]

Helpful Blogging Tips

- Today's ideal blog is around 1,600 words. Image-heavy posts should stay around 1,000.
- Short headlines are key. This allows others to retweet important posts. Hubspot reports that titles with eight words receive a 21 percent higher click-through rate as compared to longer headlines. Try keeping headlines to 70 characters so they show up in search engine results without being truncated.[1] Headlines with clarifying bracketed information such as [Infographic], [Report], [White Paper] perform 38 percent better than headlines without.[2] For example a headline might look like this: How Businesses are Using Microinfluencers on Instagram [Podcast]

- Posts with images receive 94 percent more views, so include photos, infographics, GIFs, memes, and video to complement the blog.
- Take part and encourage conversations. Negative comments can be an opportunity to develop good customer relations. Become part of the blogging community by participating on other blogs.
- Be authentic. Your online community will see through marketing strategies.

---

[1] Wainwright, Corey. "How to Write Catchy Headlines and Blog Titles Your Readers Can't Resist." HubSpot Blog. June 12, 2017. https://blog.hubspot.com/marketing/a-simple-formula-for-writing-kick-ass-titles-ht.
[2] Wainwright, "How to Write."

Getting Started

The decision to initiate a corporate blog should not be taken lightly. It is a long-term communication strategy commitment. It takes time and resources to start a blog, develop the voice of the blog, and build an active community.[28] Many companies are thrilled to launch a blog, but after the initial excitement fades, the corporate blogs often die off.

The standard life cycle of a blog can be quite dim. Initially, organizations are excited and post two or three blogs per week, which then decrease to once a week, and then to once a month, before being abandoned altogether.[29] By setting realistic goals, this doesn't have to be the outcome. When a company decides to embark upon blogging, there are ten simple steps that it needs to first consider:

1. *Determine the Blog Team:* A blog cannot be sustained by one person alone. It requires a team of people to support the efforts of the blog.[30]
2. *Determine the Blog's Purpose:* Blogs can be used in a variety of ways, but a company should focus on a short list of purposes for the blog; otherwise the intent can be diminished or confusing. Decide what messages you would like readers to take away from your blog. These messages can help build brand awareness, expand reach, encourage loyalty, foster customer satisfaction, increase sales, assist in times of crisis, and cultivate thought leadership.[31]
3. *Determine the Blog's Target Audience:* The blog's overarching goal will help you establish the target audience. Research the habits of the target audience. Do its members comment and participate in the online community, or are they lurkers?[32]
4. *Determine the Persona and Voice of the Blog:* Every blog has a persona and voice. Blogs are not traditional marketing pieces. They are less formal in nature, project a personality, have a distinct point of view, and contain no corporate-speak. Blogs need to be well written. The best blogs engage us and make us want to participate in them. It may take time to find a company persona and voice. When starting a blog, ask multiple people at the company to try their hands—human

resources, engineers, customer service, product development, customers, and vendors. The individuals who are good bloggers will gravitate to the top, while the others should cease blogging for the company. Every now and then try to incorporate blog posts from C-suite executives. Their voices should round out the corporate blog.[33]

5. *Develop the Meaning for the Blog:* Determine the type of content the blog will contain.[34] Create categories that will be covered on a consistent basis. For example, NYC PR Girls has eleven categories that it routinely blogs about, including PRofiles, events, PR, and life in New York City.[35] How-tos, narratives, lists, and video posts are also often found in successful blogs.

6. *Develop an Editorial Calendar for the Blog:* Develop an editorial calendar to keep the blog on track and maintain consistency within the blog.[36] As a rule of thumb, new blogs should post two to three times per week. Once an organization writes twenty-one to fifty-four blog posts, blog traffic generation increases by up to 30 percent.[37] Adhering to this schedule is partially why many corporate blogs are abandoned. Know what is coming up over the next week, month, and year to help bloggers stay on top of their posts. Michele Linn has created a great tip sheet for establishing editorial calendars (http://bit.ly/ContentCalendarTips).

7. *Develop a Publication Schedule for the Blog:* Editorial calendars are useless without publication schedules. Publication schedules clearly assign deadlines for the final publication date.[38] Tuesday and Wednesday are the best days for a company to share content. The average blog post will receive the most traffic between nine thirty and eleven a.m. Eastern Standard Time.

8. *Develop the Rules for the Blog:* All blogs should have rules.[39] These outline the social media guidelines, the types of acceptable posts, and the consequences for rule breakers. Provide prospective bloggers with clear guidelines from the outset. This will help eliminate confusion for your bloggers and your blog community.

9. *Develop a Content curation Plan for Your Blog:* "Content curation" is one of the hottest buzz phrases in the industry. Beth Kanter defines it best as "the process of sorting through the vast amounts of content on the web and presenting it in a meaningful and organized way around a specific theme."[40] A curator's duties include determining the best content and selecting the most relevant content to share with the online community.

10. *Develop a Promotional Plan for Your Blog:* Once you click "Post," only the people on your team actually know that there is new content available. To grow your blog, you will need to promote it.[41] Keyword searches, RSS feeds, URL shorteners, and status updates on other company social networking sites are some of the most common elements in a promotional plan. Additionally, you can promote your new posts in your email signature or send them out directly to your customer list.

Blogging is an easy channel of communication with your customers, prospects, employees, and general stakeholders, and creation of a blog account is free and simple. Blogs are one of the few platforms whereby you own, create, and curate company- and product-related content. The goal of a blog is to establish a conversation between the writer and the intended audience via comments. With this in mind, setting aside twenty to thirty minutes each week to promote these conversations is not asking much.[42] Marko Saric, a blogger and curator for HowToMakeMyBlog, suggests that bloggers should develop a post distribution routine to ensure consistency. Approximately 50 percent of a blogger's time should be devoted to the creation of content, with the remaining 50 percent reserved for active promotion. Keep in mind that companies can grow their presence on the social web over time through *interaction* and *engagement* with their larger community.

CONTENT MARKETING ROUTINE
after publishing your post

Promotional efforts start after you've published your post. If this work is not done, your post will most probably go unnoticed no matter how good it is. Visitors will not come automatically - follow this routine to drive traffic to your content.

 Tweet out the headline and the link to make your Twitter followers aware of the new post. Include an image for more attention!

Post the link with the image attached on your Facebook page. Displaying the image on your wall instead of the link thumbnail works best in terms of reach and engagement.

 Follow the same process on your Google+ profile. You should also join relevant Google+ communities, be active in them by sharing your knowledge, and then post your link once in a while as well.

Publish the post on your LinkedIn profile as well.

Submit the post image to relevant Pinterest boards. Make sure to include a headline in all the images that you put on your site.

Stumbleupon is still a nice source of traffic and you should aim to stumble all the posts that you publish in hopes of getting some visitors from there.

Keep an active Tumblr account with the main objective being for it to be a traffic driver to your site.

 Some of the articles might do well in certain subreddits on Reddit. Reddit has the potential to drive thousands of visitors to you!

 Send personal tweets and emails to certain influencers that you think the post might be interesting to in hope of getting them to share it with their networks.

Link to your new post from other relevant posts in your archive!

 Comment on the most recent posts of relevant sites that have good traffic numbers. Leave valuable comments only!

You can even write and submit guest posts to relevant and popular sites in which you would include the link to my new post.

 Depending on the niche you are in, there will be several community sites that allow you to submit content. Sites like Hacker News. There's a Hacker News type site out there for every niche.

REVIEW & REPEAT

 After several hours, take a look at the results, feedback, and data on initial push. It is useful to know before proceeding! Aim to repeat the process on selected profiles several times over the next few days!

For more blogging inspiration, visit howtomakemyblog.com

Drive traffic to your company's content by cross promoting on multiple platforms. *Source*: Infographic courtesy of Marko Saric (http://howtomakemyblog.com).

Podcasting

Organizations tend to forget the versatility of podcasts when planning their overall social strategy. Similar to blogs, podcasts are based on content that you own. This means that you have complete control over what you create and share. Users should create podcasts with the audience in mind and steer clear of direct marketing of their products. Podcasts allow companies to record seminars and conferences, spotlight customer success anecdotes, invite cohosts, create a monthly talk show, MC round-table discussions, or feature a panel of subject-matter experts.[43] With podcasts the content options are limitless, with creativity as the main driver of valuable content.

The process to create, edit, and publish podcasts is a straightforward and simple endeavor. The infrastructure necessary to record a podcast is a computer or tablet, a microphone, and great content. Today's computers are preassembled with the necessary tools that make creation of a podcast very easy. Podcasts are versatile in format (.m4a, .mp3, .mp4, .mov, .wav), which means that anyone can listen anywhere. The potential reach of a podcast is vast.[44] Your audience can listen to a podcast at the gym, walking the dog, or driving to work. The key to this social channel is that it provides a platform for uninterrupted quality time with your listeners. As a bonus, subscribing listeners are notified each time you post new content.[45] Since each podcast has its own distinct RSS feed, many are connected to podcatchers. The intent of podcatchers is to read the RSS feeds and automatically download media files for users to review at their convenience.[46] Podcatchers can download audio files in MP3 format, videos, newsfeeds, text, and photos. Some podcatchers even move the files to a

Podcasting Statistics

Edison Research found that podcasting continues to boom.

- Four in ten Americans tune in to a podcast regularly.
- Research indicated that 112 million Americans have listened to a podcast. Of those, 67 million Americans listen to podcasts monthly while 42 million listen to podcasts weekly.

- Podcast fans listen to five shows per week, and the average listener subscribes to six podcasts.
- Two thirds of podcasts are listened to on a phone or tablet.

Source: Edison Research, "The Infinite Dial 2017," March 30, 2017, http://www.edisonresearch.com/infinite-dial-2017/.

user's MP3 player automatically, while others download each file to a separate folder. Either way, the delivery of messaging and material directly to individual listeners is a huge benefit of podcasts.

By developing a voice for your company, podcasts can help further cultivate relationships with your customer base. The key to all social media is the ability to be authentic. The audible word has a much stronger connection with people than the written word. Podcasts allow for audiences to hear speakers' emotions and connect with their personalities.[47] Genuine connections build loyalty. The host must engage the audience and entice listeners to return. Diction, sincerity, and attitude play a significant role in the creation of a podcast.[48]

Additionally, take time to reward and acknowledge loyal listeners. Often listeners email the host or post their opinions in comment sections. It is important to incorporate these insights into your podcasts on a regular basis. By doing so, you will establish trust with the online community and positively affect the company's social presence.[49] Listeners feel a heightened sense of validation when they believe that their contributions matter.

The ability to share a podcast has also never been easier. The format is embeddable and easy to share within websites and blogs and can be incorporated across all social platforms that the company utilizes.[50] Also, do not forget to upload all completed podcasts onto iTunes. Millions of people search iTunes daily, seeking new content, so it is important that your podcast is available to be searched for by the larger audience.[51]

Public Relations and Social Media Podcasts That Resonate

For Immediate Release (FIR),[52] hosted by Neville Hobson and Shel Holtz, is a series of podcasts that focus on topics in communication and PR. Subscribers can listen to the biweekly podcast The Hobson and Holtz Report and learn about the current happenings in the online communication and PR circles. Hobson and Holtz also interview experts in the technology and organizational communication arenas, review popular books on PR and communication, and offer podcasts from PR meetings and conferences.

The Public Relations Society of America (PRSA) broadcasts Voices of Public Relations, a series of podcasts from guest bloggers. Podcast topics include advocacy, media relations, "On the Record . . . Online," and even some case studies. The intent of the PRSA podcast format is to connect PR professionals with experts in the field.[53]

Business Wire broadcasts the All Things Press Release podcast.[54] This is a series of three-minute-or-less podcasts that address FAQs posed to Business Wire editors and account staff. Tips, how-tos, and guidance based on industry experience are discussed courtesy of the Business Wire staff and outside counsel. Popular podcasts include "How to Write a Good Headline," "Getting Your Press Release into Google News," and "When's the Best Time to Send a Press Release."

The Social Pros Podcast: Real People Doing Real Work in Social Media,[55] with creators and hosts Jay Baer, Jeffrey Rohrs, and guest contributor Zena Weist, broadcasts thirty- to sixty-minute podcasts that highlight various preeminent social media strategists, FAQ sessions, and specialized "Four Your Information" segments, wherein guests share their insights and thoughts on four questions asked by the host.

The connection that makes these podcasts unique is that, while the hosts are all experts in their fields, they also all own businesses. Take notice—none of these hosts hawk their wares to their listeners. Through genuine conversations, they produce interesting messages whereby listeners can learn and share with others.

Podcasting in Europe

European counterparts are also paying attention to the value of podcasts. Once regarded as a niche medium with minimal appeal, podcasting is now seen as a way to connect with consumers. According to Mike Russel from New Media Europe, "Almost everyone has a podcast these days, including some high-profile celebrities who are typically associated with mainstream media. Over the past decade, podcasting has grown beyond its humble roots and evolved into one of the most popular broadcasting techniques."[56]

There are thousands of podcasts available on the web, with more being added daily. With tools like Oculus Rift coming to market, we can expect to see podcasts taken to the next level as they become increasingly immersive and interactive.[57]

Socializing Business

As organizations move toward a social, integrated way of conducting business, PR professionals and social media strategists must rethink a customer's journey and relationship with a brand. Blogs and podcasts allow customers to engage and interact with brands that they know and trust in ways that move them from passive to active interaction with companies. It is time for a sweeping change, a reorganization of how companies share what they know with their consumers. Adoption of a more social, integrated customer experience using an evolved communication process will drive companies to better position themselves as part of customers' experience with their brands.[58]

As our society becomes more mobile, consumers now gravitate toward and desire on-demand content. Blogs and podcasts are excellent social tools that allow businesses to connect with consumers and promote themselves. These tools can also go a long way to establishing you as a thought leader within your industry. The right choice of topics can nicely harmonize with the strengths of your company, as well as promote thoughts and ideas that you and your target audience are passionate about. That passion, and the time committed to establishing a deeper connection with your customers, will shine through and provide ample content to share as the use of these tools evolves within your business.

Louise Delage and the Sobering Truth of Her Success on Instagram

This case study originally appeared on the blog Laz's Lounge by Brandon Lazovic.

Meet Louise Delage. She's a twenty-five-year-old Parisian who shares fun moments of her daily life on Instagram, ranging from spending time with friends, enjoying the outdoors, eating at restaurants, and cuddling with her cat Jean-Claude.

Despite entering the social media scene in August 2016, Louise Delage gained more than 60,000 followers in a matter of weeks, armed with nothing more than relevant tags, stunning photos, and a cheery smile. Her success isn't entirely surprising, considering Instagram boasts more than 800 million monthly users; many of these users are young women just like Louise Delage, and numerous brand accounts market to this audience.

From sitting at the beach with glasses of rosé, eating lunch and drinking red and white wines, sipping on champagne in bubble baths, or attending social events holding mimosas, every post blends with one another.

In her final update Delage shared a video with a shocking reveal: she's a fictional character who's part of an ad campaign called "Like My Addiction."

Research/Diagnosis

The Paris agency BETC created the campaign for Addict Aide, an organization raising awareness of alcoholism among young adults and providing resources for those who are affected by excessive alcohol consumption.

According to Addict Aide, one out of every five deaths that occur among young adults annually are caused by addiction.

Many of Louise Delage's followers failed to notice that almost all of her 150 pictures showed her with a drink in hand. Stephane Xiberras, BETC president and creative director, thought it would be interesting to "create a person people would meet every day but whom we'd never suspect of being an addict."

Objectives

"The more people stage their ideal life on social media, the more that serves to hide a not-so-ideal reality," said Xiberras in an interview with *Adweek*.

Three images were posted at peak traffic times in the morning, afternoon, and evening, with each post accompanied by nearly thirty relevant hashtags for food, outdoors, vacation, and travel. BETC went as far as to mimic fashion bloggers to recreate attitude, filters, and poses for the pictures.

The campaign was also boosted by creating efficient bots to follow specific accounts on Delage's behalf for follow-backs; influencers with 20,000 to 100,000 followers were contacted to promote Delage and her account.

Strategies

While it was based entirely on organic and earned reach, Louise Delage's acquisition strategy was deeply rooted in "native Instagram content and user habits, building an acquisition strategy around four pillars: content, hashtags, bots and a KOL [key opinion leader] strategy," according to Xiberras.

Tactics

Using one platform, Instagram, Xiberras utilized shared media to make an impression.

Implementation

Timing was a critical factor as the BETC ended the campaign within a specified time frame instead of dragging their audience along until someone called them out. The reveal video also aimed to inform viewers and raise awareness of addiction instead of giving a sense of misdirection or feeling duped.

Reporting

In terms of metrics, the campaign was a success: Addict Aide received more than five times its usual traffic after the big reveal, more than 140 articles were written on the story, and Louise Delage became a trending topic on Twitter in France. "Like My Addiction" won 17 Lions—coveted and well-respected awards in the creative communications, advertising, and related fields—at the Cannes Lions International Festival of Creativity, which is the largest gathering of worldwide advertising professionals, marketers, digital innovators, and designers in the world.

The Louise Delage account stills boasts 110,000 followers, exceeding BETC's KPI [key performance indicators] of 8,000 followers and 50,000 likes; as the campaign went viral, it garnered more than 1 billion impressions and 9.8 million hits in earned media without spending any money on advertising.

Even though "Like My Addiction" is considered to be a resounding success, Xiberras felt as though it could have been conducted better, stating that it's difficult on Instagram to differentiate between fiction and reality.

"We hoped for more followers to take notice of Louise's behavior," he said. "There were a few people who sensed the trap—a journalist among others, of course—but in the end, the majority just saw a pretty young girl of her time and not at all a kind of lonely girl, who is actually not at all that happy and with a serious alcohol problem."

Source: B. Lazovic, "Louise Delage and the Sobering Truth of Her Success on Instagram," Laz's Lounge, November 27, 2017, accessed December 15, 2017, https://www.brandonlazovic.com/louise-delage-instagram-success/.

Learn Social Media and Public Relations

Apply the principles learned in this chapter to the scenarios below.

- Find a corporate blog, then answer the following questions: What is the blog's title and purpose? Is this clear to an outside audience? Who are the bloggers? What are their credentials? Are bios of the bloggers available? Is there an email or contact section? How often is the blog updated? What is the regularity of updates? Are comments from the blogging community answered? If so, how quickly? If not, why not? How well is the blog organized? Is the template effective? Are there social sharing buttons? Are the blog's policies clearly stated? Are they easy to find? Are they followed?

- David Burkus (http://davidburkus.com), Sarah Miller Caldicott (http://www.forbes.com/sites/sarahcaldicott/), and Gijs van Wulfen (http://www.forth-innovation.com) were named as part of the official top twenty innovation blogs 2016. Go to their blogs and read some entries. Consider what makes these blogs stand out.

- Imagine you are the PR and social media specialist for your university. You've been assigned to develop a podcast. The topic is up to you. Brainstorm to decide what you will cover, who the target audience is, and what tools you will need to create the podcast.

Notes

1. B. Gates, "Content Is King," *Internet Archive Wayback Machine*, January 3, 1996, http://www.microsoft.com/billgates/columns/1996essay/essay960103.asp.
2. M. Hall, "Content Curation: The Art of a Curated Post [Infographic]," Curata (web log), August 21, 2017, http://www.curata.com/blog/content-curation-the-art-of-a-curated-post-infographic/.
3. K. Howell, "Content Curation Explained" (lecture, October 2, 2017 Syracuse University), PowerPoint presentation lecture notes.
4. J. McGill, "How to Develop a Content Strategy: A Start-to-Finish Guide," HubSpot Blog, 2017, https://blog.hubspot.com/marketing/content-marketing-plan.
5. McGill, "How to Develop a Content Strategy."
6. E. Moreau, "The Top 10 Most Popular Blogs Online," Lifewire, June 11, 2017, https://www.lifewire.com/top-most-popular-blogs-3486365.
7. Moreau, "The Top 10 Most Popular Blogs Online."
8. Moreau, "The Top 10 Most Popular Blogs Online."
9. Moreau, "The Top 10 Most Popular Blogs Online."
10. Moreau, "The Top 10 Most Popular Blogs Online."
11. Moreau, "The Top 10 Most Popular Blogs Online."
12. Moreau, "The Top 10 Most Popular Blogs Online."
13. Statista, "Number of Bloggers in the United States from 2014 to 2020 (in Millions)," 2017, https://www.statista.com/statistics/187267/number-of-bloggers-in-usa/4.
14. Statista, "Number of Bloggers in the United States from 2014 to 2020 (in Millions)."

15 L. Safko, *The Social Media Bible: Tactics, Tools and Strategies for Business Success* (New York: Wiley, 2010), chap. 7; E. Terra, "What Is a Podiobook?" *Podiobooker*, September 21, 2012, http://blog. podiobooks.com/frequently-asked-questions.

16 P. Smudde, "Blogging Ethics and Public Relations: A Proactive and Dialogic Approach," *Public Relations Quarterly* (2005): 34.

17 B. Solis, *Engage: The Complete Guide for Brands and Businesses to Build, Cultivate, and Measure Success in the New Web* (New York: Wiley, 2011).

18 Writtent, "Top Blogging Statistics: 45 Reasons to Blog," March 18, 2017, https://writtent.com/ blog/top-blogging-statistics-45-reasons-to-blog/.

19 E. Robertson, "The 80/20 Rule for Social Media Success," Marketing of a Different Color, August 2012, http://www.marketingofadifferentcolor.com/2012/08/the-8020-rule-for-social-media-success.

20 Smudde, "Blogging Ethics and Public Relations."

21 W. Waddington, *Share This: The Social Media Handbook for PR Professionals* (West Sussex, UK: Wiley, 2012), chap. 11; K. Hanson, "Should the Boss Be Blogging?" *Strategic Communication Management* 10 (2006): 6–7.

22 Robertson, "The 80/20 Rule for Social Media Success."

23 Solis, *Engage*; Robertson, "The 80/20 Rule for Social Media Success"; N. Harbison and L. Fisher, "40 of the Best Corporate Blogs to Inspire You," *Ragan's PR Daily*, September 13, 2012, http://www.prdaily.com/Main/Articles/40_of_the_best.

24 See the Southwest blog at http://www.blogsouthwest.com.

25 Solis, *Engage*.

26 See the Dell corporate blog at http://dell.to/14dfqUo; Robertson, "The 80/20 Rule for Social Media Success."

27 Nielsen Company, "Buzz in the Blogosphere: Millions More Bloggers and Blog Readers," last modified March 8, 2010, accessed July 26, 2013, http://bit.ly/16i9ZC1.

28 Nielsen Company, "Buzz in the Blogosphere."

29 Nielsen Company, "Buzz in the Blogosphere."

30 H. Cohen, "9 Must-Have Elements for Company Blogs," Content Marketing Institute, November 24, 2010, http://contentmarketinginstitute.com/2010/11/company-blog-elements.

31 Solis, *Engage*.

32 Waddington, *Share This*, chap. 11.

33 Solis, *Engage*; Robertson, "The 80/20 Rule for Social Media Success."

34 Smudde, "Blogging Ethics and Public Relations."

35 See the NYC PR Girls website at http://nycprgirls.com.

36 D. Jackson, "4 Steps for Creating a Social Media Calendar," Sprout Social, October 2, 2017, accessed December 27, 2017, https://sproutsocial.com/insights/social-media-editorial-calendar/.

37 Writtent, "Top Blogging Statistics."

38 Writtent, "Top Blogging Statistics."

39 R. Luttrell, "Throw Out Your Social Media Policies!" Gina Luttrell PhD, July 26, 2013, http:// ginaluttrellphd.com/2013/07/26/throw-out-your-social-media-policies.

40 B. Kanter, "Content Curation Primer," Beth's Blog, October 4, 2011, http://www.bethkanter.org/ content-curation-101.

41 Jackson, "4 Steps for Creating a Social Media Calendar."

42 Safko, *The Social Media Bible*.

43 J. Van Orden, "7 Reasons to Create Your Own Podcast," How to Podcast Tutorial, last modified 2013, accessed August 7, 2013, http://www.howtopodcasttutorial.com/seven-reasons-to-create-your-own-podcast.htm.

44 C. King, "6 Podcasting Tips from the Pros," Social Media Examiner, September 8, 2012, http:// www.socialmediaexaminer.com/6-podcasting-tips-from-the-pros.

45 Safko, *The Social Media Bible*.

46 Terra, "What Is a Podiobook?"

47 Safko, *The Social Media Bible*.

48 Van Orden, How to Podcast Tutorial IS.

49 Van Orden, How to Podcast Tutorial IS.

50 Solis, *Engage*.

51 Safko, *The Social Media Bible*, chap. 10.

52 See the FIR Podcast Network at http://forimmediaterelease.biz/index.php.

53 R. Mottola, "PRSA 2013 Health Academy Conference Preview with Founders of Healthy TXT," Public Relations Society of America, April 18, 2013, http://podcast.prsa.org/podcast.

54 iTunes, "All Things Press Release," https://itunes.apple.com/us/podcast/all-things-press-release/ id323723658?mt=2.

55 Convince and Convert, "Social Pros Podcast," http://www.convinceandconvert.com/social-pros-podcast.

56 M. Russell, "Mike Russell, Author at New Media Europe," New Media Europe, accessed December 27, 2017, https://newmediaeurope.com/author/mike-russell/.

57 New Media Europe, "A Brief History of Podcasting," http://newmediaeurope.com/2015/a-brief-history-of-podcasting.

58 M. Fidelman and D. Hinchliffe, "Rethinking the Customer Journey in a Social World," *Forbes*, November 26, 2012, accessed August 8, 2013, http://www.forbes.com/sites/markfidelman/2012/11/26/rethinking-the-customer-journey-in-a-social-world.

Social Networks

7

In today's digital age, the frequency of individuals using social networking sites to connect with brands they love increases daily. Influencers initiate conversations with other influencers about what's trending, what's hot, what's new, who's who, and where to go for the best sushi. These conversations allow some brands to excel at connecting and resonating with their social users, while other brands flounder in the social web of confusion. This chapter focuses on the most popular social networking sites and the companies who understand their audiences.

KEY LEARNING OUTCOMES

1. Classify and separate each social networking platform.
2. Learn the unique features of the major social networking platforms.
3. Contextualize how brands use social media to connect with key target audiences.

SOCIAL MEDIA EXPERT

Ben Silbermann (@8en, website: www.pinterest.com)

As the CEO of Pinterest, Ben Silbermann notes that the idea behind Pinterest came from his love of collecting as a child. "Collecting tells a lot about who you are," he said, and when they looked at the web, "there wasn't a place to share that side of who you were."[1] Today, Pinterest has become a social networking platform that does more than help people discover and save creative ideas. It drives awareness, increases website traffic, boosts in-store and online sales, and connects people with the brands they have come to rely upon.

---

[1] M. Panzarino, "Pinterest's Ben Silbermann on turning his collection hobby into a product and not making money," The Next Web, May 29, 2013, https://thenextweb.com/insider/2013/05/30/pinterests-ben-silbermann-on-turning-his-collection-hobby-into-a-product-and-not-making-money/.

Setting the Stage

It seems that we are introduced daily to a new social networking site or tool on the social web. Some have staying power, some linger a bit, and some simply fizzle out as quickly as a new one gains traction. Currently there are hundreds of social networking sites on the social web. This chapter focuses on some of the predominant social networking sites today.

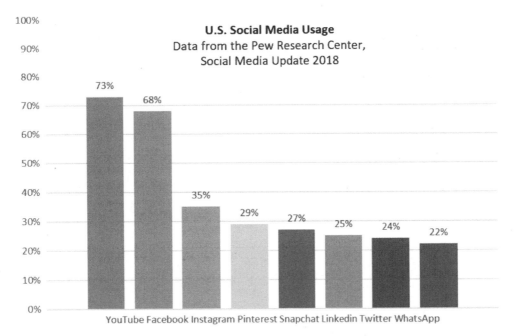

U.S. Social Media Usage
Data from the Pew Research Center,
Social Media Update 2018

The 2018 Pew Research Center survey of social media use among adults finds that the online landscape highlights a mix of long-standing platforms and newly emerging networks. *Source:* Smith, Aaron, and Monica Anderson. "Social Media Use in 2018." Pew Research Center: Internet, Science & Tech. March 01, 2018. http://www.pewinternet.org/2018/03/01/social-media-use-in-2018/.

With so many avenues to approach and design a brand strategy, it is always beneficial to the success of the strategy to plan ahead. Social media strategies should be synergistic with the overall corporate communications, public relations (PR), and marketing plans. Successful social strategies include elements from every department within the company. A few elements to keep in mind as you begin to design your social media strategy include the following:

- *Goal Plan:* When companies decide to embark upon a social strategy, including setting up a Facebook fan page, creating a Pinterest board, or initiating a Twitter account, they must first define what they want to achieve. Set clear goals and be sure to consider how this activity fits within the overall communications strategy. You also need to take the time to determine whether your customers utilize the particular social networking site(s) that you plan to utilize.
- *Content Plan:* Formulate a plan for maintenance of your content. Social sites must be continually maintained or consumers will become uninterested and leave. Your social strategy should outline the frequency that devised content will be uploaded—hourly, daily, weekly, or monthly. Consistency is key; however, posting relevant content is equally important.
- *Conversation Plan:* Companies must determine the types of conversations that they are seeking to have with their consumers. It is also helpful to consider any anticipated responses that will materialize. Is a retweet good enough, or is the expectation to converse back and forth between customers and your brand? Is liking a post on Facebook okay, or does the company want consumers to share the information with their audiences too?
- *Operation Plan:* Who is going to manage the social site? Planning is always fun, but once the planning is over, someone must curate content and maintain the site. Protocols, reputation management guidelines, and rules for conduct are all essential.

Social Network, Social Networking Site, Social Networking

There are three common terms often confused with one another: "social network," "social networking site," and "social networking." Author Gohar Khan simplifies the three[1]:

- Social networks are groups of nodes and links formed by social entities.
- Social networking sites are specific software or social media tools designed to facilitate

relationships. Facebook is the most commonly known social networking site.

- Social networking is the act of forming, increasing, and maintaining relationships on the social sphere.

---

[1] G. F. Khan, *Seven Layers of Social Media Analytics: Mining Business Insights from Social Media* (Leipzig: Verlag Nicht Ermittelbar, 2015).

- *Evaluation Plan:* As with all PR planning, the "evaluate" stage is critical. One method of measurement is to record the number of conversation starters. For example, you can track the number of status updates, videos, or links that a company shares to generate conversations. Companies can also track the number of fans, increases in fans, likes, and posts generated by fans. Measuring outcomes that correlate with corporate goals and communication goals is also a good way to evaluate the success of a social strategy.

Social strategies should support the overarching goals of the communications plan and those of the company. Any metrics collected should be weighed against those goals to understand the level of success that each initiative has achieved.

Facebook

With more than 1.37 billion people using Facebook and more than 2.07 million active daily users, Facebook is considered one of the most influential social networking sites in the world.[1]

Facebook provides users with the ability to share information and communicate with family and friends, while also promoting openness and connectivity. More than 4.75 billion pieces of content have been shared daily since 2013.[2] This includes web links, news stories, blog posts, status updates, photos, and more. Facebook provides a place to not only share information but also to interact with it. News organizations, for example, allow people to post their stories directly to their Facebook walls to share with friends. Brands use Facebook to build communities and engage with consumers in a more personal and meaningful manner. Facebook is also accessible through mobile phones, iPads, and other tablet devices. It makes sense to include Facebook in a company's social strategy, considering that the average Facebook user is connected to eighty pages, groups, and events.[3]

Back to Basics

Understanding the fundamentals will go a long way in establishing a strong presence on Facebook. Certain terminology is used frequently, and therefore it is important for PR professionals and social media strategists to have a firm grasp of the language used and its meaning. A list of the most frequent terms used when referring to Facebook is provided below[4]:

Brand Page/Profile—the official presence of a business, artist, political official, brand, cause, or product where the owner shares information and interacts

SOCIAL MEDIA CHEAT SHEET
(for brands)

		PROS	CONS
	FACEBOOK The largest social network. 1.28+ billion users. 4.75 billion pieces of content shared daily. Virtual necessity for brands investing in social. DEMO: 65% 35+ yrs old; 60% female.	- Fans are 79% more likely to purchase than on other networks. - Contains advanced ad targeting capabilities for massive audiences. - Powerful and valuable analytic insights.	- Low organic reach (pay to play). - Saturated by brands, so it's difficult to stand out.
	TWITTER 271 million active users post text, links, images, and 6 second videos (Vines) in 140 characters or less. DEMO: 18-29 yrs old, increasingly female.	- Strong customer service tool. - Strong analytics.	- Expensive, limited ad platform. - Short lifespan of posts.
	INSTAGRAM Primarily mobile app with 200+ million users who share pictures and short videos. DEMO: 37% 18-29 yrs old; 68% female.	- Untapped audience by many brands. - Facebook owned, so great potential.	- No links, analytics, or scheduling capabilities. - Advertising capabilities in their infancy.
	PINTEREST Online collaging resource for sharing inspiration and bookmarking links. 70 million users. DEMO: 79% female.	- Strong, receptive audience with buying power. - Generates over 400% more revenue per click than Twitter and 27% more than Facebook.	- Not effective for brands with limited web presence or e-commerce. - Skews highly female.
	GOOGLE PLUS Niche social network of 300 million users (though not very active). DEMO: 31% are 25-34 yrs old; 62% male.	- Great SEO benefits because it's owned by Google. - Ties to Google AdWords and YouTube.	- Uncertain future. - Largely inactive user-base.
	LINKEDIN Network of 300 million users. Exists for company information, updates, and recruiting. Demo: White collar, urban or suburban users; balanced between genders.	- Best used to establish your brand as industry leader/authority - Valuable recruiting tool.	- Unlikely to drive sales, unless B2B.
	SNAPCHAT Mobile app for sharing pictures between friends. 100 million users and rapidly growing. DEMO: 71% under 25 yrs old; 70% female.	- Find your customers where they live.	- Resource intensive. - Creativity required.

The social media cheat sheet provides a quick guide that simplifies the pros and cons of each major social network. *Source*: Infographic courtesy of Likeable Media (www.likeable.com).

with fans on Facebook. Pages create a culture that allows businesses to interact and engage with their fans one on one.

EdgeRank—an algorithm used to determine the content that appears in a person's newsfeed.

Fan—a Facebook user who "likes" a corporation's business page.

Friend—(v) to add a person as a connection to your personal profile; (n) a personal connection on Facebook.

Friend List—an ordered sorting of friends.

Group—an organized group of users with a common connection or similar interests, for example, "coworkers" or "family." Groups can be public or private.

Insights—the metrics used to analyze demographic data about the user's audience. Insights also highlight how people see, discover, and respond to posts.

Like(s)—(v) to become a fan and "like" a business's page or to "like" a comment posted by a friend or business; (n) the number of users who "like" your page.

Network—a collection of Facebook users, who may be related to a school, location, place of employment, or category such as "engineer," "nurse," or "educator."

Newsfeed—the center column of a user's home page. The newsfeed is continually updated with status updates, photos, videos, links, likes, and app activity from friends and pages that users follow. This section can be broken down by "top news" or "recent news."

Personal Profile—pages for individuals, not businesses, who have an account from which they are able to share information and interact with brands.

Timeline—a collection of the photos, stories, and experiences that users or brands post.

Constructing Your Brand Page on Facebook

Setting up a brand page on Facebook is fairly straightforward and easy. Facebook has very simple and uncomplicated instructions for novices (http://bit.ly/CreateA-PageFB). Brand pages offer "insights" that include statistical data that can be useful in measuring growth. As a company's social strategy develops and matures over time, data and analytics will become increasingly important. Which promotions work and which may need tweaks and promotional "reach" can be evaluated through insights.

A brand page also affords a company an additional opportunity to highlight important information that the customers might find important. The company address, telephone number, website, and email address, as well as other social networking sites that the company is on, are all excellent pieces of information that a company should include. The company logo should be the profile photo for the brand page. Aldi, the NFL, Maybelline, Dick's Sporting Goods, Mastercard, the *New York Times*, and even television shows such as *The Good Doctor* and *Saturday Night Live* are examples of brands that incorporate their logos as their profile photos. This helps reinforce the company brand. A company may also elect to set up customized Facebook landing pages that require users to "like" the company page before they are able to access certain features. Some brands like Pier One Imports require users to "like" their pages before they can receive a coupon during certain promotions.

Attractive, Interactive, and Fresh

Brand pages should be attractive to your audience and provide enough information to generate interest in your products, services, and company. One of the benefits of a brand page is that it allows for mutual interaction. Set up a photo gallery, update the company status regularly, post videos, share links, and invite consumers to events. Facebook events can be used to promote anything from product demos to Internet shows, community events, and open houses. Invite users to the event so that they can then share it with their friends. This is an excellent technique to generate buzz about upcoming special occasions. Keep content fresh. Including fun, creative posts is important, but be sure to follow the 80/20 rule, also known as the Pareto rule: 80 percent of the time the content should be relevant to your audience, with the remaining 20 percent specific to the company or products.[5] Companies understandably want to make fans aware of their products and services, but it is important to make use of customer stories, photos, videos, and other interesting and informative responses when establishing the community.

Customized URL Address

Custom URLs make it easy to direct people to your brand page. Facebook allows brands to choose a specific URL address. For example, Dick's Sporting Goods uses https://www.facebook.com/dickssportinggoods/, where "dickssportinggoods" is the customized portion of the show's Facebook URL. Companies should use the same username, or a very similar username, on all social networks to reinforce consistency within the brand. Keep it short, so that consumers can remember it. Bit.ly allows for users not only to shorten links but also to customize them.

Badges, Widgets, and Apps

Once a user likes a company brand page, a company then has access to that fan on a consistent basis. Badges, widgets, and apps are excellent techniques to connect on a more in-depth level. There are four types of badges for sharing different information. "Profile" badges are used to share profile information, a "like" badge showcases pages that users have liked, a "photo" badge shares Facebook photos, and a "page" badge advertises a company page on Facebook.

Brands will often want to expand the audiences that their Facebook pages reach. Adding third-party widgets from Facebook's App Center allows companies to run contests on their pages, collect data with forms, import external feeds, and customize content through HTML coding.[6] Facebook apps allow for a deeper incorporation into the core Facebook experience and even tap into Facebook algorithms to help reveal the best content for users.[7] Apps fully integrate with Facebook.com, the newsfeed, and the notifications—all of which drive traffic and engage users.

Live Streaming

The challenge with video marketing is creating catchy and attractive videos when faced with the realities of human and financial constraints.[8] Debuting in 2016, live streaming allows users to stream live videos using only a smartphone camera. This allows any Facebook user the unparalleled ability to engage and connect with your followers in real time.[9] Brands such as Martha Stewart and Kohl's have paved the path to success by using Facebook's live-streaming feature. Martha Stewart leverages the technology by streaming various how-to videos, recipes, and daily goings-on with Martha Stewart. Kohls partnered with Tone It Up to generate buzz for their live #GetActiveWithKohls campaign. Members of Tone It Up took to the airwaves to promote the cause by completing a live workout.[10]

Top Fan Brand Pages

Even with the rise in popularity of live video, fan pages remain an important aspect of social media planning. Generating buzz using creative incentives such as "liking" a page or reaching a certain number of "shares" allows fans to become brand advocates. Fans naturally want to engage with brands that resonate with them. By sharing a post or liking a company status update, a fan is promoting your business.

The first priority of a PR or social media practitioner is to listen to customers and communicate by engaging in conversations with them. Unlike traditional advertising or marketing, a Facebook strategy requires a deeper and more meaningful level of interaction. Here are some brands that are building formidable relationships on Facebook:

1. *TOMS Shoes:* The brand has tapped into its core belief system of the one-to-one principle. It follows the 80/20 rule by balancing fan responses and interactions with promotion of its products.
2. *Burberry:* This brand excels at hitting its target market with content that its users want. Elegant, simple, and stylish images present everything fans love about the brand. The company also connects with fans by showcasing past campaigns from previous years.
3. *Starbucks:* This Facebook brand page includes photos and updates from local stores. The company connects with fans by illuminating the intimacy of friends enjoying the coffee experience together.
4. *Ford:* The brand excels at having meaningful conversations with fans. The company promotes content that highlights the history of the Model T to Ford enthusiasts of today. Fans can download wallpaper or earn badges to declare their allegiance to their favorite Ford car—the Mondeo, the Mustang, and even the Escort.

Facebook and Google can give each company a run for their money if it were simply a numbers game. Both boast high active users, but what does that really tell us about using each as part of a strategic social media and PR plan?

Google

Within the PR industry Google is met with mixed reviews. If one were to simply look at the numbers, it would appear that it makes sense to include Google as part of a full social media plan. However, Google has struggled as a social networking site. Consumers have not readily taken to Google+ Circles and its ability to separate friends from "friends." What does this mean for a practitioner? Discount Google all together? Not exactly. Because Google offers easy integration across all of its platforms and services, including Google Search, Google Analytics, Gmail, and YouTube, practitioners should use Google where it makes the most sense. For PR professionals and social media strategists, the ability to pull data and analytics from these rankings provides a brand with the power to create strong and formidable campaigns.

One of the most important features aside from Search is Google Analytics, which can help PR professionals advance their reporting abilities.[11] Arguably, Google Analytics is one of the predominant tools when it comes to understanding insights about your digital efforts and how they support the overarching goals of the organization. Google Analytics can provide *a lot of* data. Using Google Analytics appropriately, a PR professional can tease out important data and develop targeted communication, allowing for better overall business decisions. Bernard Marr, author of *Data Strategy*, believes that turning data into action transforms an organization for the better.[12]

Data-driven strategies and social media analytics will be explored more thoroughly later in the book.

Twitter

Another social tool, Twitter, is often incorporated into a social strategy because it is a great way to start a conversation with your target market and build and manage connections with customers, prospects, bloggers, and a myriad of other influencers.

Launched in 2006, Twitter is a powerhouse on the social sphere. People clamor to connect with one another, update their statuses, learn about new products, share ideas, and create connections on Twitter. Twitter is one of the best social media channels for customer engagement.[13] With more than 500 million active users sending more than 500 million tweets per day, Twitter has become a crucial social media tool.[14] Businesses, both big and small, use Twitter for a variety of reasons, including lead generation, customer service, and even competitive intelligence. The rationale for introducing Twitter in the social strategy will vary based on individual company goals and outcomes.

Twitter is known as a "microblogging" service. The once succinct 140-character limit was eliminated by the company in favor of a more robust 280-character limit. Twitter noted that the "longer character count allowed users to express more of their thoughts without running out of room to tweet."[15] This was met with mixed reviews. According to Sara Perez, the controversy surrounding the decision is founded in the principle "that one of Twitter's defining characteristics is the brevity of users' posts. Many argued that the increase to 280 characters would make Twitter less readable, as longer tweets filled their timelines. Others suggested that Twitter's focus on a feature no one really asked for was diverting its attention from more critical problems—like the rampant abuse, harassment and bullying it's become known for unfortunately."[16] Only time will tell how brands will use the 280-character count to connect with their target audience.

The Business of Twitter

There are numerous lists available that identify the ways in which businesses are using Twitter to connect and, yes, even monetize their strategies. PR practitioners should lead the company strategy on Twitter by tweeting useful resources, insightful ideas, and helpful tips that will ultimately benefit their followers. Establishing company representatives as leaders within an industry is common in PR. Tweeting company resources, including white papers, blogs, and ebooks, is an excellent way to illustrate that a company representative is a thought leader. Following social media strategies and connecting with others on the social web is not just about your company. Take the time and commit the effort to link other resources within communications to your consumer base beyond those only written by the company.

In the business realm, using Twitter is more than merely tweeting content. A company Twitter page is like any other piece of collateral. It must be branded. The first thing a company should do when initiating a Twitter handle is to upload an image as the profile picture that represents the company and what the company has to say. Many companies opt to use a branded logo. Some small businesses or sole proprietors opt to use a photo of the person who maintains the Twitter account. Regardless of the image chosen, it should represent the professional image of the company. The profile background and header image should blend together well, since they also represent the brand. You want to make it easy for users to find what they are seeking when they search for you or your company on Twitter. It is important to detail your real name and location or the name of your company and

ABCs and 123s of Twitter

Similar to the other social networks, Twitter also uses a set of common terms, symbols, and language—often dictating how users behave. The following are key terms that all Twitter users should know:

Twitter Handle—an individual's or entity's username. This is the name used to represent an individual or a company on Twitter. For example, Edelman, the world's largest PR firm, tweets from the Twitter handle @ EdelmanPR.

@ Symbol—probably the most common symbol used on Twitter. This signifies that you are commenting or conversing with another Twitter user directly.

RT—retweet. When a user RTs a fellow user's tweet, it is essentially like forwarding that tweet to all of the people in that user's own Twitter stream. In business, RTs spread the information that a company wants to share with others, including links to articles, blogs, newspapers, websites, journals, contests, and coupons. When retweeting, a user should always credit the original user.

Hashtag—used to aggregate a conversation surrounding an event, topic, or theme. For example, this book uses #LRNSMPR to share links about social media and PR. Hashtags are created by combining the "#" symbol with a word, phrase, or acronym. When a tweet contains a hashtag, it then becomes searchable.

Like—represented by a small heart icon in a tweet. These are most commonly used when users like a tweet. Liking a tweet can let the original poster know that his or her content resonated with you, or you can save the tweet for later.

DM—direct message. A private message from one Twitter user to another. A DM can only be sent if both Twitter users follow one another.

Status Update—a tweet.

Twitter Stream—a list of a user's real-time Twitter updates.

Twitter Chat—an event held entirely online and intended as a forum for people to exchange ideas and discuss a specific topic. Twitter users connect with other like-minded Twitter users. Twitter chats are casual events that do not require registration and are generally organized by an individual or small group, an organization, or company. The intention of any Twitter chat is to be educational, conversational, and informative. Twitter chats are not forums to promote or sell products. A popular Twitter chat among PR professionals and students is #PRStudChat. This event is designed to bring together PR students, professionals, and educators for energetic conversations surrounding the PR industry and to provide opportunities for learning, networking, and mentoring. Monthly charts are organized by cofounders Deirdre Breakenridge (@dbreakenridge) and Valerie Simon (@ valeriesimon).

Twitter List—a curated group of Twitter users that is organized by the commonalities among its participants. Lists help individuals and companies organize their followers into categories or groups. This allows a user to easily view tweets from a specific group without having to scan an entire feed.

Blue Verified Badge—lets people know that an account of public interest is authentic.

URL Shorteners—used to shorten and share links. The most frequently used shorteners include Bit.ly (www.bitly.com), Google URL Shortener (http://goo.gl), and TinyURL (www.tinyurl.com).

Source: R. Luttrell, "Twitter Basics," Gina Luttrell PhD, July 30, 2012, http://ginaluttrellphd.com/2012/07/30/twitter-basics.

where it is headquartered. Finally, write the best, most succinct bio that you possibly can. What captures your company attitude? Companies should have fun and be creative when writing the 160-character biography. Some companies include other Twitter handles managed by the company and even Twitter chats that the company hosts. Moosejaw, the Michigan-based outdoor apparel company, uses its logo and the quippy tagline "The most fun outdoor retailer on the planet" for its Twitter image.

The Coca-Cola Company has distinct accounts for specific products and independent channels. Twitter users who follow @CocaColaCo can learn about what's happening within the company itself. Those who follow @Coca-ColaZero can get the latest updates on their favorite soda, while users who follow @WorldofCocaCola can experience the story of the company, interact with the Coca-Cola polar bear, and learn more about the more than one hundred flavors the company offers across the globe.

Moosejaw
@MoosejawMadness

The most fun outdoor retailer on the planet.

◎ Michigan
⌐ moosejaw.com
▦ Joined February 2009

Tweet to   Message

Managing a company brand on Twitter is fairly straightforward and is accomplished by monitoring what is happening with your brand and what is going on within your industry. Staying abreast of the conversations on Twitter helps brands connect more intimately with their customers, while at the same time eliminating surprises, including disgruntled customers and faulty products. When a company appoints an individual to manage its Twitter account, that person should be knowledgeable, a good listener, and trustworthy.[17] Twitter is not an advertisement, marketing campaign, or fad. Any company that enacts a Twitter strategy would benefit from appointing individuals whom it trusts completely with its brand reputation, since Twitter users expect to interact with a real person.

Bonding with Followers

The value of any interaction on social media is the conversation and relationship that is cultivated with real people and real customers. Using Twitter, there are plenty of ways to interact with your customers and engage in meaningful conversations.

- Special offers and coupons are often used. Companies can easily tweet exclusive offers to their followers. A benefit of using Twitter to support this strategy is that when the offer is compelling enough, the follower will not only redeem the offer but also share it with his or her followers. A good habit to get into is to link back to a company landing page where customers can download the coupon, ebook, or free code to the latest webinar the company has hosted. When companies steer customers back to a specified webpage, they create an opportunity to expose customers to the company website, where they may be inclined to look at or purchase other products.

- Customer service is often an avenue of connection on Twitter. When customers have questions for the company, they rely on Twitter. When customers have complaints, they rely on Twitter. According to AJ Agrawal, entrepreneur and *Forbes* contributor, "Companies who use Twitter as a customer service portal typically see a 19% lift in the satisfaction of their customers. Most of us, as customers, value customer service more than anything else. We hate having to wait to solve a solution over the phone, expect prompt responses and want to walk away from problem having found a solution. What's more, with 75% of us loving the instant gratification that social media brings, contacting companies on social is making more and more sense."[18] One of the leading brands supporting excellent customer service via Twitter is the team at Nike. They monitor the @NikeSupport Twitter handle, where their sole purpose is to respond to customers who need help. They boast a 73 percent response rate, which is three times higher than the closest brand.

- Team recruitment isn't saved for LinkedIn alone. Recruiting and hiring managers turn to Twitter to post open positions, leverage their network of followers, and view potential employee profiles.
- Philanthropic endeavors permeate the social sphere on Twitter. Twitter has been used to raise hundreds of thousands of dollars for charities and benevolent causes. In addition, Twitter has been a critical component to spread awareness about social issues. For example, the world came together to globally support the complex struggles of the Egyptian and Libyan populations using Twitter.

The key here is to look around the next time you wonder what you should tweet. Is there anything of note happening in the office that your customers may want to see? Maybe you could share a sneak peek at the latest photo shoot or the guest speaker who is spending a day at the office. Simply pull out that smartphone, snap a photo, and tweet it. Perhaps your company has an upcoming conference or webinar it is hosting—tweet the link to that event. Tweet the company's latest blog post. You could also post a link to another industry leader's content that your customers may find relevant. Finally, and this is especially important in building brand awareness, just chat with your network. After all, Twitter is "a real-time information network that connects you to the latest information about what you find interesting."[19]

LinkedIn

As consumers continue to flock to the social sphere in droves, so are businesses and brands, because it has been demonstrated time and again that these sites drive traffic, increase authentic engagement, and build brand loyalty. The recent changes that LinkedIn implemented created more opportunities for businesses to launch a brand page, and the results are paying off.

An astonishing 467 million members in more than 200 countries and territories are on the professional social networking site LinkedIn.[20] This social network boasts 106 million unique monthly U.S. visitors and is available globally in 24 languages.[21] If you look a bit closer at these statistics, professionals are signing up on LinkedIn at a rate of approximately two new members per second.[22] There are more than 40 million students and recent college graduates on LinkedIn, making them the fastest-growing demographic.[23] This makes LinkedIn the world's largest professional social network. Creating a company profile with a company page on this network just makes sense.

Professionals come to LinkedIn for a variety of reasons. Some are looking for a new job, while others join groups to network with. LinkedIn's membership includes individuals spanning numerous sectors, including employees, potential customers, purchasing managers, clients, and users who are simply interested in observing what is going on in industries. LinkedIn members typically follow companies to keep abreast of new developments, compare products and services, track potential business opportunities, and keep a lookout for job openings. When members want to know more about a company, they seek out company pages and access specific profiles.

Central to the Brand

Businesses should consider their company pages as anchors within LinkedIn. A company's page is the first place a member lands to see company status updates, the latest blog post written by thought leaders within the business, Twitter updates, and special offers, and to network with other professionals. Company pages bring life to a brand, reveal the human side of a business, and reach millions of professionals through word-of-mouth recommendations. Businesses can manage and measure all facets of the company brand on LinkedIn, including product brands and employment brands. There are four tabs on every company page on LinkedIn: overview, careers, products, and insights.

Overview Tab

The overview tab is akin to the front receptionist in a typical brick-and-mortar business. A receptionist will often greet visitors and make them feel welcome. A company page should accomplish the same goal. This is the first impression that a newcomer will have of your business. A high-level overview of the company should be included on the overview tab along with a cover image that represents the company and brand. Be mindful of how the company description is written and the images used to represent the company. Any text and photography should be consistent with the company's brand position across multiple channels. Unilever (http://www.linkedin.com/company/unilever) has a created a strong image that represents not only some of the brands that it sells but also its people, philanthropy efforts, and followers. The overview tab gives members the opportunity to connect with a company on various levels:

- Follow the company to stay abreast of significant developments, updates, employment opportunities, and landmark events.
- Access the latest news through the company Twitter feeds and blog posts.
- Connect with employees of the company.
- Access essential data on the company.
- View the "employee statistics" area to gain a better understanding of the company makeup. There is no better ambassador for a company than its own employees. Connecting with employees humanizes a company.

The feed on LinkedIn is a company's way of communicating important messages to its audience. Some businesses are more effective than others at using images to tell their stories, providing rich content, writing compelling status updates, and engaging in meaningful dialogue with their target audiences. Hays, a staffing and

Get Inspired: Five Steps to a Successful Company Page on LinkedIn

1. *Be Creative:* Be creative with how you present your company. Upload an image that welcomes visitors to the company page and reinforces the presence of the brand. Create and share videos that resonate with your target audience. Members are more likely to share information that they think their sphere of influence will appreciate.

2. *Start Conversations:* Post regular updates that spark conversations with members.

3. *Share with Others:* Share your status updates and encourage members within your company to add the company page to their personal profiles. It should become common practice for employees to "like" and "share" the content published on the company page. Sharing drives traffic to the company page and increases the number of people who see your content updates.

4. *Show Off a Little:* Add your product or services so that LinkedIn members can see what you have to offer. Include recommendations to further highlight the reasons why your products and services are special.

5. *Extend Your Reach:* Feature relevant groups to reach a broader audience.

recruiting company (https://www.linkedin.com/company/3486/); Schneider Electric (https://www.linkedin.com/company/2329/); Hotmart, a platform to sell digital products, (https://www.linkedin.com/company/2960917/); and Woolworths Group (https://www.linkedin.com/company/295257/) are some companies that understand the best practices for creating an effective company page.

Careers Tab

Premium careers pages, a paid subscription section within LinkedIn, allow businesses to promote general job opportunities as well as post specific jobs that target candidates using an automated job-matching system. This tab also allows a company to highlight awards, showcase the company's best employees, and even determine various career paths available within the company. Customized modules like this help complete the corporate story by providing a company with an opportunity to share its mission, vision, and goals.

Products Tab

The company products tab is particularly important because it accomplishes three goals: it (1) enables a business to showcase its best products and services to a highly targeted audience, (2) creates a place to feature product recommendations, and (3) facilitates meaningful conversations with current and prospective customers.

It would be prudent for a business to take advantage of the features provided in this tab. One such feature allows a company to capture the significant features of its products by incorporating powerful images and video clips that promote interactivity. Some businesses also include the contact details of the people behind the products in case members would like to connect directly with a designer or simply learn more, buy a product, or contract with a company for work. Companies that understand how to connect with their members on LinkedIn create personalized content that is geared toward that specific target market. Using this technique, companies retain the ability to show different content to different members based on their preferences and needs. Currently LinkedIn offers users up to thirty specific audience segments (based on date), including segmentation by industry, geography, company size, and more. Companies need to capitalize on the fact that recommendations from family, friends, and peers are greatly influential in our decision-making process.[24] By featuring recommendations from trusted third-party entities, organizations, and LinkedIn members, companies can potentially benefit from these influences related to specific products or brands.

Insights Tab

Analytics are invaluable to all social media strategies. Analytics allow most PR professionals and social media strategists to track the successes and failures of their campaigns. Each LinkedIn company page is outfitted with an insights tab that is only visible to administrators. Company administrators can analyze the number of visits to their company pages and the demographics of followers, and they track new followers, see which areas have the most hits, and monitor overall page growth. Using these analytics, administrators can easily populate graphs, providing insights regarding traffic, user-pattern page clicks, likes, comments, shares, and percentages related to a number of valuable metrics.

Proof Is in the Pudding

Successful companies lead by example. LinkedIn is a great illustration of how a social networking platform can best utilize each offered feature to support business

LinkedIn Lingo

LinkedIn is a social networking site dedicated to professionals and businesses alike. The following glossary of commonly used terms is provided to help ground users in the LinkedIn lingo.

1st Degree Connections: These are users that you choose to connect with personally. In general, these are the individuals whom you have established a personal relationship with prior to connecting on LinkedIn. These can be school-related connections, previous colleagues, or personal friends.

2nd Degree Connections: These are contacts of a 1st degree connection.

3rd Degree Connections: These are contacts of a 2nd degree connection.

Activity Feed: This feature of LinkedIn displays the current activity of any of your connections—generally other users or groups that you are a part of. This would also include activities related to joining or starting groups, comments that you have made, changes to your profile, and application downloads.

Activity Broadcasts: This includes content that appears on the Activity Feed and is visible for other users to see and comment on. This section can be edited.

Anonymous Viewers: These are LinkedIn members who have chosen to keep part or all of their profiles private.

Applications: Applications allow members to integrate other social media networks with their LinkedIn account, including Twitter, Facebook, and WordPress.

Basic Account: This is a free LinkedIn account.

Connection: A connection is another LinkedIn member who has accepted your invitation to connect, network, and view each other's profiles and networks.

Groups: Groups allow professionals to develop their careers by sharing expertise, experience, and knowledge.

Invitation: This is a request from an existing member or individual not on LinkedIn to join or make a professional connection.

InMail: These are private messages that allow a member to directly contact any LinkedIn user, while protecting the recipient's privacy. This is a fee-based service.

Job Seekers Account: LinkedIn members can choose between three levels of fee-based job-seeking accounts: basic, standard, and plus. The aim of this service is for the member to gain increased exposure to potential employers.

LION: This acronym, meaning "LinkedIn open networker," is sometimes visible on a member's profile. It simply means that the particular member agrees to connect with anyone, regardless of industry or connection.

Network: This is a group of users who can contact you via connections up to three degrees away.

Open Link Network: Premium members can join this network, which allows any LinkedIn member to send them an InMail free of charge, regardless of relationship.

Premium Accounts: This is an upgraded LinkedIn account where members can pay a monthly or annual subscription fee. Paid account benefits include InMail, better profile search results, expanded profiles, and larger storage space.

Recommendations: Similar to letters of recommendation, recommendations are references that are written to recommend a colleague, business partner, or someone whom you have done business with.

initiatives. On average, LinkedIn posts fresh, engaging content approximately 150 times each month to its members. Fresh videos, images, status updates, and blog posts keep members coming back for more and incidentally also promote increased sharing among members. From a social site whose original goal was to provide networking opportunities and recruit talent, LinkedIn has become a powerhouse in search, content, and influence.

Pinterest

Another social media platform, Pinterest, has seen its adoption continually increase since its inception and now takes its place as a "go-to" social media tool alongside other veteran social networking sites like LinkedIn and Facebook.

Pinterest has quickly become one of the biggest social traffic referral sites, recording more traffic than YouTube, Google+, and LinkedIn combined.[25] The astonishing growth of Pinterest has led to widespread media coverage and an abundance of articles, blog posts, forum discussions, how-to podcasts, and videos about how this new social network is taking the social web by storm. Keenly adept at what other social networks have done so well, Pinterest connects people and triggers them to share and communicate, while at the same time facilitating *discovery* rather than having users search for what they want.

The fastest social site to garner 10 million visitors per month in the short history of social media, Pinterest's rise to the top has communications professionals, tech junkies, and social media thought leaders amazed at the power it commands. Strictly speaking, Pinterest is a social network that allows users to visually share, curate, and uncover new interests by "pinning" videos or images to their own pinboards. Through pictorial representations, brands can connect with pinners who share interests and preferences that the brand represents. Pinterest is a social network meant to "collect and organize the things that inspire" its users.[26] With thirty-two categories of pinboards, brands have the ability to connect on many levels. There are five types of pinners:

> *The Influencing Pinner:* Influencers' activity affects the decisions of those who follow them. If an influencer pins or repins an image from your brand, others are likely to follow suit. Influencing pinners recommend products, websites, contests, and social connections that they believe other Pinterest users will also enjoy. These individuals have the ability to sway the decision-making power of their followers.
>
> *The Purchasing Pinner:* These pinners express themselves through pictures and images relevant to items that they have purchased or plan to purchase.
>
> *The Almost Purchasing Pinner:* Pinners who use Pinterest as a social bookmarking site or simply as a wish list fall into this category. These users pin images as a reminder of what they want to do, buy, plan, share, or come back to at a later date.
>
> *The "In It for the Long Haul" Pinner:* Pinners in this category use Pinterest to explore and conduct research on products or projects that they know will eventually be purchased or implemented. Pinners who are "in it for the long haul" know what they want. For example, perhaps they are planning a wedding. These individuals know that they need invitations, but they do not quite know what type of invitation they like. They will create a board and save images that approximate what they are looking for. These users will keep collecting pins until they find the perfect pin.
>
> *The Instantaneous Pinner:* Instantaneous pinners are precise in what they search for on Pinterest—for example, "hand-painted, classic, do-it-yourself wedding invitations" rather than "wedding invitations."

Pinterest Promoted Pins

One of the biggest changes for all businesses, small and large, occurred when Pinterest opened up Promoted Pins to everyone. Now any company seeking to grow its business through Pinterest can develop a strategy around Pinterest Ads and

Promoted Pins. According to Ash Read, the data around this new endeavor has been encouraging. Companies that used "the Pinterest Ads Manager received an average of 20% more (free) clicks in the month after the start of a Promoted Pins campaign."[27]

Pinteresting Campaigns

Branded profiles allow businesses to develop promotions that encourage users to follow the profiles of individual brands and pin items from their websites. Whole Foods Market, an early adopter of Pinterest, has amassed close to 330,000 followers on this platform.[28] With fifty-seven boards ranging in topic from organically grown foods—"How Does Your Garden Grow?"—to gift-giving ideas—"Great Gifts (. . . You May Not Think Of)"—the company presents itself to a variety of audiences. However, Whole Foods Market does not overly promote its products within these boards. Its pins relate to the core values of the company: being all-natural, sustainable, and organic.

When defining a social strategy for Pinterest, brands should focus on creating genuine interactions that result in a community of dedicated and loyal followers. Think of pins in terms of "likes" and every comment and follow as a symbol between two people building a long-term friendship.[29] The social strategy for Whole Foods Market is to pull content from blogs and other online sites that align with its mission.

Mastercard's acceptance campaign during Pride Weekend in New York City engaged pinners from all over. The #AcceptanceMatters campaign was two-fold: Mastercard being accepted around the world and spreading awareness about the acceptance of people. By introducing the hashtag #AcceptanceMatters, Mastercard immediately resonated with a number of Pinfluencers. Without a single pinboard follower at the outset of the campaign, Mastercard tallied 171 new followers over the course of the campaign.[30] More importantly, over the following nine-week period, the company generated more than 24.5 million media impressions, resulting in 13,000 repins and an outreach that was simply unprecedented.[31]

Perhaps one of the most successful Pinterest campaigns to date is the creation from the brilliant minds at Honda. The You Deserve a Pintermission campaign promoted the CR-V's young, hip, live-life image by reaching out to five influential pinners and challenging them to a #Pintermission.[32] They were asked to take a twenty-four-hour break from Pinterest so they could bring something from their personal pinboards to life. To help the influential pinners complete the activity, Honda gave each $500.

It's that easy.
#AcceptanceMatters
#CommissionedByMasterCard

Once the pinners were selected, Honda uploaded personalized posters to individual boards within the company's profile. Honda also had the pinners create their own #Pintermission boards and add Honda as a collaborator. The results from this initiative were astounding, primarily because these five "chosen" pinners were so influential within the target community. The #Pintermission boards attracted more than 4.6 million visitors, resulting in more than 5,000 repins and nearly 2,000 likes. The campaign was so popular that it migrated to Twitter, resulting in hundreds of tweets and generating more than 16 million media impressions.

Pinterest Patois

Although other social networking sites require mastery of a long list of essential definitions, Pinterest only has a few phrases that matter.

Follow: Following means that a user wishes to pay attention to whatever another user is posting. Two levels of following exist:
  • *Following the Overall User:* Any time a particular user posts anything on Pinterest, it will show up on your newsfeed.
  • *Following an Individual Board:* Any time something new is pinned to that specific board, it will show up on your newsfeed.
Pin: This is an image added to Pinterest using the "Pin It" button. Pins are generally uploaded from your computer or from a URL. A pin can be an image or a video. Pins typically link back to the site that they originate from.
Pinboard (aka Board): A board is a themed collection of pins. Pinners can create as many boards as they wish and as many categories as they can think of. Boards can be edited at any time.
Pinning: This is the act of adding an image to a board.
Pinner: This is a user who shares content on Pinterest.
Repin: This is the act of reposting another Pinterest user's image to one of your own boards (similar to retweeting).

Watch John Watts, Honda's head of digital marketing, discuss why the campaign was so successful: http://bit.ly/HondaPintermission.

These types of campaigns illustrate that contests can be powerful draws using Pinterest if they are executed correctly. They create a more engaged fan base, broaden a brand's online reach, and foster longer-term relationships.

Snapchat

Younger users are typically a rich resource for what's hot and what's not. In fact, much of the success that the company UsTrendy has realized is because founder and CEO, Sam Sisakhti, implements the social platforms his interns use. So, when his interns started praising Snapchat, he took notice.[33]

As noted throughout, not every organization needs to have a presence on every social media platform. Even fewer need to be on Snapchat. However, if your business is targeting younger consumers falling in the thirteen-to-twenty-four age demographic, you might want to pay attention.

Snapchat has now become a mainstream social platform with more than 160 million daily active users. Recently the company has taken measures to evolve and respond to the market. Perhaps not surprisingly, these users are considered *highly* engaged, with the majority of users consuming every post that is available. With an average commitment to the app of twenty-five to thirty minutes every day, it is no wonder that Snap commands the attention of 41 percent of the eighteen-to-thirty-four age demographic. In order to rise above the rest on Snapchat, content must be creative and fun and actively engage the audience.

Here are a few examples of top brands investing time and creative efforts into developing a strategy around Snapchat[34]:

X-Men: X-Men committed a considerable effort to promote the release of the upcoming *X-Men: Apocalypse* movie. Not only did they create *all* of the sponsored filters for the event, but every filter available on Snapchat during the day of the release was X-Men related. Even though the analytics are not yet available for this effort, it is estimated that this initiative may have received upwards of 1.5 billion views! Not too shabby!

World Wildlife Fund: Using the creative #LastSelfie hashtag campaign, the World Wildlife Fund leveraged Snapchat to raise awareness specific to numerous endangered species.

Charlie and the Chocolate Factory: One of the most innovative Snapchat campaigns to date came from the *Charlie and the Chocolate Factory* musical. Below is a screenshot from the Facebook page of the musical, which entices fans to find the "hidden" Snapchat geofilters that have been hidden all over New York City. If a fan finds one and sends the account a snap, they can win free tickets, goodies, and more.[35]

Major League Soccer: The professional soccer league devoted an entire week to its Snapchat "takeover," an instance when another person or organization takes over a Snapchat account. Within this promotion MLS turned over the responsibility of the MLS branded Snapchat account to a different star from the league over the course of a week. In the days leading up to the "takeover," each MLS star promoted the event using his own social media account and then engaged with fans using creative, fun activities and content using the MLS account on his day. With this in mind, a "takeover" could potentially be a great way to build and enhance a Snapchat following.

Four

Important Snapchat Metrics

Four Metrics Your Brand Should be Using to Increase Your Chances of Reaching your Goals

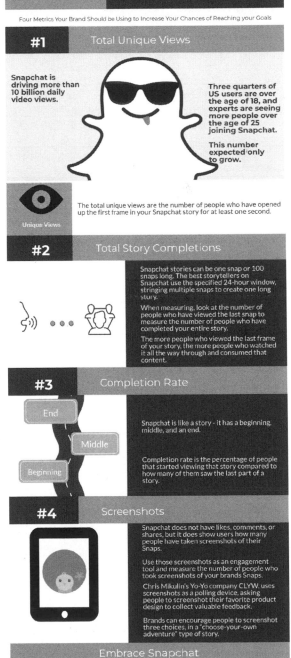

#1 Total Unique Views

Snapchat is driving more than 10 billion daily video views.

Three quarters of US users are over the age of 18, and experts are seeing more people over the age of 25 joining Snapchat.

This number expected only to grow.

Unique Views

The total unique views are the number of people who have opened up the first frame in your Snapchat story for at least one second.

#2 Total Story Completions

Snapchat stories can be one snap or 100 snaps long. The best storytellers on Snapchat use the specified 24-hour window, stringing multiple snaps to create one long story.

When measuring, look at the number of people who have viewed the last snap to measure the number of people who have completed your entire story.

The more people who viewed the last frame of your story, the more people who watched it all the way through and consumed that content.

#3 Completion Rate

End

Middle

Beginning

Snapchat is like a story - it has a beginning, middle, and an end.

Completion rate is the percentage of people that started viewing that story compared to how many of them saw the last part of a story.

#4 Screenshots

Snapchat does not have likes, comments, or shares, but it does show users how many people have taken screenshots of their Snaps.

Use those screenshots as an engagement tool and measure the number of people who took screenshots of your brands Snaps.

Chris Mikulin's Yo-Yo company CLYW. uses screenshots as a polling device, asking people to screenshot their favorite product design to collect valuable feedback.

Brands can encourage people to screenshot three choices, in a "choose-your-own adventure" type of story.

Embrace Snapchat

The Chitchat of Snapchat

Snap—when used as a verb, refers to taking a picture or video with Snapchat and sending it to another individual. Snap, when used as a noun, refers to the actual picture or video that is received from another user. Snaps cannot be viewed for longer than ten seconds.

Stories—collections of snaps that are specifically added to the story and are available for twenty-four hours.

Filters—applied to a snap after it is taken to change the snap's appearance. Filters have also been added to allow users to show their location, their speed, or the time or temperature when the snap was taken. Video filters have also been added that recognize an individual's face and create fun videos.

Geofilters—special overlays for snaps that can only be accessed in certain locations.

Replay—a feature that allows a user to view a snap again. The replay feature can only be used once a day.

Front-Facing Flash—allows a user to snap in the dark using a front-facing camera by lighting up the screen while taking a snap.

Best Friends—a list that Snapchat creates of the friends with whom you exchange the most snaps. The number of best friends shown can be adjusted using the settings.

Snapstreak—used to highlight when you have snapped a person back and forth for two or more days. If one person does not send a snap within twenty-four hours, the streak will break. The Snapstreak is represented by a flame emoji next to the friend's name.

Trophy Case—gives users virtual trophies that can be unlocked when they achieve a goal on Snapchat. Examples of goals that unlock trophies are sending a video snap, using a filter on a snap, and reaching a 10,000 Snapchat score.

Snapchat Score— the total number of snaps that a user has sent to friends. Friends can see the score and compare their own.

Discover—a feature that allows users to see stories from news outlets or locations around the world. ESPN, Comedy Central, the Food Network, CNN, and other outlets supply interactive snaps with users and can keep users up to date with things that apply to the outlet.

Sources: "Snapchat FAQ," Snapchat, accessed November 11, 2015, https://support.snapchat.com/a/geofilter-faq; Derek Kerr, "The Language of Snapchat" (class presentation, "Fundamentals of Social Media," October 1, 2015).

Snapchat Reinvented

As with most social platforms, with growth come changes. Recently CEO Evan Spiegel revamped the app to clearly separate interactions between friends from the items users read. Snap conversations and a user's friends' Stories are on the left, and content from companies, the public, and curated Stories are on the right. Why this big change? Well, Spiegel said, "The combination of social and media has yielded incredible business results, but has ultimately undermined our relationships with our friends and our relationships with the media. We believe that the best path forward is disentangling the two by providing a personalized content feed based on what you want to watch, not what your friends post."[36]

By splitting the feed, Snapchat can continue to benefit from algorithms, but it has also made a commitment to users. Those on the app can find content they truly want to engage with, something Facebook and Twitter struggle to deliver currently. And according to blogger Pete Pachal, Snapchat also has "a curated set of media and real editors, which help insulate it from the worst evils of socially driven content, like false stories going viral."[37]

Social Networks: The Platform/Social Networking Sites: The Channel

Loyalty is the foundation for successful relationships. The connection between a business and its customers is no different. Customers who are loyal to a specific brand, product, or service tend to stay loyal throughout their lives. They even become brand champions and look for ways to share their love of a brand with others. The dynamics between a customer and a business have created an ever-evolving relationship that promotes and fosters loyalty.

People connect with brands on social networks using various social networking sites because they want to learn something about a brand, share valuable content with others, define who they are, grow and cultivate their online relationships, and support causes that resonate with them. Social media campaigns help businesses accomplish these goals while also building brand and company loyalties. Selecting the correct social platform to promote a business and incorporating the necessary elements that make sense is also core to building a successful social strategy or campaign. Genuine, authentic interactions with consumers can be a company's best asset for enhancing relationships and expanding a brand. Social networking sites are easy, available channels for customers to reach out to a brand and, in turn, for a company to respond.

Theory into Practice

Flatliners Attempts to Create Buzz before Box Office Debut

Research/Diagnosis

To create buzz and drive box office sales prior to the remake of Joel Schumacher's 1990 cult psychological thriller/horror Flatliners, *Sony Pictures launched an all-immersive social media campaign.*

Objectives

In the month leading up to the premier, Sony Pictures engaged fans on just about every platform—Facebook, Twitter, Instagram, Pinterest, Snapchat, and even Spotify.[1] The objectives of the campaign were to:

- Create a connection for original fans and entice new fans to embrace the reboot
- Drive popularity and support for the launch of the film
- Increase the engagement by fans in the various social media channels
- Hit record sales by moviegoers for opening night

Strategies

To meet the objectives, it was critical that *Flatliners* rise above the clutter and noise often found on the social sphere to not only bring back original fans but create a new fan base. To that end Sony Pictures attempted to generate excitement and media attention by implementing a campaign that relied heavily on social media.

Tactics

Sony Pictures attempted to grab the attention of moviegoers by implementing these specific initiatives:

Owned/Shared: By creating content on specific *Flatliners* social media accounts, fans could share and take part in the campaign. Movie trailers were posted on Instagram and Twitter, while a special Snapchat filter was developed allowing users to share their live experience virtually. According to Rachel Grate, "Snapchat is ideally suited to drive the sense of FOMO ('fear of missing out') that spurs ticket sales and buzz."[2] The social promotion did not stop there. Sony Pictures also worked with Spotify to create the "Pick Your Pulse" Spotify playlist. The social media post read: "Find the perfect

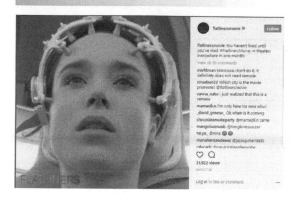

playlist that matches your heartbeat with the #FlatlinersMovie, 'Pick Your Pulse' @Spotify playlist! http://pickyourpulse.com." Finally, all posts used the hashtag #FlatlinersMovie to unify the conversation across all channels.

Earned: Nina Dobrev, who plays the character Marlo, made the rounds by appearing on late-night television to promote the movie. Jimmy Kimmel posted a photo of himself with Dobrev on his Twitter account with a shout-out using the movie's hashtag, #FlatlinersMovie.

Owned/Shared: Sony Pictures also launched a sweepstakes to win tickets to the *Flatliners* premier in Los Angeles. The posts were shared on Twitter with directions to enter to win.

Owned: A short movie trailer was created and distributed to media and posted on various social networking sites approximately four weeks before the premiere to pique interest and coverage. See https://www.youtube.com/watch?v=a1S52y5ZVIY.

Implementation

In the four weeks leading up to the premier, Sony Pictures consistently posted on the movie's social media accounts multiple times per day. Some posts garnered several thousand likes, comments, and shares.

Reporting

Unfortunately, not all campaigns are successful. Despite the enormous effort to promote the *Flatliners* reboot, critiques of the film were devastating. Movie critic Adam Nayman from *The Ringer* called the movie an "agonizingly dull remake,"[3] while Glenn Kenny from the *New York Times* wrote that the movie was "just meh."[4] Box office sales were dismal too. "Flatliners essentially flatlined this weekend, earning just $6.7 million in its opening weekend. Even for a cheap horror film, that's terrible, and at $19m (double the budget of Split) it's not exactly a cheap horror film."[5]

---

1   K. McCavitt, "7 Thrilling Posts That Will Make You Want to Go See 'Flatliners' This Weekend," September 27, 2017, https://krmccavi.expressions.syr.edu/2017/09/27/7-thrilling-posts-that-will-make-you-want-to-go-see-flatliners-this-weekend/#.WgOy88anHIV.

2   R. Grate, "Why You Should Use Snapchat for Your Event—And How to Do It," Eventbrite US Blog, August 4, 2017, https://www.eventbrite.com/blog/snapchat-for-event-marketing-geofilter-story-ds00/.

3   A. Nayman, "The 'Flatliners' Remake Is Agonizingly Dull," *The Ringer*, September 29, 2017, https://www.theringer.com/movies/2017/9/29/16388050/flatliners-2017-review.

4   G. Kenny, "Review: Why the New 'Flatliners' Is Just 'Meh,'" *New York Times*, September 29, 2017, https://www.nytimes.com/2017/09/29/movies/flatliners-review.html.

5   S. Mendelson, "Box Office Failures Of 'Flatliners' and 'LEGO Ninjago' Show the Limits of Remakes and Brands," *Forbes*, October 2, 2017, https://www.forbes.com/sites/scottmendelson/2017/10/02/box-office-failures-of-flatliners-and-lego-ninjago-show-the-limits-of-remakes-and-brands/#7f5d1c483744.

#LRNSMPR

Learn Social Media and Public Relations

Apply the principles learned in this chapter to the scenarios below.

• Each social networking site discussed in the chapter has its own unique characteristics. Imagine you work for a business to business (B2B) organization. Consider which platforms would work to promote your company to its key audience.

• Look up the social media profiles for three brands. Examine their social media activities over a month's time. What campaigns have they run? Do they appear to be successful? Do you see room for improvement?

• How have you used social media to communicate with an organization? What were your objectives when reaching out?

Notes

1. Facebook Newsroom, https://newsroom.fb.com/company-info/.
2. Zephoria Inc., "Top 20 Facebook Statistics—Updated October 2017," October 19, 2017, https://zephoria.com/top-15-valuable-facebook-statistics/.
3. Zephoria Inc., "Top 20 Facebook Statistics."
4. R. Wilson, *Share This: The Social Media Handbook for PR Professionals* (West Sussex, UK: Wiley, 2012), chap. 7; A. Sibley, "An Introduction to Facebook for Business," HubSpot, last modified 2013, accessed August 23, 2013, http://hubspot.uberflip.com/i/152427.
5. R. Luttrell, "Are You Abiding by the 80/20 Rule?" Gina Luttrell PhD, August 9, 2013.
6. R. Menezes, "How to Add Widgets to Facebook," eHow.com, 2013, http://www.ehow.com/how_5086646_add-widgets-facebook.html.
7. Facebook, "Games on Facebook Overview," last modified 2013, accessed August 26, 2013, https://developers.facebook.com/docs/guides/canvas.
8. C. Austin, "9 Facebook Live for Business Examples You've Got to See," IMPACT: Inbound Marketing Strategy, Advice, and Agency, January 17, 2017, https://www.impactbnd.com/blog/facebook-live-business-examples.
9. Austin, "9 Facebook Live for Business Examples You've Got to See."
10. Austin, "9 Facebook Live for Business Examples You've Got to See."
11. C. Austin, "4 Ways to Leverage Google Analytics for PR Measurement," Cision, August 8, 2017, https://www.cision.com/us/2016/07/4-ways-to-leverage-google-analytics-for-pr-measurement/.
12. B. Marr, "Data-Driven Decision Making: 10 Simple Steps for Any Business," *Forbes*, June 14, 2016, https://www.forbes.com/sites/bernardmarr/2016/06/14/data-driven-decision-making-10-simple-steps-for-any-business/2/#23049f38589b.
13. A. York, "47 Social Media Statistics to Bookmark for 2017," Sprout Social, July 19, 2017, https://sproutsocial.com/insights/social-media-statistics/.
14. C. Smith, "By the Numbers: 24 Amazing Twitter Stats," *DMR Digital Marketing Ramblings*, August 18, 2013.
15. S. Perez, "Twitter Officially Expands Its Character Count to 280 Starting Today," TechCrunch, November 7, 2017, https://techcrunch.com/2017/11/07/twitter-officially-expands-its-character-count-to-280-starting-today/.
16. Perez, "Twitter Officially Expands Its Character Count to 280 Starting Today."
17. J. Duffy, "How to Use Twitter for Business," *PC*, April 16, 2013, http://www.pcmag.com/article2/0,2817,2383408,00.asp.
18. AJ Agrawal, "How to Have Rock Star Customer Service on Twitter," *Forbes*, February 25, 2017, https://www.forbes.com/sites/ajagrawal/2017/02/24/how-to-have-rockstar-customer-service-on-twitter/#324484dfd918.
19. Twitter, "About Twitter," https://twitter.com/about.
20. See the LinkedIn website at http://www.linkedin.com.
21. M. Chaudhary, "LinkedIn by the Numbers: 2017 Statistics," LinkedIn, April 5, 2017, https://www.linkedin.com/pulse/linkedin-numbers-2017-statistics-meenakshi-chaudhary/.
22. S. Rayson, "9 Ways to Improve Your LinkedIn Marketing," *Social Media Today*, July 22, 2013, http://socialmediatoday.com/steve-rayson/1611011/improve-linkedin-marketing-9-ways.
23. Chaudhary, "LinkedIn by the Numbers."
24. B. Solis, *Engage: The Complete Guide for Brands and Businesses to Build, Cultivate, and Measure Success in the New Web* (New York: Wiley, 2011).
25. E. Gilbert et al., "I Need to Try This? A Statistical Overview of Pinterest," in *Proceedings of the SIGCHI Conference on Human Factors in Computing Systems*, 2427–36 (New York: ACM, 2013).
26. See the Pinterest website at http://about.pinterest.com.
27. A. Read, "Where Social Media Is Headed in 2017: The Biggest Trends to Watch For," The Buffer Blog, November 21, 2016, https://blog.bufferapp.com/state-of-social-media#quickfire.
28. Pinterest Whole Foods: https://www.pinterest.com/wholefoods/.
29. L. Indvik, "How Brands Are Using Promotions to Market on Pinterest," Mashable, March 7, 2012, http://mashable.com/2012/03/07/pinterest-brand-marketing.
30. M. Wolske, "Innovation at Work: 5 Successful Pinterest Campaigns," SEO Savvy Innovation at Work: 5 Successful Pinterest Campaigns Comments, May 31, 2017, http://www.seosavvy.com/blog/innovation-work-5-successful-pinterest-campaigns/.
31. Wolske, "Innovation at Work."
32. K. Piombino, "Honda's Shoestring Pinterest Campaign Attracts Millions," *Ragan's PR Daily*, February 21, 2013, http://www.prdaily.com/Main/Articles/Hondas_shoestring_Pinterest_campaign_attracts_mill_13883.aspx.

[33] B. Solomon, "How to Use Snapchat: A Small Business Guide," *Forbes*, August 25, 2015, accessed November 2, 2015, http://www.forbes.com/sites/smallbusinessworkshop/2015/08/25/how-to-use-snapchat-a-small-business-guide/#7564dd4167bd.

[34] Wallaroo Media, "21 Creative Snapchat Campaigns from Brands to Inspire Your Snap Strategy," October 30, 2017, https://wallaroomedia.com/12-creative-snapchat-campaigns-from-brands-to-inspire-your-snap-strategy/.

[35] Wallaroo Media, "21 Creative Snapchat Campaigns from Brands to Inspire Your Snap Strategy."

[36] P. Pachal, "What the New Snapchat Update Gets Right about Social Media," Mashable, November 30, 2017, accessed December 27, 2017, http://mashable.com/2017/11/30/snapchat-redesign-what-it-gets-right/#3oYAfQHR0aqR.

[37] Pachal, "What the New Snapchat Update Gets Right about Social Media."

Visual Content on the Social Sphere 8

The overwhelming acceptance and widespread use of visual content has inspired brands to explore images, photos, infographics, GIFs, and video as a way to further connect with customers. Visual content allows companies to show, not tell, about their brands, businesses, and stories.

KEY LEARNING OUTCOMES

1. Discuss important trends surrounding photos, infographics, GIFs, and video that are transforming content marketing on the social sphere.

2. Identify ways to use visual content to communicate strategically.

3. Understand the relationship between consumer empowerment and influence using visually attractive messaging.

SOCIAL MEDIA EXPERT

Instagram cofounders Kevin Systrom and Mike Krieger

Within hours of launching the Instagram app on October 6, 2010, founders Kevin Systrom and Mike Krieger reported that more than 10,000 users had already signed up. According to Systrom, the original goal of Instagram was "to not just be a photo-sharing app, but to be the way you share your life when you're on the go."[1] Today, Instagram has more than 600 million active monthly users, and those users have shared more than 40 billion photos since 2010. On average, users share approximately 95 million photos and videos per day.[2] Just two years after its launch, in 2012, Facebook purchased Instagram for $1 billion.[3]

---

[1] C. Lagorio-Chafkin, "Kevin Systrom and Mike Krieger, Founders of Instagram," Inc.com, April 9, 2012, https://www.inc.com/30under30/2011/profile-kevin-systrom-mike-krieger-founders-instagram.html.

[2] S. Parker, "A Long List of Instagram Statistics That Marketers Need to Know," Hootsuite Social Media Management, December 13, 2016, https://blog.hootsuite.com/instagram-statistics/.

[3] Wikipedia, "List of Mergers and Acquisitions by Facebook," November 15, 2017, https://en.wikipedia.org/wiki/List_of_mergers_and_acquisitions_by_Facebook.

Images Boost Understanding and Retention

Located in the back part of your head, the visual cortex contributes to the reality around you. It can also process visuals an astounding 60,000 times faster than written language, essentially "speaking" a separate language than just using words yet decoding the meanings rapidly as well.[1] That's why using creative imagery is so important.

5 REASONS TO USE PHOTOS IN SOCIAL MEDIA CAMPAIGNS

People Are Visual Beings
Photos allow a company to tell a story that they otherwise could not have accomplished through other, more traditional mediums. Integrating photos as a means to inform your audience can create engagement and interaction.

Share Photo Streams
Since it is so easy to share photos across multiple social media platforms, encourage the company's online community to distribute photos across multiple sites.

Tag It
Tags assigned to photos are used in SEO. Tags allow users to more easily find your brand, products, and services. This not only supports growth of your base audience but also affords a more genuine level of interaction with them.

Creative Commons
Employ a Creative Commons (CC) License on the photos that a company uploads. The social web is about sharing, being both transparent and authentic. CC License gives individual creators, large companies, and institutions a simple, standardized way to grant copyright permissions to their creative work.

Chat, Chat, Chat
Image platforms, such as Instagram, allow for users to post comments on photos that are uploaded. Take the time to interact with your consumers by replying to their comments and also share what they have to say.

It is quite common for public relations (PR) professionals to use images in promoting campaigns. Brochures, newsletters, annual reports, websites, social media posts, promotional videos, and press kits include a bevy of images that complete a story, show off products, or highlight specific services. The evolution and mass acceptance of the digital camera and handheld video recording devices have played an important role in how we create strategic stories.

Impact of Photos

The advent of the point, shoot, and upload philosophy allows anyone to take high-quality images with ease, upload them to a computer, and then use them for professional or personal use.[2] Prior to the age of digital photos, the process of incorporating photos within collateral material or on a website was tedious and time-consuming. As digital photos started becoming more mainstream, but before the advent of social networks and apps like Instagram, Snapchat, Flickr, Pic Stitch, and Tumblr, consumers flocked to photo-sharing websites such as KodakGallery.com and Snapfish.com. These types of web-based photo-sharing and photo-printing services allowed users to create private accounts, upload images from their digital cameras, buy prints, and share their albums with others. Essentially, these websites paved the way for what we now use today.

Impact of Video

The introduction of video on the social web in 2003 created an area of substantial growth for PR practitioners and social strategists alike. Approximately 200 million people, or roughly 76 percent of the online population, is consistently viewing video using online and mobile platforms. Companies can step into the spotlight and generate user-specific content that resonates with their customers through creative, high-impact, well-thought-out videos.

Show, Not Tell

At any given moment there are thousands of people on the web searching for photos or videos. Research by John Medina indicates that "a person who hears a piece of information will remember just 10% of it three days later, while someone who sees that same information in a picture will recall 65% of it."[3,4] According to Reuters, more than 84 percent of communication in 2018 will be visual.[5] Additionally, Adobe indicated that posts including images on Facebook led to a 650 percent increase in engagement over typical text-based posts, and as a result, the GIF creation site Giphy noted that the platform delivers approximately one billion GIFs a day.[6] In today's clutter-filled media landscape, it is challenging to win over a reader's attention, and even more difficult to retain it. Presenting materials that are flush with visuals can be both a strategic and easy way to communicate your message in a short time. Companies utilize visual content to successfully connect with online influencers, investors, stakeholders, consumers, and prospects.

Mirroring other forms of social media, photo-sharing sites and apps allow users to share their love and affinity for a company's brand with others inside their sphere of influence. Photo sharing is another example of a powerful tool that allows direct interaction with your consumer base. The more a company shares with its consumers, the higher the likelihood that those consumers are to share with others. Two-way communication is at the epicenter of social media. Sharing photos with those online, while also encouraging them to share, comment, and interact with a company, supports the very spirit of social media. Instagram allows companies to create a community of fans who share images, build trust, and develop genuineness with consumers—just like the other social media platforms that have been discussed.

Instagram

The allure of Instagram is the ability to create, manipulate, and share photos with family, friends, coworkers, and anyone else interested in taking a peek at those sepia-tinted, vintage-style, toaster-hued digital images. With Instagram's mass appeal, unprecedented usage, and popularity, the company has positioned itself as a social network in its own right and not merely a photo-sharing app. The success and mass appeal of Instagram has not escaped the attention of many popular brands that have incorporated the platform into their social strategies. National Geographic, Nike, Victoria's Secret, and H&M are among the most popular brands on Instagram. National Geographic tops the charts with over 72 million followers, closely followed by Nike with 70 million fans, while Victoria's Secret and H&M have accumulated millions of fans through the power of images to showcase their products to their followers without selling—an important aspect of success on the social sphere.[7]

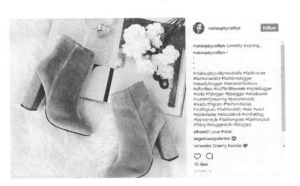

Small-business owner Caitlyn Tuzzolino launched Makeup by Caitlyn Michelle in 2012, after graduating college. She had a full-time marketing career at an accounting firm, but like most Millennials, she turned her side hustle into a thriving business.

When Caitlyn first started out, she built her own website and simultaneously launched

her Facebook and Instagram accounts dedicated to her makeup business. Since then she has used content creation more than ever to gain clients at a rapid pace. After being in business for almost five years, she wanted to be known as the go-to local professional not just for wedding makeup but for all things beauty. Her aim was to grow her following on social media, specifically Instagram. By developing a content calendar to keep her topic ideas in one place and schedule them ahead of time, she was able to stay organized. By September 2017 she began posting two to three times per day. If you examine her feed, she posts in a pattern: client, non-related beauty, client, non-related beauty, and so on. The "non-related beauty" photos typically include an image of flowers (usually pink or white), a product (Caitlyn will create a flat lay of beauty products or sometimes an outfit), or a quote (always a white background with black text). She keeps her photos light and bright to create a consistent and cohesive theme.

Each image includes thirty relevant hashtags that relate to the photo and include popular and non-popular tags. This helps people who don't already follow her discover her photo through the tags she uses. She built 600 followers over approximately five years, ballooning to more than 1,800 in just half a year due to her tactics. After a few months of research and planning, she was able to grow her Instagram following and blog audience and create a YouTube channel to help expand her brand. In less than a year, Caitlyn went from a wedding makeup artist to a social media micro-influencer and blogger with authority who now receives free beauty products to test. Her brand has grown into much more than what it was in early 2017. Her Instagram following grew by 206 percent, her blog views increased by 37 percent, and her YouTube channel is receiving a steady number of new subscribers and views daily.

There is a method to seeing results like Caitlyn has. Companies engage with customers by sharing snapshots of their products, cultures, and people in an intimate yet informal manner. There are three major features that draw users to Instagram: (1) personalization, (2) lifestyle, and (3) exclusivity.

Personalization

Much more than a photo-sharing app, Instagram has become a visual storytelling platform. Today, brands share entertaining, expressive content that conveys their best story. Gary Parkinson, a writer for Shutterstock, says that Instagram's most endearing aspect is its Stories feature.[8] When more than 200 million people actively follow Instagram Stories, it's time for brands to seriously think about their strategy. Keeping in mind a "mobile-first" audience, brands should use images and stories that stand out.

Moen, the number one faucet brand in North America, is not the brand that typically comes to mind as the best fit for Instagram Stories. Andrew Hutchinson concedes that Moen may not inspire creativity; the campaign does, "by showing the brand in a new light for Stories' younger skewing audience. Instagram says Moen used Olapic's Content in Motion tools to create the ad, made especially for Stories. This resulted in 45 percent more impressions and a fresh, new way for the brand to create engaging content more quickly and efficiently."[9] This particular campaign grabbed the attention of the customer by using impeccable imagery and video that told a complete story.

Lifestyle

Starbucks is a company that resonates well with Instagram users because followers of the company primarily control the content on this social platform. The Starbucks Instagram account predominantly features images posted by enthusiastic, imaginative fans who love and enjoy everything about Starbucks coffee. The company aims to promote the brand as part of a lifestyle choice and one that should be enjoyed with friends. It should come as no surprise that Starbucks is famous for cross-promoting its social strategies.

Exclusivity

Instagram users have also become accustomed to seeing exclusive photos, including behind-the-scenes looks at their favorite companies. Burberry is a company that frequently does this. Whether it is the latest commercial, photo shoot, or iconic images from London, Burberry fans always feel connected to the brand. As a company, Burberry recognizes the impact of this premier access and often rewards followers with exclusive content. This technique builds a community of loyal brand ambassadors.

The hit ABC television series *Once Upon a Time*, for example, has various characters take over the brand's account temporarily and post messages of their own. You don't need to be a hit TV series to do this. Any brand can create an influencer campaign. This tactic benefits companies because the takeover allows the influencer to express an approval for the brand, ultimately shaping brand perception and consumer buying choices.[10] Consequently, the influencers also benefit from the experience as they interact with a new audience, resulting in increased exposure within the social sphere.[11] More brands are also partnering with "micro-influencers." Micro-influencers have fewer followers but extremely high engagement rates on their posts.

With these success stories in mind, the first question that a PR practitioner should ask might be: How might a company best look to harness the power of Instagram? A company's Instagram account can serve multiple purposes, but above all, it should make users feel included and part of the company culture. Some tactics to consider when planning an Instagram campaign include the following[12]:

- *New Products:* Snap a quick picture of a new product, share a screenshot, or, better yet, share an image of someone using the product on Instagram. Instagram photos should be simple and can promote the desired effect using the many photo filters that are available.

- *Company Culture and Employees:* Use Instagram to humanize the company brand. Highlight the inner workings of the company culture; give followers insight into the day-to-day behind-the-scenes activity. Followers want to see who is running the company, who is tweeting them, and who is blogging—so show them. It is not necessary to post a traditional headshot. This would be too formal for Instagram. Save those for LinkedIn and the company website. Make the photo fun by using a more relaxed image. A peek behind the scenes is not a photo of someone simply sitting at his or her desk. As an example,

Many brands allow for Instagram takeovers. In this example, Mekia Cox from the hit series *Once Upon a Time* takes over the television show's account for a day.

Centresource, an interactive agency, uses Instagram to show the details of its company culture. The "Who We Are" page is a running feed of its Instagram account.

- *Trending Topics and Events:* In addition to posting images of company events, illustrate that the company is involved in and informed about events that matter to your followers. Post Instagram photos of news, fun facts, and trending topics that followers are most likely aware of and then engage with them on that topic. John Lewis, a London-based fashion brand, wanted to appeal to a younger female demographic. In partnering with influential fashion bloggers, the company launched an Instagram campaign that showcased the bloggers wearing John Lewis clothes in a series of simple fashion shoots. As a result, the brand increased its reach by a full 14 points among the twenty-five-to-thirty-four female demographic, along with a 10 percent increase in ad recall.[13]
- *Photo Contests:* Instagram users love the app because they can create fun images. Use this passion to a company's advantage. Develop and launch a photo contest in which followers can submit images and earn recognition from a brand they adore. To promote a product giveaway, RYU, the urban athletic apparel company, created an Instagram campaign centered on collecting user-generated content from their followers. Fans simply had to post an image of what they had in their gym bag, then tag the post with RYU's branded hashtag, #WhatsInYourBag. Users who shared posts with the hashtag were then entered to win prizes.[14]

Video

1.8 Million Words

According to Dr. James McQuivey of Forrester Research, video is worth 1.8 million words.[15] Imagine this: in a single frame a video can deliver the same amount of information as 3 pages of text or an astonishing 3,600 average webpages. In all, it would take a person 150 days of writing to achieve relatively the same impact that a single one-minute video has.[16]

Scientifically speaking, it is well understood that when people read, they convert text into images and emotions.[17] So it should not come as a surprise that when people receive information directly from images as opposed to text, the mind creates more connections intellectually and emotionally because the translation from word to image is not necessary. People are drawn to video for four simple reasons: we see the face as a point for gathering information and believability; the voice allows us to convert information into meaningful content; body language resonates; and movement grabs and holds our attention.[18] For PR professionals and social strategists, this is great news.

Video is most effective when implemented with the total communications strategy in mind. Companies can increase outreach to influencers, build credibility, promote brand awareness, enhance SEO, and, more importantly, create a loyal following of brand ambassadors. Just look at these statistics:

- Today, video content represents 74 percent of all Internet traffic. However, by 2019 that number will increase to 80 percent.[19]
- Four times as many consumers would prefer to watch a video about a product than to read about it.[20]
- Using the word "video" in an email subject line boosts open rates by 19 percent and click-through rates by 65 percent.[21]
- Facebook users spend 30 percent more time watching live videos than traditional videos.[22]

Idea to Implementation

Create content that is relevant. Keeping your audience in mind is essential to the success or failure of a video strategy. Videos can be shot in a variety of styles and formats. The first step for a PR practitioner is to decide which format is right for the organization. Generally, there are three overarching varieties of videos found on the web:

- *Product Demonstrations:* This type of video captures a product's best features and uniqueness while entertaining and engaging your audience. One of the most famous examples is the Blendtec blender.[23] To illustrate the amazing capabilities of the product, CEO Tom Dickson blends items like iPads, iPhones, golf balls, Justin Bieber CDs, and even his mother's dentures. The company posted these videos on its YouTube channel, and the "Will It Blend?" series exploded. The videos not only increased brand awareness but also made the Blendtec product a household name. In fact, shortly after the video series launched in 2006, sales increased over 1,000 percent. Today, the Blendtec videos receive hits, likes, and shares in the millions (http://www.youtube.com/user/Blendtec).
- *How-To/Educational Videos:* This video format shares best practices and builds trust with consumers. Ranking the highest among brands, Home Depot stands out because it publishes content about topics that are relevant to its brand without blatantly promoting or advertising the specific products it sells.[24] Home Depot strategists have established their brand as a trusted expert and resource for home renovation and repair projects while at the same time humanizing the company. Videos are hosted by and feature employees sharing a wealth of home-improvement information (http://www.youtube.com/user/homedepot).
- *Viral Videos:* Every brand wishes that its videos would go viral, but none can guarantee that particular outcome. Viral videos typically share two things in common: relatability and discussability, which is tied directly to social currency.[25] People are drawn to content that affects them deeply. The videos can be serious in nature or comical. Either way, the content is emotionally stimulating and creates a connection with the viewer, so much so that the viewer wants to discuss it and share the video with others. It is the viewers who make videos "go viral," not the actual videos. Always's #LikeAGirl (http://bit.ly/AlwaysLikeAGirlVideo), Heineken's "World's Apart" (http://bit.ly/HeinekenWorldsApartVideo), and the Sandy Hook Promise (http://bit.ly/SandyHookPromiseVideo) rank among the top viral videos—each garnering millions of views, likes, and shares.

Videos, like most forms of social media, should not "sell" anything. The most successful videos are the ones that resonate. Useful, smart, interesting, captivating, and entertaining videos tend to be the most popular. Social media strategists and PR professionals need to decide why a video should be part of an overarching strategy and then ultimately what content should go into the video. Does the company want to drive traffic to a website or landing page? Perhaps growing the number of company YouTube subscribers is the goal. Increasing blog followers and conversations, heightening brand awareness through influence, and maximizing brand engagement through completed videos watched are all plausible objectives. These milestones will become important in measuring the video's overall level of success. Content within the videos can range from a simple interview to a complex message, like the Sandy Hook Promise, which tackles the tough issue of gun control. "The Sandy Hook Promise is a national non-profit organization founded and led by family members whose loved ones were killed at Sandy Hook Elementary School on December 14, 2012. The intent of the organization is to honor all victims of gun violence by turning tragedy into a moment of transformation by providing programs and practices that protect children from gun violence."[26]

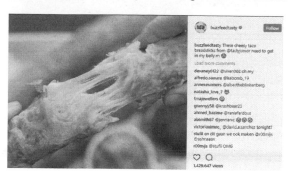

The Tasty videos from BuzzFeed have become some of the most popular content on the social sphere.

Instagram Video

Instagram had social media strategists and PR professionals buzzing as it extended its photo-sharing features to include video capabilities. This development created another avenue for companies to promote products and services, build corporate culture, and interact with their customer bases. In late March of 2016, Instagram announced that it would start rolling out the ability for Instagram users to upload sixty-second videos.

The videos that BuzzFeed Tasty creates are perfect for Instagram videos because they are visual, helpful, shareable, lighthearted, but most of all simple. Andrew Gauthier, creative director for BuzzFeed, said, "We want people to be able to watch the video and feel like they can pull it off at home."[27] Because of Instagram's decision to extend video length to sixty seconds, BuzzFeed is able to post full recipe videos along with a caption explaining how to make the recipe. Check out some of the tasty videos: http://bit.ly/buzzfeedtastyvideos.

As a result of these upgrades, marketers and PR professionals can leverage the Instagram app to connect with fans and customers, showcase their businesses' personalities, and promote artistic creativity. The power of Instagram is that it allows companies to use this video feature in countless creative ways. Shooting a product demo, answering some frequently asked questions, featuring events and special offers, creating a video portfolio of the company's products, and encouraging fan submissions are some examples of ways that a company can take advantage of video storytelling.[28] Both customers and fans want to see a humanized brand, one that captivates them and keeps them connected to the brand.

YouTube

The practicality of YouTube, for end users, is quite simple: it allows them to locate and watch videos. However, for social strategists and PR practitioners, this platform is much more. Owned by Google, YouTube is a search engine, promotional platform, social network, and community site with a loyal viewership. One unique feature that YouTube boasts is the ability to create branded channels.

The YouTube branded channels allow for the creation of a specific space for all the videos that pertain to that company. Users do not have to search to find the content they desire, because these branded channels ultimately create a set destination for customers to locate the content they seek. YouTube channels afford companies the opportunity to engage and further shape formidable relationships with their audiences using an environment that consumers know and trust.

Channels should reflect the brand itself using company images, graphics, and colors. YouTube does offer an upgrade to its channel services that helps PR and social strategists further maintain company branding. Users can benefit from this by accessing templates that can be customized and personalized to complement other social sites, the company website, and even printed collateral material. Using this functionality helps create and align content with key demographics and the company's goals, products, and mission.

It may not come as a surprise that Red Bull is one company that understands how to maximize YouTube's potential. Red Bull's overarching theme embedded

Periscope

Periscope is an app that provides users the ability to catch a live stream and encourages engagement through likes. The app provides brands with new opportunities to interact with their audiences in real time.[1] From celebrity takeovers to sneak peeks and special product offers, brands are capitalizing on the power of Periscope. In its first Periscope stream, retail chain JCPenney hosted Eva Longoria, who introduced fans to her new JCPenney bedding collection and answered questions from an exclusive launch event held in Los Angeles. DKNY uses Periscope to take fans on "inside" tours, introducing them to the faces behind the brand. GE used drones equipped with Periscope on guided tours through remote facilities as a part of its #Droneweek social event.[2]

[1] T. Dua, "5 Ways Brands Are Using Periscope," Digiday, August 17, 2015, accessed November 15, 2015, http://digiday.com/brands/5-ways-brands-using-periscope.

[2] P. Michaels, "Meerkat FAQ: Everything You Need to Know," Tom's Guide, accessed November 15, 2015, http://www.tomsguide.com/us/meerkat-faq,news-20663.html.

throughout all its communication strategies focuses on extreme sports and extreme athletes. Its Facebook page and twenty Pinterest boards feature spectacular images and videos of Red Bull–sponsored extreme sports and extreme sport athletes, while its Twitter feed is dedicated to various events and current projects. To keep its content fresh and new, Red Bull posts between one and three new videos per day—all of which are directed toward its key niche audience.

When Felix Baumgartner took his leap from the edge of space, Red Bull's live broadcast of the remarkable video pulled in more than 9 million streams of the actual dive. Aside from the historic feat, what made this video so successful was that Red Bull documented the days leading up to the jump by producing and posting more than fifteen videos that chronicled the journey. The project, Red Bull Stratos, garnered more than 366 million content views on YouTube alone.[29]

Producing Quality Videos

Video has the potential to spread copious amounts of information to a broad audience. Every detail is critical, whether you are shooting a thirty-minute video or a six-second video. When a social strategist or PR professional steps behind the camera, he or she becomes a video maker and thus is responsible for every image and message conveyed in each frame of the finalized product.

Video-sharing social media sites have their own sets of rules, time constraints, and uses. When using these platforms for filming videos, the following guidelines can be used:

1. *Audience and Platform:* This may seem obvious, but believe it or not, it often isn't. Knowing whether the video should be six seconds or sixty minutes means that you need to know your audience, which platform will work best for the content you plan to promote, and on which social media platform the video will make the most impact.

2. *Purpose and Storyboard:* Understanding the purpose and then taking the time to storyboard the idea are the first steps toward creating the framework for a company video. Even short videos need a purpose and a storyboard. Defining the purpose helps to deliver the core message. Creating a storyboard is a technique that maps out a video sequence prior to filming. Essentially it is a written plan for the content going into the video.

3. *Style and Tone:* The style of the video sets the stage. Videos can be serious, funny, cheerful, professional, or even whimsical. Regardless of the style, the

message needs to fit the overall tone. Some professionals have created videos many times over. To these individuals, conveying a style and setting the tone may be simple. However, not all social strategists or PR professionals are trained videographers. By examining videos with similar messaging or formats, professionals can catch a glimpse of how certain tones and feelings have previously been conveyed. Seeing the work of others may inspire you or give you an idea. Consider these tips:

- *Tone*—upbeat, carefree, serious minded, or staid
- *Dialogue*—"talking head" interview style or free-flowing conversation
- *Production Quality*—in-house studio or on location
- *Video Quality*—simple, online, made-it-myself video or big-budget professional production

4. *Script Writing:* Once the purpose and tone have been decided, it is time to write the script. For longer YouTube interview-style videos, write out the list of questions so that you are prepared. For more conversational videos use bulleted notes. Is it possible to pack a story into a six-second or a sixty-second video? The answer is yes! The key here will be to weave in quick edits and multiple shot angles throughout.

5. *Angles and Shots:* How the video is made has a direct effect on whether the content will resonate. Videos need to be relatable, discussable, and shareable. When filming a video, consider the best angle and perspective for each sequence. For videos that require multiple frames, characters, or scenes, it is best to script out your video in detail.[30] This includes notes related to the sets, stage actions, props, and dialogue.

6. *Images, Sound, and Lighting:* Graphics, music, and imagery also play a critical role in video. These elements support the tone, dialogue, and effectiveness of the messaging. When storyboarding the video, think about the types of still shots, b-roll footage, music, and background sounds that can be used. Lighting can make or break the quality of a video. Poor lighting creates dark, shadowy, discolored, or even gritty images. Never record a scene with a window in the background. The subjects will appear dark, and although some editing can happen, the quality of the shot is diminished. Viewers tend to accept ordinary, uninspiring graphics but have very little tolerance for poor sound. Invest in external microphones to ensure good sound quality.

7. *Editing to Final Product:* The three most commonly used desktop editing tools for YouTube videos are iMovie, Camtasia, and Windows Movie Maker. The websites associated with each of these tools provide in-depth instructions for how to use each editing product. Both iMovie and Windows Movie Maker are easy to use and have drag-and-drop tools, while Camtasia is an excellent tool for simple videos and screencasts.

8. *Sharing:* Once the video has achieved production-ready status, it is now time to publish the video for the world to see. Be sure that the original goals of the video are in line with the company's overarching social media goals. This can include calls to action, hashtags, clever captions, and tags. Since YouTube, Vine, and Instagram are embeddable, the potential for innovative storytelling is limitless.

9. *Evaluation:* Illustrating results and understanding metrics properly are important in all social media platforms because the analytics can drive social media strategies. Statigram, a tool specifically developed for Instagram users, allows brands to measure their efforts through viable metrics. With Statigram a company can manage both comments and the community simultaneously and analyze the company activity within Instagram. YouTube has built in metrics through analytics, engagement, and performance.

Create a Spark

Create a "spark" with a page, post, or video using three of Adobe's most popular apps, which are all free. According to the website, "Adobe Spark is a one-stop content shop for creating and sharing visual stories that will wow your audience on any device.

- *Spark Page:* Create beautiful web stories combining text and graphics.
- *Spark Post:* Create stunning social posts and graphics. Remix, resize, and transform your social feed in seconds.

- *Spark Video:* Radically easy way to create animated videos. No filming required; just speak your story and customize with themes, images, icons and text."[1]

[1] A. Cattell, "Welcome to Adobe Spark!" Adobe Spark, June 3, 2016, https://spark.adobe.com/blog/2016/05/19/welcome-to-adobe-spark/.

Regardless of the route, there are many options supporting inclusion of a video into a social strategy. It was not that long ago that YouTube was the only outlet for video. Not anymore. Today, videos also appear everywhere from Instagram to Facebook. Most platforms facilitate easy video capabilities and are generating quite the stir in the video-creation sphere.

Infographics

Infographics have taken the web by storm. The first infographic was developed over a decade ago. Today, infographics are pervasive throughout the social sphere because brands and audiences alike love them. Despite their unusually long length, the public cannot seem to get enough of them. Everywhere we turn, from newspaper publications to blogs, corporations, and even small businesses, everyone is using them, and there is a very good reason for that. The method by which we process and share information has significantly changed. In 2010 individuals were creating and sharing information so rapidly that the sheer volume produced every two days eclipsed the entirety of information developed between the start of human civilization and 2003.[31] As a result, it has become increasingly difficult for PR and communications professionals to get the attention of their intended audiences. The digital age has ushered in an information overload. One way of organizing a significant amount of information is through visual representation and infographics.[32] Corporations, organizations, and companies use images and graphs to highlight data in their analyses, journal articles, press releases, and newspaper stories. Infographics are widely used to convey complex information in a concise, easy-to-understand format. John Dalton suggests that practitioners follow these simple steps[33]:

1. *Clear Objectives:* As with every piece of communication that PR practitioners develop, a clear objective should be identified. By identifying the objective of the infographic, brands can determine the type of information necessary and how to present it graphically.
2. *Meaningful:* Every infographic should tell a story. Data presented in an infographic should have a relevant narrative that supports the main topic. Successful infographics are appealing, memorable, and, more than anything, understandable to the reader.
3. *Memorable Headline:* An appropriate headline can contribute to 90 percent of readers seeing (or not) an infographic.

4. *Design:* An appealing infographic will draw people to your graphic. Depending on the audience and messaging, you will use various types of data and formats when creating the infographic. Typography and colors are paramount in creating effective infographics. Successful infographics are clear and simple.
5. *Research:* Cite sources that are credible and trustworthy. A good rule of thumb is to use sources that are not older than two years old.
6. *Effective Promotional Plan:* Once the infographic is created, it is time to promote it. Infographics are part of a company's owned media strategy and can be published on a blog and other social media channels.

GIFs

GIFs, pronounced *jifs*, are nothing new, but their use is more widespread than ever throughout social media. GIF, which is an acronym for Graphics Interchange Format, was introduced in 1987 by Steve Wilhite of CompuServe as a new way to present a moving image.[34] GIFs are an image file, such as a JPG or PNG, and while they do not have sound, they are animated. Almost thirty years ago the Internet embraced the GIF. Its staying power illustrates just how relevant it is.

Their popularity can be attributed to the fact that GIFs are easy to understand, appealing, effective, mobile friendly, and platform agnostic. According to Twitter, users shared more than 100 million GIFs in 2015 through tweets and direct messages, with this trend expected to grow year after year. According to HubSpot, visual content is more than forty times more likely to get shared on social media than other types of content.[35] Because of this, many famous brands use GIFs to interact with their followers. NASA uses GIFs of satellite imagery, while Coca-Cola and Disney have their own Tumblr blog which is brimming with personal branded GIFs.[36]

When Netflix launched its first digital outdoor campaign in France, it relied exclusively on GIFs. Inspired by people's everyday lives, Netflix featured original content from shows like *Orange Is the New Black* to showcase skepticism, spoiler alerts, weather, or sales at large retailers. With more than 100 digital billboards issued, Netflix created an entertaining outdoor campaign while building a pop cultural trend into an innovative social media and PR campaign. Check out details of the campaign: http://bit.ly/NetflixGIFCampaign.

The Upsurge in Visual Social Media

The changes that occurred across almost every major social network, including Facebook, Snapchat, Instagram, and Twitter, along with an upsurge in mobile use underscore the importance of visual content. According to Kristin Twiford, content marketing manager for Libris, marketers are investing heavily in visual content. She notes that "74 percent of marketers use visual assets in their social media marketing strategies, 93 percent of senior marketers reveal that photography is either important or critical to their overall strategies, and that video is on the rise and will account for 80 percent of all internet traffic by 2019."[37] Research indicates that when people interact with brands on social networking sites, they are more likely to engage with those brands that post images over other forms of media.[38] The need for and rise in the incorporation of images is increasing. Consumers have emphatically shown that they would like to see what a company is made of. Whether it is a fashion house giving fans a peek behind the label or a chef welcoming you to his or her kitchen, photos, infographics, and GIFs are becoming a staple in social media campaigns.

Creating #Cupfusion

Reprinted with permission from the Public Relations Society of America

This case is a PRSA 2017 Silver Anvil Award of Excellence Winner

Written by Reese's with Ketchum, Havas and Soulsight

Reese's Pieces Peanut Butter Cups were scheduled for a new product launch in late summer 2016. The mashup of two popular candies—Reese's Pieces candy stuffed inside the flagship Reese's Peanut Butter Cup—could be counted on to generate interest from devoted brand fans and trade press, but no advanced drumbeats activated, no PR activities were planned. Then confusion hit. A photo of the unreleased product was leaked on a personal Facebook account without the brand's knowledge or permission, and suddenly Reese's Pieces Peanut Butter Cups were a hot topic on social media. People wanted to know if the whimsical-looking confection was real or fantasy. And if real, where could they get them? The fact was, the product wouldn't be on shelves for months. The leaked photo now had nearly 40,000 shares, and social media speculation had upstaged the planned launch. How could the brand take back control of its own product? Then again, maybe the confusion had created opportunity. Working with the Reese's brand, the PR team closely monitored the unexpected brand conversation that was surging online. Speculation was heightening interest among the brand's biggest fans, a huge asset for driving sell-in of the product to retailers. Instead of shutting down speculation and resetting to the scheduled launch date, why not fuel more speculation? Why not have a little fun by adding to the confusion? Within hours #Cupfusion was born, our totally in-the-moment social campaign that leveraged Reese's irreverent brand voice to fuel an unlikely product launch that raised the volume far above expectations.

Research/Diagnosis

There wasn't much time for research. We knew the brand's first response needed to be clever, tone right, and, most importantly, fast. The team recognized an opportunity for Reese's, a brand that already brought a little more attitude. We immediately monitored the ongoing social conversation

spreading from the leaked photo. Consumers were confused about whether the product was real—and excited at the possibility. The lack of confirmation from the brand had fueled an almost "too good to be true" chatter. The conversation was being driven by the brand's best consumers and natural social ambassadors. Their speculation was almost entirely positive, suggesting it would be better for the brand to encourage the speculation rather than end it. But our experience with organic social media also suggested that timing would remain crucial. We could generate a lot of fun and goodwill, but it could quickly turn into annoyance. We needed to monitor the mood literally by the minute.

Objectives

Business Objective: Drive sales of Reese's Pieces Peanut Butter Cups among Hershey's customers (retailers)

Communications Objective: Drive buzz around Reese's Pieces Peanut Butter Cups following an unexpected real-time social media leak

Strategy

It would have been simple to issue an official confirmation and call it a day. But we recognized a unique opportunity to play up Reese's witty brand personality while connecting and engaging with its most devoted consumers. And so #Cupfusion was born. #Cupfusion played off two concepts: the confusion of consumers who didn't know if the product was real or fantasy and the fusion of two of Reese's most beloved and iconic products, Reese's Peanut Butter Cups and Reese's Pieces candy. We would ease social media with branded memes and messages that fell just short of official pronouncements, feeding a fresh wave of speculation and sharing. The campaign would enlist an emoji-inspired graphic—Cupmoji—as its main asset, and most importantly, would maintain constant social listening and analysis to determine how far to push the prank. And when it came time to come clean about the rumors, the unexpected social media phenomenon would require an unconventional social media press conference. The target audience was Hershey's customers (retailers) and male and female Millennials.

Tactics

With a core team of internal experts and external agency partners, we launched the #Cupfusion campaign within hours. The brand began posting a series of cryptic images and GIFs on its Facebook and Twitter channels that neither confirmed nor denied the new product. Instead, the branded content playfully bantered with its fans to keep the conversation—and confusion—going.

Implementation

A quick glance at the calendar gave us two openings to play with. We quickly created a Cinco de Mayo meme of a Reese's Peanut Butter Cup piñata filled with Reese's Pieces candy, and a Mother's Day GIF of a Reese's Peanut Butter Cup telling its Reese's Pieces candy, "You're so cute, I could eat you up!" We hinted that the cup was perhaps a dream. And pretended we didn't know where all our "Pieces" were disappearing to. The #Cupfusion campaign was originally intended to last about two weeks before the brand would confirm the product. However, the integrated team was keeping a keen eye on the conversation, where Facebook fans and Twitter followers were now telling the Reese's brand not to be such a #cuptease. It was time to pivot

and fess up. The #Cupfusion ended with an official announcement in an unlikely venue. Our Facebook "press conference" invited consumers and top-tier media to tune in to the big news delivered in an irreverent GIF: "Yup . . . it's a thing." Within minutes comments and questions from fans flooded the comments section. And within hours the team launched a real-time social campaign on its Facebook and Twitter feeds, continuing the cheeky back-and-forth between the brand and its fans.

Reporting

Just as with the original leaked photo, news of the confirmation went viral. The official announcement post on Facebook received nearly 750,000 views in less than twenty-four hours—topping out at 1.3 million views. And media took notice. Within a few days the news reached more than 1.1 billion people through online news stories and in national and local broadcast segments. The online conversation generated 43 million social impressions and 2.2 million engagements. And the playful confusion led to real business results. In the weeks following the PR blitz, retailers inundated the Hershey Company sales team with calls asking how soon they could receive the now infamous Reese's Pieces Peanut Butter Cups. Since the launch of #Cupfusion, volume expectations have increased more than 200 percent, tripling original projections.

#LRNSMPR

Learn Social Media and Public Relations

Apply the principles learned in this chapter to the scenarios below.

- Using what you have learned about creating winning photos and videos, check out Tiny Kitchen and analyze its effectiveness on Instagram and YouTube. Tiny Kitchen has made everything from boneless buffalo chicken strips to tiny pho and even a teeny-tiny birthday cake. Except on Tiny Kitchen, everything is cooked in a dollhouse kitchen roughly one-twelfth the normal size of an actual kitchen. In the short time it has been around, it has amassed a cult-like following. See https://www.tastemade.com/shows/tiny-kitchen.

- Search the Internet for an infographic; then examine whether it is operational. Assess the overall functionality, title, and citations; are there multiple steps or phases; was the data used effectively; and ultimately, did you learn something?
- The Perfect GIF from Hulu: Hulu knows the holidays are emotional. Between dealing with an overcrowded house to politically charged dinners or merely celebrating the perfect gift, people must express themselves. And what better way than through GIFs—the language of the Internet?[1] This past holiday season Hulu's gift to TV fans around the world bottled the magic of the holidays in an innovative

GIF experience unlike any other. Hulu created the Perfect GIF generator, which paired users' tweets and Tumblr posts with the perfect TV GIF. Search #favepartofchristmas or #worstpartofchristmas on Twitter, and chances are you will find an endless supply of reasons for why people either love or hate the holidays.[2] In the same vein, searching Hulu users could find an equally endless supply of TV shows and episodes that echo those emotions. The primary goal for the Perfect GIF was to drive social sharing and advocacy for Hulu by creating an experience that was fun, compelling, and easy to use. Hulu also wanted to build awareness for its vast content library. The company ensured that its GIF library represented more than 70 different TV shows. "By the end of the campaign, social posts from the site garnered over 15k content shares, which contributed to 23 million social impressions and even a few 'Hulu gets me' tweets."[3] Read the full case study and identify what made this campaign so successful: http://shortyawards.com/7th/the-perfect-gif.

---

[1] Hulu and M. Marina, "The Perfect GIF from Hulu—The Shorty Awards," December 2016, http://shortyawards.com/7th/the-perfect-gif.

[2] Hulu and M. Marina, "The Perfect GIF from Hulu—The Shorty Awards."

[3] Hulu and M. Marina, "The Perfect GIF from Hulu—The Shorty Awards."

Notes

[1] P. Wilson, "How to Use Images to Enhance Your Content and Social Media," Duct Tape Marketing, November 15, 2016, https://www.ducttapemarketing.com/use-images-enhance-content-social-media/.

[2] L. Safko, *The Social Media Bible: Tactics, Tools and Strategies for Business Success* (New York: Wiley, 2010), chap. 9.

[3] J. Medina, "Rule #10: Vision Trumps All Other Senses," Brain Rules, accessed 2017, http://www.brainrules.net/vision.

[4] M. Krasniak, "Visual Content and Social Media Marketing: New Research," Social Media Examiner, May 30, 2017, https://www.socialmediaexaminer.com/visual-content-and-social-media-marketing-new-research/.

[5] M. Lopes, "Videos May Make Up 84 Percent of Internet Traffic by 2018: Cisco," Reuters, June 10, 2014, https://www.reuters.com/article/us-internet-consumers-cisco-systems-idUSKBN0EL15E20140610.

[6] A. Boatman, "4 Reasons Why Visual Communication Has a Big Impact," TechSmith Blog, October 20, 2017, https://www.techsmith.com/blog/why-visual-communication-matters/.

[7] P. Kelly, "10 Most Followed Brands on Instagram," Smart Insights, March 17, 2017, https://www.smartinsights.com/social-media-marketing/instagram-marketing/10-followed-brands-instagram/.

[8] G. Parkinson, "3 Creative Ways to Personalize Marketing with Instagram," Shutterstock Custom, February 15, 2017, http://custom.shutterstock.com/blog/2017/2/15/3-creative-ways-to-personalize-marketing-with-instagram.

[9] A. Hutchinson, "3 Examples of Instagram Stories Ads, and the Potential of Stories for Marketing," *Social Media Today*, April 26, 2017, https://www.socialmediatoday.com/social-business/3-examples-instagram-stories-ads-and-potential-stories-marketing.

[10] C. Luck, "What Is an Instagram Takeover?" Instagram Reviews, May 9, 2017, http://igreviews.org/2017/04/what-is-an-instagram-takeover/.

[11] Luck, "What Is an Instagram Takeover?"

[12] B. DiFeo, "Some Tactics to Consider When Planning an Instagram Campaign," SocialFresh, June 7, 2012, http://socialfresh.com/instagram-followers.

[13] C. Ratcliff, "How Brands Are Using Instagram Ads," Econsultancy, July 13, 2015, accessed November 15, 2015, https://econsultancy.com/blog/66689-how-brands-are-using-instagram-ads.

[14] B. Chacon, "8 Creative Instagram Marketing Campaigns to Inspire Your Business," Later Blog, September 6, 2017, https://later.com/blog/instagram-marketing-campaign/.

[15] C. Pannunzio, "SMK: Social Media Knowledge," i-Impact Group, last modified April 18, 2012, accessed September 30, 2013, http://www.i-impactgroup.com/A Video Is Worth_041812.pdf.

[16] A. Follett, "18 Big Video Marketing Statistics and What They Mean for Your Business," *Video Brewery*, April 11, 2013, http://www.videobrewery.com/blog/18-video-marketing-statistics.

[17] K. Barnard et al., "Matching Words and Pictures," *Journal of Machine Learning Research* 3 (2003): 1107–35.

[18] S. Rosensteel, "Why Online Video Is Vital for Your 2013 Content Marketing Objectives," *Forbes*, January 28, 2013, http://www.forbes.com/sites/seanrosensteel/2013/01/28/why-online-video-is-vital-for-your-2013-content-marketing-objectives.

[19] J. Mawhinney, "42 Visual Content Marketing Statistics You Should Know in 2017," HubSpot Blog, November 20, 2017, https://blog.hubspot.com/marketing/visual-content-marketing-strategy#sm.001uf512o19uzd9vqpu1yzoofjk77.

[20] Mawhinney, "42 Visual Content Marketing Statistics You Should Know in 2017."

[21] B. Houston, "Skyrocket Your Email Click-Through Rate with Video," Switch Video, April 18, 2017, accessed December 28, 2017, https://www.switchvideo.com/2017/04/18/skyrocket-email-click-rate-video/.

[22] Houston, "Skyrocket Your Email Click-Through Rate with Video."

[23] R. Parker, "Content Marketing Shoutout: Blendtec," Resonance Content Marketing, January 8, 2013, http://www.resonancecontent.com/blog/bid/169002.

[24] G. Reinhard, "YouTube Brands: 5 Outstanding Leaders in YouTube Marketing," *Mashable*, June 1, 2009, http://mashable.com/2009/06/01/youtube-brands.

[25] S. Fiegerman, "Here's Why These 6 Videos Went Viral," *Mashable*, May 15, 2013, http://mashable.com/2013/05/15/viral-video-factors.

[26] Sandy Hook Promise is a national nonprofit organization founded and led by several family members whose loved ones were killed at Sandy Hook Elementary School on December 14, 2012. "About Us," Sandy Hook Promise, 2017, https://www.sandyhookpromise.org/about#mission.

[27] L. Kolowich, "17 Inspiring Instagram Video Examples from Oreo, Spotify, BuzzFeed & More," HubSpot Blog, May 18, 2016, https://blog.hubspot.com/marketing/instagram-video-examples.

[28] DiFeo, "Some Tactics to Consider When Planning an Instagram Campaign."

[29] G. Abramovich, "The Best YouTube Brand Channels of 2012," Digiday, December 11, 2012, http://digiday.com/brands/the-best-youtube-brand-channels-of-2012.

[30] S. Bernazzani, "How to Write a Video Script [Template + Video]," HubSpot Blog, July 13, 2017, https://blog.hubspot.com/marketing/how-to-write-a-video-script-ht.

[31] J. Dalton, *A Brief Guide to Producing Compelling Infographics* (London: London School of Publishing, 2014), http://www.publishing-school.co.uk/uploads/publications/LSP_2014_Infographics.pdf.

[32] J. Porter, "Making the Case for Infographics in PR," Journalistics, June 24, 2011, http://blog.journalistics.com/2011/infographics-in-pr/.

[33] Dalton, *A Brief Guide to Producing Compelling Infographics.*

[34] T. Litsa, "12 Reasons for Brands to Use GIFs in Content Marketing," ClickZ, July 18, 2016, https://www.clickz.com/12-reasons-for-brands-to-use-gifs-in-content-marketing/99932/.

[35] Mawhinney, "42 Visual Content Marketing Statistics You Should Know in 2017."

[36] A. Durdevic, "GIF—The Biggest Digital Marketing Trend for 2017," Digital Doughnut, January 5, 2017, https://www.digitaldoughnut.com/articles/2017/january/gif-the-biggest-digital-marketing-trend-for-2017.

[37] K. Twiford, "Visual Content Marketing: 16 Tips," Content Marketing Institute, October 31, 2017, http://contentmarketinginstitute.com/2017/10/visual-storytelling-tips/.

[38] ROI Research Inc., "Performics," SlideShare, last modified July 25, 2012, accessed September 22, 2013, http://www.slideshare.net/performics_us/performics-life-on-demand-2012-summary-deck.

"Sticky" Social Media 9

Understanding online consumer behavior can be difficult with 3.5 billion active social media users worldwide. Developing highly targeted social content to drive unique online experiences is becoming a larger part of today's public relations (PR) practitioner's job. This chapter focuses on specific elements needed to create content that is memorable, shareable, and "sticky."

KEY LEARNING OUTCOMES

1. Differentiate between "viral," "sticky," and "contagious" content.

2. Learn to focus on storytelling as it applies to social currency, social media influencers, and shareability of the message.

3. Appreciate the importance of developing memorable content that is simple yet inviting.

SOCIAL MEDIA EXPERT

Chip Heath (website: http://heathbrothers.com/about/)

Chip Heath, author of *Made to Stick: Why Some Ideas Survive and Others Die*, asserts that ideas that make it are what he calls "sticky." Sticky ideas share six common traits: they are simple, unexpected, concrete, credible, emotional, and come in the form of a story.

Creating Shareable Social Content

For some practitioners, the ultimate goal of a good social media campaign is to achieve "viral" status. The challenge here is that increasing brand awareness using social media channels grows progressively more difficult every day. Facebook now sees 100 million hours of video daily, Twitter users send 6,000 tweets per second, 25 million LinkedIn profiles are viewed every day, 95 million photos and videos are posted to Instagram every day, 76 percent of top brands and 40 percent of digital marketers use Pinterest, and around 400 million Snapchat stories are created per day.[1] Breaking through the noise can seem virtually impossible.

Luckily, there are numerous savvy companies that are utilizing creative tactics and have exploded into the mainstream by executing fresh, catchy campaigns that encourage consumers to share content within their social spheres. We know this type of content as either "viral," "contagious," or "sticky." What's the difference?

Viral: This includes any PR, marketing, or social media technique that encourages users to pass messages on to other users, potentially creating exponential growth in the messages' visibility and effect.[2]

Contagious: This involves users' spreading or tending to spread messages from one to another through social media, PR, and marketing mechanisms. The idea is to get people talking, sharing, and telling others using word of mouth.[3]

Sticky: This is content that is developed to gain the user's attention and increase the possibility that he or she will share the content with others.[4]

Regardless of the definition, the end result is the same—professionals need to create content that is both memorable and shareable. This raises the question: Are there existing steps that companies can take to ensure that their brands, images, and content will grab the attention of the intended audience? Most people identify viral content as something that just "happens." Viral videos are often considered flukes that only happen once; however, that's not necessarily the case.

Jonah Berger and Malcolm Gladwell are two influential thought leaders who are researching this exact topic. Berger believes that all successful viral campaigns contain triggers that get people talking.[5] Similarly, Gladwell believes that there are forces that cause social phenomena to "tip," or make the leap from small groups to big groups.[6] Gladwell calls one of those factors "stickiness." An idea, concept, or product is considered sticky when it is remembered, repeated, and acted upon by many people.

A closer examination of Berger's research reveals six main factors that help explain social pandemics, while Gladwell identifies three. There is overlap in the findings of both researchers. So, who is right? Is content contagious or sticky? Can it be both? Logic would tell us that both researchers are right, and yes, there are steps that companies can take to create shareable, sticky, contagious content. Between Berger's six factors on social pandemics and Gladwell's three, we can identify four overarching areas of importance when developing shareable content:

1. Storytelling
2. Social Currency
3. Influencers
4. Shareability

Each person on the social sphere has an audience. That audience has an audience with an audience of audiences. When messages are shared, they spread quickly, depending on how large a person's social group is. This spreading and sharing is part of the sticky, viral, and sharable aspects of social media.

Storytelling

Stories have been and continue to be the most useful and persuasive tools when communicating with others. A successful PR professional must be able to describe something in a compelling way. Great storytellers can find unique, emotion-filled angles to capture the interest of their intended audiences. Savvy PR integrates language and visual cues to engage targeted publics, leading them to discover something new about a brand, product, or service. With the onset and universal adoption of the digital age, PR professionals have new tools and opportunities to express their brands. Today, an organization can share its brand's story using a variety of social media platforms, including Facebook, Twitter, Instagram, YouTube, Snapchat, and many others.

Although pulling together coherent narratives may seem challenging, it is certainly not impossible. A practitioner is responsible for developing custom content that communicates a particular angle or story, provides some level of engagement and value, and identifies the company as a brand that can be considered the go-to source for related information in the future.[7] Stories must be told in a way that consumers deem relatable and trigger an emotion that resonates with them. What experience do you desire for your customers to share within their social spheres? The information that you are trying to convey about your organization or brand should be included in this story. Remember, stories are a quick and easy way for audiences to consume information in a meaningful way. Many of the most effective stories often originate from sound research and have a particular audience or perspective in mind. Prior to launching any campaign, practitioners should devote considerable time to planning its execution and associated content.

The #LikeAGirl campaign created and executed by the Always brand of Procter & Gamble is an exceptional example of storytelling. This campaign examined the emotional side of what it means to do something "like a girl." According to A&AD, the creative agency tasked with developing the campaign,

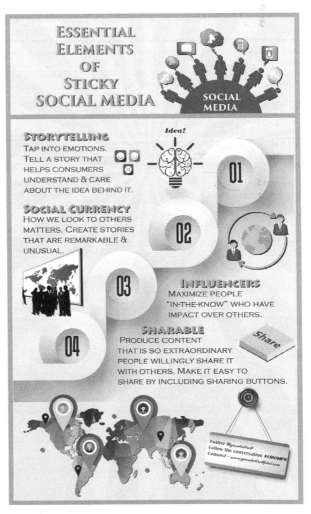

> the Always brand has been committed to empowering girls and educating them about puberty-related topics for decades. However, the brand's purpose was not immediately apparent to the newest generation of consumers: Millennials. The challenge that Always faced was to develop a new, fresh, and meaningful message about "confidence" that would resonate with the next generation of consumers. Always was interested in creating a campaign that not only leveraged the brand's legacy but also reinforced why the brand was "relevant to me" today.[8] Research revealed that more than half of women claimed that they experienced a decline in confidence at puberty. The opportunity was clear—empowering girls during this time of their lives, when confidence is most susceptible to influence, would provide a powerful, relevant, and purposeful role.

The campaign's "story" was to turn a phrase widely accepted as an insult into an empowering message—#LikeAGirl. The idea quickly snowballed into a global initiative. The creative team set out to redefine confidence in a way that was much more relevant, yet remain true to the brand and turn the phrase "like a girl" from insult

These four elements are necessary when creating sticky social media campaigns.

The Always Like a Girl campaign strives to change the meaning of "like a girl" from an insult to a compliment.

into empowerment.[9] The campaign was built around a social experiment to show the impact that the phrase "like a girl" had on society—especially on pre- and postpubescent girls. The centerpiece of the campaign was a video (http://bit.ly/AlwaysLikeAGirlYouTube) that recorded the interpretation of the phrase "like a girl" from people of all ages.

As a secondary strategy supporting the video element of the campaign, the hashtag #LikeAGirl was introduced as a rallying cry.

Always continues to evolve the campaign by updating elements yearly. The first iteration of the campaign was #LikeAGirl Rock; it was changed to #LikeAGirl Unstoppable and then to #LikeAGirl Fueled by Failure. The latest iteration of the campaign is #LikeAGirl Keep Going.

From the initial iteration of this campaign to the present day, PR has played a huge part in amplifying the impact and reaching the appropriate media outlets and influencers.[10] Ultimately, the Always #LikeAGirl initiative generated considerable global awareness and influenced the way that people interpreted the phrase "like a girl"—initially achieving more than 85 million global views on YouTube from more than 150 countries. Prior to the video only 19 percent of women between the ages of sixteen and twenty-four held a positive association with the phrase "like a girl." Following the video an astonishing 76 percent of this population said that they no longer perceived the phrase negatively.[11] Furthermore, two out of three men who watched the video noted that they would now think twice before using the phrase "like a girl" in a derogatory manner. Six months after the campaign was initiated, Always ran a sixty-second television spot highlighting the initiative during sporting events, including the Super Bowl and the World Cup. At the time, the video realized a total of 53 million views during a World Cup year, when many ads were dominated by high-profile athletes.[12] This brand-defining moment helped Always further solidify the company as one of the preeminent thought leaders in empowering women and as a true innovator. The most recent #LikeAGirl Keep Going has garnered a following of more than 3.3 million.

There is incredible value that great storytelling can bring to a campaign or news story. Successful initiatives tend to contain similar elements, including an amazing storyline, emotional appeal, and context, which together trigger experiences that stay at the forefront of the consumer's mind. Now that we have a better understanding of the components necessary to create and develop good stories, we need to investigate the mechanisms behind why people share them with others.

Social Currency

Being "in the know" makes people feel special, influential, and admired. In general, people like to discuss topics that make them look intelligent in the eyes of their peers and want to be thought of highly by those around them—a fact that often finds its way into what we talk about.[13] Think about it: we tell funny jokes because we want others to see that we are witty or share our intimate knowledge about the latest celebrity scandal because it makes us seem cool. Not surprisingly, "people prefer sharing things that make them seem entertaining rather than boring, clever rather than dumb, and hip rather than dull."[14]

When we possess information related to a unique topic that others may not be aware of, we have what is termed "social currency." Social currency allows an individual to enhance his or her own identity, status, or recognition. Therefore, people tend to share things that make them look good. Research has shown that more than 40 percent of online topics are about personal experiences or relationships.[15] As PR professionals, it is our job to create that fantastic experience that inspires a sense of importance, thereby providing consumers with the opportunity to share with others.

Let's take a look at another example. Nearly all women purchase and wear bras. This item is considered a staple in most women's daily wardrobe. You can imagine that competing for the attention and loyalty of women all over the world is priority number one for companies playing in this space. So how does an established brand like Victoria's Secret break through the clutter and get people talking?

Add diamonds, of course!

The price of an average bra is approximately $65 at the traditional higher-end retailers, while the price plummets to around $13.90 at the major mass retailers.[16] Back in 1996, when Victoria's Secret began creating bras with million-dollar price tags, consumers began to talk, and, well, they haven't stopped. As a result, the Victoria's Secret Fantasy Bra has since become the centerpiece of the annual Victoria's Secret fashion show. Designed by renowned jewelers such as Damiani and advertised as the "ultimate" holiday gift, the bras are available for purchase for only one year following their debut. The most expensive Fantasy Bra was valued at $15 million and holds the Guinness World Record for the most expensive lingerie ever created. Modeled by Gisele Bündchen in 2000, the luxury item was made of red satin decorated with more than 300 carats of Thai rubies.[17]

In this initiative, Victoria's Secret focused on a specific piece of clothing and, by adding diamonds and gemstones, created something that was newsworthy. The response over the years has been nothing less than extraordinary. The brand now makes an annual announcement identifying the next Victoria's Secret "Angel" who will don the expensive, sparkly undergarment. The bra, as well as the coveted role of "Angel," has become iconic with loyal patrons of the brand. The Victoria's Secret Fantasy Bras are recognized as some of the most show-stopping lingerie in history. The ornate designs have served as the dazzling finale of almost every highly anticipated fashion show since 2001.[18]

Even if you never purchase one of these bras, you will most likely talk about them and share what you know with others. Countless media outlets pick up the story annually to discuss the price tag, the jewels, and the person who will be wearing the piece. And let's be honest—it is only a bra after all. This is a "sticky" story oozing with social currency, and that is what entices us to share it. Victoria's Secret found a way to make a more or less mundane object remarkable. It uses scarcity (the bra is only available for a limited time) and exclusivity to make people feel like insiders who are receiving information that others do not necessarily have access to.

Now, not all brands can simply take a piece of clothing, add diamonds, and garner similar reactions; however, any brand can utilize exclusivity and scarcity as a tactic. Let's look at Coach Outlet and Bath & Body Works.

Coach Outlet often runs periodic sales lasting from twenty-four to forty-eight hours that offer deep discounts on the normal cost

Lais Ribeiro, a Victoria's Secret Angel, wears the 2017 $2 million bra called the "Champagne Nights Fantasy Bra."

WELCOME

You've arrived at the members-only Coach Outlet online shop, where you'll enjoy access to our limited-time events.

Please provide your email address.

ENTER EMAIL

| | SUBMIT |

of Coach merchandise. The exclusivity element here is that consumers need a personal invite to capitalize on the deals.

And an email address that is on Coach's exclusive list.

The website that Coach utilizes for this promotion is unlike a traditional shopping website where anyone has access to purchase. Invited consumers can only purchase items during a specific period using the link contained within a special email. Consumers are not allowed to share or forward the email; otherwise it will deactivate. It only works for shoppers "on the list." A few years ago the company provided an opportunity to those customers already "in the know" and "on the list" to invite others to become part of this specialized community. When friends shop, the original member receives $10 to shop. These incentives can add up quickly, especially if you are receiving 50 percent off Coach bags, jewelry, and accessories.

Garnering an equal level of buzz and exclusivity, Bath & Body Works initiated a First Look promotional email campaign that invites customers to provide their email addresses in order to join the company's First Look mailing list. This allows subscribers to receive exclusive glimpses of upcoming items, exclusive offers, and fun surprises. Only those individuals lucky enough to receive these special email notifications are aware of secret sales or new fragrances before they hit the mainstream.

Victoria's Secret, Coach, and Bath & Body Works are a few brands that know how to make their customers

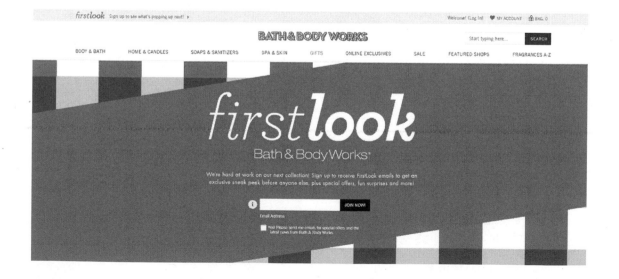

feel special. Select consumers are provided with an exclusive benefit to share with others—something so unique that it is sticky, thus providing the consumer with social currency.

Influencers

For stories to catch the attention of media outlets, there needs to be a catalyst that broadens the appeal to a larger audience. This is where influencers play a critical role. If an idea were solely contagious, it would only depend on the channel to spread the story. Something that is sticky factors in not only the channel but also the specific audience necessary to disperse the message to the masses. These influencers circulate the message by communicating, influencing, and persuading other individuals or groups to act.

Influencers are people who possess extensive social networks. They are often successful business executives, politicians, celebrities, or folks who are simply connected to an "in crowd." These individuals are integral to the process of spreading ideas because their influence stems from a particular expertise, level of popularity, or reputation. Within their pervasive group of friends and acquaintances, influencers can communicate a message rapidly to a readily available, receptive audience.

On the entertainment front, celebrities are often considered influencers due to their high visibility. Think about it: when a celebrity uses a product, the maker of that product gains enormous exposure. Bloggers should also be considered important influencers because they are seen as authentic and have loyal followings. As with a celebrity, when an influential blogger recommends a product, it seems more trustworthy than traditional advertising efforts.[19] Not surprisingly, entire companies now exist that help promote this connection of messaging and influencers. IZEA, a company that specializes in influencer relations, connects brands with influential content creators and publishers to spread messages. Influencer marketing is one of the most useful and efficient ways for brands to reach their target audience. According to a study by *Adweek*, 75 percent of brands engage with influencers as a part of their main marketing strategy.[20]

Manhattan-based beauty startup Glossier owes much of its success to over-the-top, enthusiastic fans and and micro-influencers. Taking a page from the creative folks at Dove, rather than using celebrities to promote its products, Glossier relies on ordinary women to spread awareness. Highly engaged fans sharing the company's products make up 90 percent of Glossier's revenue.[21] This strategy is brilliant. Essentially, it has an "army of Glossier girls" who follow the brand's every post, and in turn forward the brand's messages to their followers on social media and in real life.[22] According to Glossier CEO Emily Weiss, "What's very motivating to us is this idea of every single woman being an influencer. That power of the individual person—just the girl—is infinite."[23]

To launch its new Encore luxury model car, Buick worked Pinfluencers, influential Pinterest users, outside the car industry who could showcase the new vehicle from a different perspective.[24] They dubbed the campaign "Pinboard to Dashboard." The Pinfluencers created boards that illustrated how they would want the interior and exterior of the new model to look. Winning over younger car buyers while maintaining Buick's image as a luxury brand, the campaign generated more than 17 million unique visitors and followers across Pinterest, Twitter, Facebook, and Instagram. Check out some of the playful pins at http://bit.ly/BuickPinboardDashboard.

What happens when Mercedes joins forces with a famous Instagram dog and virtual reality technology? Why, sheer genius, of course. Called the #MCPhoto-Pass, the campaign centered on developing cinematic video content for Mercedes's YouTube Channel. To accomplish this, the company sourced professional photographers to produce photos of Loki the Wolf Dog and his owner Kelly Lund driving a 2017 Mercedes GLS through the snowy mountains of Crested Butte, Colorado.[25] They installed 3D cameras inside and out of the vehicle to make it appear as though Loki the Wolf Dog was running through the snowy terrain, while the inside cameras give an up-close and personal tour of the GLS. Seeking to offer a fresh perspective on Mercedes-Benz, the #MBPhotoPass campaign created videos that brought together a variety of influencers from Loki to world-class chef Chris Coomb. In addition to the videos, Instagram photographers captured images of the excitement and glamour associated with the Mercedes brand. The campaign generated 173 million impressions, 2.3 million likes and comments, and $4 million worth of earned media coverage.[26] Catch some of the footage from Loki and Kelly: http://bit.ly/LokiMercedes.

The common thread in each of the preceding examples is that the influencers were all encouraged to tell a unique story and provided the social currency and specific channel to share the message. People communicate information in a virtual, online environment for many of the same reasons that they share in real life. We are driven by our personal desire to create or strengthen relationships with other people by sharing information with others—especially if we believe that the knowledge we have is new or unfamiliar.

Shareable

Former President Barack Obama continually creates shareable content, whether he intends to or not. In August of 2017 the former U.S. president tweeted a photo of himself smiling up at a racially diverse group of children. The caption read "No one is born hating another person because of the color of his skin or his background or his religion," a quote from Nelson Mandela. This tweet became the most-liked tweet of all time. Why? Because he shared it during what some consider the most controversial time in modern U.S. history, when current President Donald Trump blamed "both sides"—white supremacists and counter protesters—for the tragic, racially charged events that unfolded in Charlottesville, Virginia.[27] At the time of this writing, Obama's photo had more than 70,000 comments and been liked 4.6 million times and retweeted by 1.7 million people.

This wasn't the first time the former president "broke the Internet." As he was confirming the polling results of his reelection bid in 2012, he also cemented his place in social media history at the same time. Once the election results were announced, President Obama posted a photo of himself

Former President Barack Obama's anti-racism tweet becomes the most popular image in history on Twitter.

hugging his wife, Michelle, to his official Facebook and Twitter accounts.[28] The photo, titled "Four More Years," has since become the most frequently tweeted and most liked in Twitter and Facebook history.

These examples clearly highlight that there exists a direct connection between shareable content and high social engagement—which is apparent when something achieves "viral" status.[29] The more compelling and provocative the content, the more likely it is to be embraced and distributed across multiple networks.

Simply stated, experiences prompt people to communicate with others. Brands can tap into this urge to share by creating content that starts the conversation. The New York Times Customer Insight Group published a study that highlights four key factors that cause people to share content. These key motivations include[30]

- defining ourselves to others
- bringing valuable and entertaining content to others
- growing and nourishing relationships
- getting the word out about causes and brands that we care about

To motivate consumers to share, practitioners need to make it easy to share the content. Sharing buttons enable visitors and content viewers to easily communicate your company's content with their social media connections and networks. Adding these buttons to content pieces allows a company to expand its reach to new audiences and generate new visitors.[31] PR practitioners should get into the habit of adding social media sharing links and buttons to every piece of content created, including landing pages, web pages, individual blog articles, and email efforts.[32]

Turkey Joints—*Yum!* Wait, What?

You read that correctly: Turkey Joints are delicious. These are a little-known delectable treat from the small town of Rome, New York. As the leaves turn burnt orange and the temperature in the air becomes crisp, candymakers Spero and Sharon Haritatos of Nora's Candy Shop turn out their signature candy for the holiday season. Turkey Joints are made of "Brazil nuts and chocolate suspended inside a sweet and thin edible wrapper that best resembles ribbon candy. The nuts make the treats bumpy and uneven—and look a little bit like a bone joint."[33] Each jar is specially packaged to stay airtight behind the shimmering gold-and-green label.

The Haritatos family began making Turkey Joints almost one hundred years ago, in 1919. The process is a family-held secret, and each chocolate treat is still made by hand. According to Tina Caputo, "No one knows for sure where the idea for the bone-shaped candies came from, but they've been a local Thanksgiving and Christmas tradition for decades."[34] An employee of the candy shop who manages in-store and online sales said, "I don't know how many jars we sell during the holidays, but I will say it's a lot. All I know is, at the end of the holiday season I am extremely tired!"[35]

Nora's Candy Shop's popular candy creation, Turkey Joints.

According to Chip Heath, "When we talk about sticky, what we're talking about is an idea that people understand when they hear it, and that they remember later on. And that changes something about the way that they think or act." Turkey Joints embody a sticky story. Consider this:

- *Unique Story:* The candies have been made by hand since 1919 and nobody knows how, except the Haritatos family. They are highly sought after during the holidays, which creates excitement and scarcity of the product.
- *Social Currency:* The name itself evokes wonder and intrigue. Once someone hears about this product, a question immediately follows: A Turkey Joint, what is that? Next, people usually ask what they taste like. The taste is so unique it is difficult to describe. Some liken the flavor to cotton candy, but most tell others they must try one and experience for themselves just what a Turkey Joint is.
- *Shareability:* Once a person tastes the sugary confection, they are now a part of the small group that is "in the know." They have experienced a Turkey Joint and have a unique story to share with others. Plus, as natives of Rome move away, the Turkey Joint tradition spreads. With the migration the unique tale of a Turkey Joint is shared.
- *Influencers:* Nora's Candy Shop boasts a website, but their mystique makes them desirable and highly sought after. The candy has been written about by local and regional journalists, covered in *USA Today*'s Eats section and by a variety of bloggers spanning the globe; NPR host Rachel Ward; and Dan Myers, the senior Eat/Dine editor for *The Daily Meal*. But when the James Beard and International Association of Culinary Professionals Award–winning author Brad Thomas Parsons posts an Instagram photo of the taxonomy of a Turkey Joint, you know the treat has hit cult-like status.

Search #turkeyjoints on both Twitter and Instagram and the phrase "Turkey Joints Candy" on Pinterest to see for yourself what all the buzz is about. You may notice that images are typically from the months of November and December. That's because Turkey Joints are a staple and often a holiday tradition shared among family and friends. I know that as a child I could not wait to open that jar and bite into the scrumptious hard candy shell only to be met with the mouthwatering clash of rich chocolate and savory Brazil nuts. See https://www.turkey-joints.com/.

Go Forth and Create Sticky Content

With the numerous avenues available for the distribution of messaging, there is an equal number of ways to create socially shareable, sticky, and contagious content in support of these communications. As you apply the best practices within this chapter to a strategic PR and social media campaign, be sure to measure exposure, engagement, influence, impact, and advocacy to understand how consumers are talking about a company or brand. Reporting and evaluation allow companies to track what is and is not working to continually improve the quality of their content.[36] Social media analytics and the importance of data are discussed in the next chapter.

Theory into Practice

Women's March: Worldwide Solidarity

Born out of an expression of resistance, a simple Facebook post turned into a global moment.

> This is an outpouring of energy and true democracy like I have never seen in my very long life. It is wide in age. It is deep in diversity. And remember the Constitution does not begin with "I, the president." It begins with "We, the people."
>
> Gloria Steinem, political activist and feminist organizer

Research/Diagnosis

When it became clear that Hillary Clinton did not win the 2016 presidential election, Teresa Shook, a retired lawyer and the woman who launched the Women's March on Washington, turned to the pro–Hillary Clinton "Pantsuit Nation" Facebook page and posted that a women's march was in order. Since nobody else took the lead, she educated herself on how to make a Facebook group and began to organize. When she went to bed, "a few dozen friends had said they would attend. By the time she woke up, 10,000 people had RSVP'd to what would eventually become the Women's March on Washington."[1]

At the same time, on the opposite side of the country, fashion entrepreneur Bob Bland, the woman behind the "Nasty Woman" and "Bad Hombre" T-shirts, was organizing her own event. Within a day Shook and Bland were working together. Shook eventually declined to take a central role in planning the March; however, she was instrumental in this historic civic movement.

When asked what prompted her to take a stand, Shook said, "I wasn't that political. Something happened in me with this administration that woke up my love for people and humanity and what this country stands for. We're prepared to just keep letting our voices be heard and not relenting. We have to make it really uncomfortable for the Trump administration."

Other women, including Tamika Mallory, Linda Sarsour, Breanne Butler, Teresa Perez, and Janaye Ingram, eventually joined forces to plan the event. The women now make up the Women's March Board. "We want to ensure that this country knows women are not happy," cofounder Tamika Mallory said. "And when we get angry, change happens. We make things happen."[2]

It is now a full-fledged nonprofit organization; the website reports that the "Women's March was the largest protest in U.S. history, and reached seven continents. The mission of Women's March is to harness the political power of diverse women and their communities to create transformative social change." They are dedicated to ending violence and standing up for reproductive rights, LGBTQIA rights, disability rights, workers' rights, civil rights, immigrant rights, and environmental justice.

Objective

The objective was simple—come together for one day, January 21, 2017, and peacefully assemble to challenge newly elected President Donald J. Trump's agenda. In an interview one of the organizers, Breanne Butler, said, "We're doing it his very first day in office because we are making a

womensmarch   ···

1.21.17

♡ ◯ ◁   ◻

29,198 likes
womensmarch LET'S DO THIS.
View all 507 comments
christiebrinkley 🖤🤍✋🤍👍
JANUARY 21

🏠   🔍   ⊞   ♡   👤

Source: Woman's March Social Media Pages

statement. We are here and we are watching. And, like, 'Welcome to the White House.'"

Strategy

The organization firmly believes that "Women's Rights are Human Rights and Human Rights are Women's Rights." This was the original tenet for which they came together to March on Washington: women's rights = human rights. With so many people responding, the organizers predominantly utilized social media to connect with like-minded individuals and Eventbrite to track attendance.

Tactics

Each social media platform had a specific purpose. Perez said, "Instagram is inspirational but less interactive. Think posts with messages like 'Resist. Rest. Repeat.' Twitter is a good spot to share what partner organizations are up to, and Facebook serves as peak interaction. It's impossible to talk to everyone, everyone, all the time—but Facebook helps."[3]

> *Shared:* To help drum up support, Facebook and Twitter were initially the main channels utilized for communication. These platforms allowed potential marchers to locate the latest information and logistics and connect with others who were planning on attending. Organizers exploited the Internet's extraordinary powers to rally protesters. Perez said,

> Social media streamlined the organization of the women's march, making it easier for people to join the movement. About 45,000 protesters with disabilities participated in the Washington march because they used social media ahead of time to make sure the demonstration was accessible. Facebook gave organizers a way to get a feel for who was interested in attending, as well as what information they needed, how the logistics were changing, and what issues were relevant. In addition to interested participants, they were able to create groups to work with local and state organizers, and partner organizations.[4]

> *Owned:*

> *Website:* As the March grew, organizers built a website to keep people informed.

Source: Woman's March Social Media Pages

> Here protesters connected with others, found lodging and public transportation, downloaded posters and informational kits, and learned how to organize locally.

> *Women's March on Washington App:* Organizers launched an official app that provided information about the day's scheduled speakers, the march route, transportation, accessibility concerns, and safety, as well as an Instagram-inspired feed where marchers could share photos from the day.[5]

> *Messenger Chatbot:* If participants had simple questions such as when the March started or what routes were open, they could also have utilized a specially developed bot designed by the San Francisco–based development firm doubledutch.[6]

Implementation

The implementation process took just seventy-five days. Between November 8, 2016, and the March on January 21, 2017, the organizers held planning meetings, developed social media posts and media kits, lined up speakers, obtained permits, and set up a multitiered FAQ page.

Reporting

The Women's March was the largest one-day protest in U.S. history. Civil and peaceful, it drew 1 in every 100 Americans to march to protest Trump and his agenda.[7] An estimated 2.6 million activists took part in 673 marches in all 50 states and 32 countries ranging from Belarus to New Zealand, with the biggest taking place in Washington, D.C.[8]

womensmarch

Women's March on Washington
DoubleDutch

GET

App Support

Activity Feed
Agenda
Speakers
Attendees
Exhibitors
Sponsors
Bookmarks
Photo Feed
Leaderboard
Surveys
Map
Search

WOMEN'S
MARCH

Liked by jenmorrisonlive and 3,180 others
womensmarch The official #WomensMarch on Washington app is here. Download it today! (Link in bio.)
View all 150 comments
JANUARY 17

Source: Woman's March App

When the Women's March posts on social media, a single post can garner more than 25,000 to 41,000 likes and hundreds of comments, shares, and reposts. In followers alone, the organization's account has 715,000 Instagram followers, 544,000 Twitter followers, and 808,000 Facebook followers. The social media accounts are used not simply to get messages out but also to connect with followers and engage in conversations. Comments are responded to and community action is evident.

Earned media was not the spotlight that propelled this movement forward. From its inception the March was a social media phenomenon. This case study illustrates that when people are passionate about a cause, they will unite, and today social media is the connective tissue that binds action together. In the months since that historic day in January, the March has received much coverage. The media has helped amplify the message. The *New York Times, Chicago Tribune, Washington*

Business Journal, HuffPost, The New Yorker, Vogue, Teen Vogue, and *Time,* among others, as well as bloggers from all over the world, reported on the impact the March had and its continued influence.

Along with the co-organizers, on the day of the March, celebrities including America Ferrera, Madonna, Ashley Judd, Michael Moore, and Scarlett Johansson stood beside activists such as the iconic Gloria Steinem, Cecile Richards, Amanda Nguyen, Melissa Mays, Angela Davis, and LaDonna Harris, among other influential, powerful, modern suffragists.

To date, the Women's March has become more than just a one-day event. Immediately following the March, organizers rolled out a campaign to continue the momentum. They dubbed these "10 actions for the first 100 days."[9] These included sending post-cards to senators, hosting huddles, enacting a day without women, engaging young activists, holding workshops, and even donating to the cause.

In its first year the organization hired a full-time executive director; planned and held the Inaugural Women's Convention in Detroit, Michigan; stood up against the NRA, the ending of DACA, and voter suppression; developed Women's March EMPOWER, an initiative of Women's March Youth that provides young people with the tools needed to create high school and college chapters that guide students in making a positive impact in their communities; and wrote the book *Together We Rise.*[10]

On January 21, 2018, in Las Vegas, Nevada, the organizers once again brought together thousands of women and allies to celebrate the one-year anniversary of the Women's March and to launch their collective 2018 Women's March agenda: #PowerToThe Polls.

1   P. Stein, "The Woman Who Started the Women's March with a Facebook Post Reflects: 'It Was Mind-Boggling,'" *The Washington Post,* January 31, 2017, accessed December 29, 2017, https://www.washingtonpost.com/news/local/wp/2017/01/31/the-woman-who-started-the-womens-march-with-a-facebook-post-reflects-it-was-mind-boggling/?utm_term=.47a4012eb531.

2   A. M. Salazar, "Organizers Hope Women's March on Washington Inspires, Evolves," NPR, December 21, 2016, accessed December 29, 2017, https://www.npr.org/2016/12/21/506299560/womens-march-on-washington-aims-to-be-more-than-protest-but-will-it.

3   E. Carson, "How Facebook, Twitter Jumpstarted the Women's March," CNET, April 20, 2017, accessed

December 29, 2017, https://www.cnet.com/news/facebook-twitter-instagram-womens-march/.

4 Carson, "How Facebook, Twitter Jumpstarted the Women's March."

5 K. Tiffany, "The Women's March on Washington Has an Official App for Live Updates," The Verge, January 20, 2017, accessed December 29, 2017, https://www.theverge.com/2017/1/20/14338774/women-march-on-washington-app-information-schedule.

6 T. Chappellet-Lanier, "Need Last-Minute Women's March Info? Try This Chatbot," Technical.ly DC, January 20, 2017, accessed December 29, 2017, https://technical.ly/dc/2017/01/20/womens-march-info-chatbot/.

7 M. Broomfield, "Women's March against Donald Trump Is the Largest Day of Protests in US History, Say Polit-

ical Scientists," The Independent, January 23, 2017, accessed December 29, 2017, https://www.independent.co.uk/news/world/americas/womens-march-anti-donald-trump-womens-rights-largest-protest-demonstration-us-history-political-a7541081.html.

8 H. M. Przybyla and F. Schouten, "At 2.6 Million Strong, Women's Marches Crush Expectations," USA Today, January 22, 2017, accessed December 29, 2017, https://www.usatoday.com/story/news/politics/2017/01/21/womens-march-aims-start-movement-trump-inauguration/96864158/.

9 Women's March, https://www.womensmarch.com/actions/.

10 Women's March, https://www.womensmarch.com/empower/.

Learn Social Media and Public Relations

Apply the principles learned in this chapter to the scenarios below.

- Compare and contrast the four areas of sticky content that you learned in this chapter—storytelling, social currency, influencers, and shareability—with Chip and Dan Heath's six tenets of sticky content. Discuss the similarities and differences. Examine where there is crossover. Create your own categories for what makes something "sticky." Watch this video to understand more about the Heath brothers' philosophy: http://bit.ly/MakeItStickVideo.

- With revenue trending downward, Kmart needed to do something to get customers talking—and shopping. Teaming with creative agency FCB, it created the Ship My Pants online video campaign.[1] Embracing juvenile wordplay, this message was a clever way to inform customers that out-of-stock items in Kmart stores may now be shipped directly to a consumer's home for free. Enthusiastically, one elderly shopper proclaims, "I just shipped

my pants, and it's very convenient!" Another announces, "I just shipped my bed!" Some viewers called it "gross" and "vulgar," but the video triggered 20 million YouTube views, at one point realizing one share for every nine views. Kmart and FCB followed Ship My Pants with the equally funny Big Gas Savings campaign. Watch the videos: Ship my Pants: http://bit.ly/1QskW9f; Big Gas Savings: http://bit.ly/1ppjcre.

- Candy Corn M&Ms, watermelon-flavored Oreos, and the annual limited-edition Prada handbag are examples of brands attempting to create a story around a distinctive product. When brands launch and create items that are limited-edition, are they developing sticky content? Support your responses with examples from the text.

---

1 Jason Ankeny, "How These 10 Marketing Campaigns Became Viral Hits," Entrepreneur, April 23, 2014, accessed November 22, 2015, http://www.entrepreneur.com/article/233207.

Notes

1 J. Bagadiya, "151 Amazing Social Media Statistics You Should Know in 2017," Social Pilot, 2017, https://www.socialpilot.co/blog/151-amazing-social-media-statistics-know-2017.

2 "What Is Viral Marketing?—Definition from WhatIs.com," SearchCRM, 2015, accessed November 22, 2015, http://searchcrm.techtarget.com/definition/viral-marketing.

3 Jonah Berger, Contagious: Why Things Catch On (New York: Simon & Schuster, 2013).

4 Berger, Contagious.

5 Berger, Contagious.

6 Malcolm Gladwell, *The Tipping Point: How Little Things Can Make a Big Difference* (Boston: Little, Brown, 2000).

7 Steve Armenti, "6 Principles for Creating Contagious Social Content," *Content Standard*, November 11, 2013, accessed November 23, 2015, http://www.skyword.com/contentstandard/enterprise-marketing/6-principles-for-creating-contagious-social-content.

8 D&AD, "Case Study: Always #LikeAGirl," June 26, 2014, accessed November 23, 2015, http://www.dandad.org/en/case-study-always-likeagirl.

9 D&AD, "Case Study: Always #LikeAGirl."

10 D&AD, "Case Study: Always #LikeAGirl."

11 D&AD, "Case Study: Always #LikeAGirl."

12 Salesforce Blog Authors, "The 30 Most Brilliant Social Media Campaigns of the Last Half of 2014," Salesforce Blog, December 31, 2014, accessed November 23, 2015, https://www.salesforce.com/blog/2014/12/the-30-most-brilliant-social-media-campaigns-of-the-last-half-of-2014-152015.html.

13 Berger, *Contagious*.

14 Berger, *Contagious*.

15 A. Smith and M. Duggan, "Online Dating & Relationships," Pew Research Center, October 20, 2013, accessed November 23, 2015, http://www.pewinternet.org/2013/10/21/online-dating-relationships.

16 E. Olson, "Finding the Right Fit, with Technology's Help," *New York Times*, August 16, 2012, accessed November 24, 2015, http://www.nytimes.com/2012/08/17/business/media/finding-the-best-fitting-bra-with-technologys-help.html?_r=0.

17 C. Lankinston, "As Victoria's Secret Unveils Two Fantasy Bras, FEMAIL Takes a Look Back at the History of the World's Most Expensive Lingerie," *Mail Online*, November 4, 2014, accessed November 24, 2015, http://www.dailymail.co.uk/femail/article-2819365/A-Victoria-s-Secret-unveils-two-Fantasy-Bras-FEMAIL-takes-look-history-world-s-expensive-lingerie.html.

18 Lankinston, "As Victoria's Secret Unveils Two Fantasy Bras."

19 Marketing-Schools.org, "Influencer Marketing," 2012, accessed November 25, 2015, http://www.marketing-schools.org/types-of-marketing/influencer-marketing.html.

20 S. Main, "This Report Shows Just How Effective Influencer Marketing Can Be for Brands," *Adweek*, April 27, 2017, http://www.adweek.com/digital/this-report-shows-just-how-effective-influencer-marketing-can-be-for-brands/.

21 S. Cheung, "10 Examples of Innovative Influencer Marketing Campaigns," Sensei Marketing, September 11, 2017, https://senseimarketing.com/10-examples-innovative-influencer-marketing-campaigns/.

22 Cheung, "10 Examples of Innovative Influencer Marketing Campaigns."

23 Cheung, "10 Examples of Innovative Influencer Marketing Campaigns."

24 Cheung, "10 Examples of Innovative Influencer Marketing Campaigns."

25 Cheung, "10 Examples of Innovative Influencer Marketing Campaigns."

26 Cheung, "10 Examples of Innovative Influencer Marketing Campaigns."

27 Shear, Michael, and Maggie Haberman. "Trump Defends Initial Remarks on Charlottesville; Again Blames 'Both Sides'." *New York Times*. August 15, 2017. https://www.nytimes.com/2017/08/15/us/politics/trump-press-conference-charlottesville.html.

28 Cision, "Shareable Content—the Key to Social Media Engagement Success," May 2, 2015, accessed November 25, 2015, http://www.cision.com/us/resources/white-papers/shareable-content-the-key-to-social-media-engagement-success.

29 Cision, "Shareable Content—the Key to Social Media Engagement Success."

30 J. Bullas, "10 Ways to Create Contagious Content for Your Social Media Marketing," Jeffbullas.com, October 20, 2014, accessed November 25, 2015, http://www.jeffbullas.com/2014/10/21/10-ways-to-create-contagious-content-for-your-social-media-marketing.

31 P. Vaughen, "The Ultimate Cheat Sheet for Creating Social Media Buttons," HubSpot Blog, October 30, 2014, accessed November 25, 2015, http://blog.hubspot.com/blog/tabid/6307/bid/29544/The-Ultimate-Cheat-Sheet-for-Creating-Social-Media-Buttons.aspx.

32 Vaughen, "The Ultimate Cheat Sheet for Creating Social Media Buttons."

33 T. Weaver, "Turkey Joints: See Where This Iconic Upstate Candy Is Made," NewYorkUpstate.com, May 6, 2016, http://www.newyorkupstate.com/utica/2016/05/turkey_joints_see_where_this_i.html.

34 T. Caputo, "The Holiday Candy Tradition These New Yorkers Love," *Zester Daily*, November 19, 2013, http://zesterdaily.com/thanksgiving/turkey-joints-holiday-candy-tradition-new-york-loves/.

35 Caputo, "The Holiday Candy Tradition These New Yorkers Love."

36 Bullas, "10 Ways to Create Contagious Content for Your Social Media Marketing."

Measuring Social Media's Impact and Value

10

The success that social media has achieved within mainstream business activities highlights the importance of measuring the outcomes of these campaigns. Traditionally, up to 5 percent of a typical public relations (PR) budget is allocated to the measurement and interpretation of campaign-related metrics. Today, companies expect their PR and social media professionals to quantify the impact and value.

KEY LEARNING OUTCOMES

1. Appreciate the importance of measurement in social media and PR.
2. Understand that analytics begins during the planning process and continues throughout the campaign, rather than after the campaign ends.
3. Become familiar with social media models and frameworks and grasp how they work.

SOCIAL MEDIA EXPERT

Zeynep Tufekci, Ph.D. (@zeynep)

Zeynep Tufekci is an associate professor at the School of Information and Library Science at the University of North Carolina at Chapel Hill. Her research centers on the construction of technology and society. As a techno-sociologist, she focuses on social movements, civics, privacy and surveillance, social interactions, big data, and algorithmic decision making.[1]

---

[1] School of Information and Library Science, University of North Carolina at Chapel Hill, "Zeynep Tufekci," https://sils.unc.edu/people/faculty/zeynep-tufekci.

Significance of Social Media Analytics

Social media analytics is an integral aspect of PR and social media planning because the main purpose is to enable informed and insightful decisions based on data.[1] Thomas Davenport and Jeanne Harris, authors of *Competing on Analytics: The New Science of Winning*, define analytics as "the extensive use of data, statistical and quantitative analysis, explanatory and predictive models, and fact-based management to drive decisions and actions," while at the same time provide a framework for business intelligence as "a set of technologies and processes that use data to understand and analyze business performance."[2] Practitioners use the data derived from social media to answer questions such as

- Who are the influencers on our social pages?
- What is the overall sentiment surrounding conversations on our social pages?

- In what ways can our company leverage social media to promote our overarching goals?
- Which platform(s) are driving the most engagement?
- When are our users reading our content?
- Which platforms drive traffic to company-owned channels?
- What are the best keywords to use to drive engagement?
- How are our competitors performing?
- How does the company best analyze social media data to improve customer service, products, or services?
- What are our paid, earned, shared, and owned (PESO) channels telling us and how can we harness that information to make informed decisions?

Gohar Khan, in his book *Seven Layers of Social Media Analytics: Mining Business Insights from Social Media*, notes that there are three forms of analytics.[3]

1. *Descriptive Analytics:* What happened? Insights into the past.
2. *Predictive Analytics:* What could happen? Insights into the future.
3. *Prescriptive Analytics:* What should the company do? Possible actions/outcomes.

Descriptive analytics accounts for the majority of social media analytics today. Here practitioners are focused on gathering and describing social media data to populate update or status reports. According to Khan, examples of this type of analytics include the number of likes, tweets, and views, as well as user comments. User comments are used to decipher sentiment or identify trends. Similarly, predictive analytics are used to predict future events such as a customer's decision to purchase or forecasting sales figures based on historical visits to the company website.[4] The goal of prescriptive analytics is to improve an organization's performance through a series of mathematical techniques including machine learning, algorithms, and computational modeling to decide the best plan of action.[5] Keith Peterson, president and CEO of Halo, notes that "prescriptive analytics are relatively complex to administer, and most companies are not yet using them in their daily course of business. When implemented correctly, they can have a large impact on how businesses make decisions, and on the company's bottom line. Larger companies are successfully using prescriptive analytics to optimize production, scheduling and inventory in the supply chain to make sure they are delivering the right products at the right time and optimizing the customer experience."[6]

Social media measurement and analytics can be a stand-alone position at a company, agency, or within the PR and marketing department. However, there are times when practitioners will be called upon to anticipate and analyze campaigns. This chapter is meant to provide an introduction to and overview of analytics, and not as an in-depth examination into social media analytics.

Social Media Measurement

Listening, as we have learned throughout the book, is a vital component of social media. When an organization actively listens to its respective audiences, it can assess what is being said about the company, an individual, a brand, or a product on the social sphere. These conversations produce copious amounts of unstructured data, which can seem somewhat uninterpretable and overwhelming. Just ask the individuals who spend their time trolling through Twitter feeds Facebook comments, pins, and posts; reading comments from blogs; and examining message boards or forums. Phew! It's exhausting just thinking about that! It is difficult enough to closely follow these conversations, let alone interpret the content and make sense of the information as an origin for action. Listening to and monitoring social media–driven conversations allows a company to gather data, create metric-driven reports, and identify important action items. As a company collects this data, direct correlations can be made based on the results of its campaigns or initiatives. However, this does not mean that this task is easy by any stretch of the imagination.

Measuring the success and impact of social media initiatives is not as simple as adding up the number of "likes" or "shares." In fact, measuring the effectiveness of a social media campaign and overall strategy can be extremely daunting. Experts like Bernadette Coleman have developed a series of equations to calculate everything from user lifetime value to impression value and social media expenditures in order to valuate social media efforts. For example, companies that would like to calculate their social media expenditure might use the following formula:

Expenditures (E) = hard costs + cost / time spent + sunk cost

Those companies interested in calculating their lifetime user value, however, might instead use

User lifetime value (U)
= (gross distribution per customer) × Σ (yearly retention rate)^i
/ (1+ yearly discount rate)^i − (retention cost per customer per year)
× Σ (yearly retention rate)^p / (1 + yearly discount rate)^p + 0.5[7]

While the formulaic approach can be confusing, other models and frameworks are more straightforward. Don Bartholomew (@Donbart), senior vice president of digital and social media research at Ketchum, is largely considered one of the industry's "resident experts" on measurement. His work[8] and the efforts of both the International Association for Measurement and Evaluation of Communications (AMEC) and the Conclave, a volunteer group representing different associations, organizations, and academia, are contributing to the development of a set of generally accepted standards within the communications industry.[9] In June 2013 the Conclave released the "Complete Social Media Measurement Standards" in an attempt to provide a framework around some generally accepted measurement principles. The full report can be found using the following link: http://bit.ly/SMConclave. Highlights contained within this report include:

Content and Sourcing: This area of the report attempts to capture information regarding content sources to provide transparency and ease of comparison across analyses.[10] This section highlights how to analyze content from multiple sources (channels), including Twitter, Facebook, Instagram, YouTube, and Pinterest, among others. Key metrics that are calculated to understand reach, engagement, influence, and opinion/advocacy are also examined in this section. Even the coding for understanding sentiment is addressed.

Reach and Impressions: This section serves as a basis for defining data collection in social media so that subsequent metrics and other standards can be calculated consistently. In-depth definitions and explanations of "item," "mention," "impressions," and "reach" are provided. Mention, impression, and reach can be defined as follows:

• A "mention" refers to a brand, organization, campaign, or entity that is being measured. Mentions are typically defined in social media using Boolean search queries. These queries may include "AND" as well as "OR" statements to capture specific brands, campaigns, or subject matter topics, as they pertain to the goals of the search objective. Furthermore, mention queries may also include "NOT" statements to filter off-topic mentions from the data set.

- "Impressions" represent the number of times an item has an opportunity to be seen and reach people, based on the simple addition of those audiences that have had the opportunity to see it. Perhaps better called "potential impressions," this term represents the gross number of opportunities for items to be seen, regardless of frequency of display, method of accessing the item, or audience duplication. It will typically count the same individuals multiple times and will include individuals who had the opportunity to see the item, but did not in fact see it at all. A virtue of this metric is that it is somewhat comparable to metrics used in traditional media. The term "displayed" applies across channels, browsers, devices, and other methods by which an individual might see an item.
- "Reach" is the total number of unique individuals who had the opportunity to see an item. Reach is typically a constructed metric that is based on the number of impressions, refined to eliminate the duplication of individuals who have had the opportunity to see the item through multiple media channels, or access points (e.g. laptops and hand-held devices) and to eliminate repeated serving of the item other than valid reproductions of that item across digital media.[11]

Engagement and Conversation: "Engagement" and "conversation" are words commonly used by social media professionals, yet they are rarely defined with any type of consistency to guide sound measurement. Within this section of the report, definitions and differentiations between engagement and conversations are provided. For example, the report states, "Engagement counts for such actions as: likes, comments, shares, votes, +1s, links, retweets, video views, content embeds, etc. Engagement types and levels are unique to specific channels, but can be aggregated for cross-channel comparison."[12] Conversation, on the other hand, measures items such as blog posts, comments, tweets, Facebook posts/comments, video posts, replies, and so on.[13]

Opinion and Advocacy: Since not all practitioners are experts in market research, robust parameters and comprehensive examples regarding measuring sentiment, opinion, and advocacy are provided within this section of the report. The Conclave offers the following distinctions:

- Sentiment is a component of opinion and advocacy. Sentiment is the feeling the author is trying to convey, often measured through context surrounding characterization of object.
- Opinion is a view or judgment formed about something, not necessarily based on fact or knowledge. Standard indicators of opinion standards have not yet been achieved, but typically opinion is definitively articulated and associated to the speaker.
- Advocacy is a public statement of support for or recommendation of a particular cause or policy. Advocacy requires a level of expressed persuasion. The key distinction between "advocacy" and "opinion," is that advocacy must have a component of recommendation or a call to action (CTA) embedded in it.[14]

Influence: Buzz words like "influencers" and "influential" are regularly used in social media planning. The Conclave adopted the following language surrounding these terms: a "key influencer" is "a person (or group of people) who possess greater than average potential to influence due to attributes such as frequency of communication, personal persuasiveness, or size of and centrality to a social network, among others."[15]

Social Blade: PR's Newest Best Asset

Blogger and PR newcomer Alison Verp notes that as PR practitioners, we must extract relevant information from social media analytics sites to increase the magnitude and power of our own outreach. This is typically done by analyzing internal accounts; however, it is equally crucial to have an external benchmark for comparison. There are a variety of analytics websites that allow you to compare social media accounts, SocialBlade being a new favorite. SocialBlade grants organizations access to statistics on any public YouTube, Twitch, Twitter, Instagram, or Dailymotion account. This analytics platform allows organizations to see the company's following in real time, ranks company account following, shows the average posts and reposts, and makes future projections for the accounts. Organizations can compare up to three accounts at a time. PR practitioners can utilize SocialBlade to compare influencer followings and make informed decisions about who will maximize social media impressions. Additionally, statistics of successful accounts available on this platform can be used as target numbers to improve the following on company-owned accounts. Competitive analysis is a core advantage for any company. Using SocialBlade's comparison feature, organizations can use competitor's accounts as an indicator of the health of their own social media accounts.

Impact and Value: It is widely accepted that both "impact" and "value" represent the ultimate outcome of any social media or campaign effort.[16] Too often, these terms are interchanged and confused with return on investment (ROI). The Conclave reports that "impact within social media is the effect of a social media campaign, program, or effort on the target audience, while value is the importance, worth, or usefulness of something."[17] As with all planning in PR and social media, measuring impact and value should be connected to the overarching goals and objectives outlined by the organization or plan.

Social Media Models and Framework

For decades, communication models have been linear and almost formulaic in nature. There are countless examples that support this claim; we will look at three of the more widely adopted models. John Marston's R-A-C-E Four-Step Model for Public Relations is considered very straightforward.[18] The components include *r*esearch, *a*ction, *c*ommunication, and *e*valuation. Practitioners commonly begin with the research phase, continue to the action and communication phases, and then ultimately end with the evaluation phase in a linear fashion. R-O-P-E, another commonly adopted model used in communication planning, follows the same blueprint—practitioners start with *r*esearch, create *o*bjectives, *p*lan, and finally *e*valuate the outcomes. Schramm's Communication Model is the final example we will examine. Again, this model follows a linear process. Wilber Schramm is a pioneer in communication theory. He developed the one-way linear model of communication, which sought to explain how meaning was transferred between both individuals and organizations. Meaning, in the context of this model, includes five basic elements: source, encoder, signal, decoder, and destination.[19] Schramm's model emphasizes that the source and

| Source | Encoder | Signal | Decoder | Destination |

| Noise |

Wilber Schramm proposed the model of communication in the 1950s.

Understanding Media Platforms: Paid, Earned, Shared, Owned

Seasoned PR professionals can have difficulty distinguishing between various forms of media in the digital age. An easy way to remember and understand the differences in the media landscape is by using the acronym PESO, which stands for "paid, earned, shared, and owned."

Paid refers to the social channels a company pays to leverage its message. For example, promoted tweets, banner ads, Facebook or LinkedIn advertisements, pay-per-click search ads, sponsorships, and ads in magazines or on radio are all considered paid media. The company has not *earned* the coverage; rather, it has *paid* for it.

Earned is where the customers become the channel for a company through word of mouth or achievement of viral status. Think of traditional PR efforts. The resident PR manager writes a narrative around the company's latest product launch and then pitches that story to both new and traditional media channels, including blogs. The resulting news coverage, broadcast hits, and blog posts are deemed "earned" media, since the company did not pay the news writers, bloggers, or other media outlets for coverage. Therefore, the coverage was earned and resulted from the efforts of the PR practitioners to gain coverage in both online and offline media channels.

Shared refers to the instances wherein consumers are working in conjunction with a brand to create, share, and promote the brand's content. This occurs only when a brand cultivates passionate and loyal followers who want to engage not only with the brand but also with a larger audience as well.

Owned is a term for channels that a company owns and controls. These include the company website, a Facebook brand page, blogs, ebooks, infographics, an official Instagram account, Pinboards specifically maintained by the company, and Twitter accounts.

Source: L. Odden, "Paid, Earned, Owned and Shared Media—What's Your Online Marketing Media Mix?" Top Rank Marketing (blog), 2011, http://www.toprankblog.com/2011/07/online-marketing-media-mix.

receiver continually encode, interpret, decode, transmit, and receive information while also filtering out noise.

Schramm's model revolutionized how individuals thought about communication between senders and receivers.[20] These three models continue to be taught in universities across the globe and are still widely used in PR planning and practice today. However, in today's digital age of communication, these models continue to provide challenges when tasked with measuring outcomes. There simply are no standards.

Since PR activities are regarded as a series of actions, changes, and functions that generate results, the same can also apply to social media and social strategies. Social media impacts the way that content is created, distributed, and consumed. It should not come as a shock that measuring these efforts takes great change.[21]

Social Media Metrics Model

Googling "how to measure social media" will result in hundreds of pages of advice. In this text you are presented with the framework for what one day may be generally accepted practices. Referencing the Conclave report and approximately fifteen other social media and communications models, Don Bartholomew and members of AMEC set out to develop a social media metrics model that takes into account the different stages of social media measurement.[22]

The social media metrics model presented can be considered a recommended approach that strives to create standard metrics for measuring social media. Incorporating models and developing intuitive frameworks are integral to properly

Suggested Social Media Metrics Model

EXPOSURE	ENGAGEMENT	INFLUENCE	IMPACT	ADVOCACY
Create potential audience exposure to content & message.	Interaction that occurs in response to content on an owned channel **'engaging *with* you'.** Also *earned* social conversation **'talking about you'.**	Ability to cause or contribute to a change in opinion or behavior.	Effect of a social media campaign, program or effort on the target audience. Also Value - the financial impact.	Act of pleading or making the case for something. Includes positive sentiment and one of the following: • A recommendation • A call to action to purchase • Suggested usage or suggested change to opinion.

AMEC, the global trade body and professional institute for agencies and practitioners who provide media evaluation and communication research, and Don Bartholomew of Ketchum developed the suggested social media metrics model. *Source*: This and the following two images are reproduced by kind permission of AMEC, the global trade body and professional institute for agencies and practitioners who provide media evaluation and communication research, and of Don Bartholomew, Ketchum.

conducting any measurement. A five-step social media measurement process accompanies this model to integrate all aspects.[23]

1. Step one of the social media measurement process begins with practitioners establishing measurable objectives that are aligned with desired business outcomes and key performance indicators.
2. Step two digs deeper and further defines the specific metrics required to assess performance against any and all measurable social media objectives. Performance targets should be set for each metric during this step.
3. Step three requires populating the selected social media model with the metrics specified and defined in the previous step.
4. With the measurement approach having been defined earlier in the planning process, step four focuses on the gathering and analysis of data. Practitioners should always strive to evaluate the performance against the objectives and targets.
5. Finally, report the results to stakeholders and interested parties as step five.

Social Media Valid Frameworks

Throughout the process of developing a set of accepted metrics and consistent definitions to aid in measuring the success of a social media initiative, Bartholomew and others have proposed a less complicated arrangement that captures social media metrics from three specific areas: programmatic, channel specific, and business. Bartholomew explains that "programmatic metrics directly tie to social media objectives while channel-specific metrics are the unique metrics associated with specific social media channels—tweets, RTs, MTs, Followers, Likes, Diggs, Talking about This, Pins, and Re-Pins, and finally, business metrics illustrate the business impact of the campaign or initiative."[24] Additionally, "paid, earned, owned" and "paid, earned, shared, owned" media metrics were also considered and enable businesses to measure integrated programs containing a variety of differing elements.

One can now see why the creators of social media–based measurement models have abandoned the one-size-fits-all framework that could be instituted across differing business platforms. Business goals and objectives vary; therefore, a flexible and easily adaptable, one-size-fits-most approach is appropriate.[25] This approach allows for companies to focus the framework to their specific business objectives. Within the fifteen-plus models that were studied by Bartholomew and AMEC, the ideas related to post-purchase engagement and advocacy were repeatedly identified. As a result, these elements are also included in this recommended approach. Finally, engagement and influence have always been key concepts in social marketing and measurement; consequently, these elements are explicitly used in this mode.

The following images illustrate the types of metrics used.[26]

	EXPOSURE	ENGAGEMENT	INFLUENCE	IMPACT	ADVOCACY
PROGRAM METRICS	**Total OTS for program content**	**Number of interactions with content** Interaction rate **Hashtag usage**	**Increase % association with key attributes** Change in issue sentiment	**New subscribers** Referral traffic to website **White paper downloads**	**Recommendation/ Total Mentions %**
CHANNEL METRICS	**Number of items** Mentions **Reach** Impressions CPM	**Post Likes** Comments **Shares** Views **RTs/1000 Followers**	**Net promoter % by channel**	**Unique visitors to website referred from each channel**	**Organic posts by advocates** Ratings/Reviews
BUSINESS METRICS			**Purchase consideration %** Likelihood to recommend % **Association with brand attributes**	**Sales** Repeat sales **Purchase frequency** Cost savings **Number leads**	**Employee ambassadors** Brand fans/advocates

The AMEC Social Media Valid Framework: Program, Channel, Business.

	EXPOSURE	ENGAGEMENT	INFLUENCE	IMPACT	ADVOCACY
PAID	• Impressions • Reach • Frequency • Viewability • Digital Display • Video views • Completed Views	• Engagements (paid social) • Click-through • Page views (page landings) • Interactions: expand, unmute, replay, enter data, etc.	• Awareness • Purchase consideration • Purchase intent • Likelihood to Recommend • Brand attributes or equities	• Visit website • Attend event • Sales conversion • Download coupon • Leads captured • Promotion redemptions	• Mentions in Earned channel • Recommendations • Review • Ratings
OWNED	• Unique visitors • Visits	• Return visits • Page views (per visit) • Interactions: clicks, views, use tools • Subscriptions • Links	• Consideration • Purchase intent • Tell a friend • Likelihood to Recommend • Brand attributes or equities	• Sales • Leads • Information requests • Download paper • Download app • Cost savings	• Recommendations • Ratings • Reviews
SHARED	• Organic Impressions • Organic reach • Number of followers	• Likes • Comments • Shares • Replies • Retweets • Etc.	• Consideration • Purchase intent • Tell a friend • Likelihood to Recommend • Brand attributes or equities	• Visit store • Attend the event • Sales • Vote for issue • Satisfaction • Loyalty	• Ratings • Reviews • Recommendations • Recommendations rate
EARNED	• Number of posts • Impressions • Message delivery	• Hashtag use • Mentions • Contest entries/participants	• Awareness • Consideration • Purchase intent • Associations with issues/topics	• Visit website • Attend event • Download coupon • Leads captured • Promotion redemptions	• Recommendations • Ratings • Reviews

Based on the AMEC Social Media Valid Framework: Paid, Owned, Shared, Earned. *Source:* Adapted from Bagnall, Richard. (2014). Metric That Matter: Making Sense of Social Media Measurement. Presented at Public Relations and Corporate Communications Summit, Agra, India.

The methodologies and guidelines surrounding social media measurement are still evolving. When attempting to establish a measurement strategy for your company's social media efforts, expect moments of trial and error. But do not panic. Over time you will begin to see correlations between your social media strategies and the company's key performance indicators. Use the models presented within this chapter to help your organization develop a powerful measurement strategy that meets the specific needs and provides the necessary metrics.

Theory into Practice

T.R.I.P. through the Multiverse

The Lights Out + Aeronaut Brewing Co.
  Reprinted with permission from Adam Ritchie of Adam Ritchie Brand Direction

For nearly twenty years consumers haven't been willing to pay for new music. They're not going into music stores for it, and if they discover it online, it has all the excitement of dragging and dropping a gallon of milk onto their online grocery order. The tactile and emotional elements of new music discovery have vanished. And if you're an independent music creator in a constant struggle with obscurity, you have little hope for label support. Releasing a new album feels like hacking a dull machete through the overgrown app jungle of the Internet.

The agency was asked by indie rock band The Lights Out to help promote their forthcoming album. The album had an interesting concept: each song was a report back from an alternate universe. The music and production were highly professional. But with hundreds of albums released every day (more than 100,000 each year), there was little chance media and consumers were going to find, or care about, a bootstrapped album from an unsigned, obscure band.

We had to do something radically different. In one stroke, with almost no money to spend, we needed to figure out a way to establish national awareness of this band from scratch, generate buzz around their new album, *and* get consumers to actually buy it—requiring a change in consumer behavior that would go against decades' worth of established expectations and buying habits.

Research/Diagnosis

We interviewed music fans and music makers in the band's home market of Boston, asking them where they get their music news, where they get their pop culture news, and where they go for music. It turned out almost none of them regularly visited music stores anymore. If they did, they were shopping for a new release from an already-established band, a reissue of a classic album they already owned, or to browse for vintage vinyl. On-site research at music stores revealed growing shelf space dedicated to pop culture merchandise; shrinking shelf space dedicated to music; and almost no shelf space for unsigned, independent artists. Spotify playlists were the primary consumer discovery tool of choice. However, to be eligible for the most prominent Spotify playlists, artists need to have thousands of followers. This band had less than a dozen.

But when we asked our research group of music fans and musicians about their shopping habits, an interesting trend emerged. The same people who once visited the music store every week were now visiting the beer store at least that often, browsing the cold case. Industry research on craft beer drinkers showed that the majority of their purchase decisions are made at the point of sale. It also showed that craft beer drinkers are adventurous and always look for the new brew they haven't tried yet.

If consumers weren't going to discover this album in a music store or online—and certainly weren't going to pay for it even if they did—we were going to put it somewhere we knew they'd find it, on a product they were already used to paying a premium price for.

We were going to release this album on a beer.

Objectives

The objective was direct and straightforward: achieve national media exposure for an unsigned indie band within three months of its new album release.

Strategies

We convinced the band to let us take a rough cut of the album to Aeronaut Brewing Co.—a brewery founded by scientists from Cornell and MIT—whose sci-fi-meets-arts culture and "beers that tell a story" meshed with the themes of the record. We asked Aeronaut if they would listen to the music and create a beer that would pair flavor with sound. Despite no previous ties to the brewery, the idea "spread like wildfire" through their organization. They agreed.

Aeronaut passionately approached it like a science project. We guided them in the development of a beer to serve as fuel for a pandimensional traveler, with the music as the soundtrack for a journey between realities. Fully embracing the theme of the record, they even used Galaxy hops in the recipe.

We worked with their label artist to capture elements from the band and brewery while staying true to both. We put a social media trigger on the label and used back-end technology on the band's Twitter account, so each time the social media trigger was posted by a consumer, the consumer would receive a message back from the band, telling them what they were doing right now in a parallel universe, and a link to the album. Putting a download code on the cans would have been easier. But it wouldn't have been good enough. We wanted to make consumer retrieval of the album fun, interactive, and socially visible.

We called the unified album/beer "T.R.I.P."—short for "The Reckonings in Pandimensionality"—which was going to be the name of the album. It was a new kind of product that offered a full sensory experience with sound, taste, touch, visual, and smell.

Usually a PR agency is given a product to promote. This was a case of a PR agency actually inventing the product. We created the silver bullet. We needed to run a campaign.

Tactics

We wrote auto-responses for the chatbot we installed on their Twitter account, telling consumers who purchased the beer and posted the social media trigger what they were doing right now in a parallel world, and giving them the album.

We produced a YouTube trailer explaining the collaboration to consumers and media. We brought in the chair of a leading music industry school as a third-party spokesperson, offering the business perspective on why an idea like this is critical in the careers of bands in a post-label world.

We broadened our media horizons and untethered ourselves from usual suspects in music media. We tailored versions of the story for food, beverage, beer, pop culture, lifestyle, business, technology, design, science, and visual arts titles.

We prepared a series of announcements to roll out over the course of the campaign, including live interactive events, where the band would rappel from a reality-splitting wormhole projected seventy feet in the air onto the stage to perform the album. Every several weeks we released a new track or video, announced a show, or added another new element to maintain momentum.

Implementation

We needed every one of these touchpoints. The album was released on November 12, 2016, in the middle of three holiday vacations, a contentious presidential election, fallout/protests in the wake of the inauguration, and finally the Super Bowl—possibly the noisiest, densest, most challenging launch climate in recent memory.

When the campaign needed a progressive media hook, we pledged a portion of proceeds to the ACLU. We even shifted our outreach to the UK during election week, in what felt like flying an airplane around a weather system. We positioned the product as the perfect beer/album for consumers "who felt like they just woke up in an alternate reality." Even National Beer Can Appreciation Day was used as an angle to shift attention back to beer at a time when all anyone wanted to talk about was politics.

Reporting

If the campaign wasn't original, we wouldn't have stood a chance.

We fought hard and earned exposure in MarketWatch, *Adweek*, Uproxx, *Paste* magazine, *Food & Wine*, *Men's Journal*, the A.V. Club, and more—reactively earning placements as far away as Russia, Finland, and Thailand. More than 100 million media impressions were earned through outreach alone, unheard-of coverage for a previously unknown band.

It was important that this campaign be viewed not as a gimmick but as a legitimate new way for artists to release new music. We succeeded in getting this message across ("How the beer aisle suddenly became a record store"—MarketWatch; "Out of this world"—Men's Journal; "Unconventional ingenuity"—The A.V. Club; "A new high in album dropping"—Uproxx).

The media recognized the effort to reintroduce the immersive, "quest" aspect and excitement of physical discovery of new music, citing the project's innovation. Reporters posted pictures to social media of the beer albums we sent them. Competing releases from established artists, without a food/beverage component, suddenly appeared flat.

Consumer fans of craft beer and music ran to beer stores and posted social media images of themselves hoisting the beer/album in the air. The same consumers who research showed would never have purchased or streamed the album were putting on their shoes, going to a store, and buying it.

Nearly 2,000 cans of the album were brewed and shipped to stores. They sold out within weeks, inspiring the brewery to release a second batch of the album, twice the size—which also sold out.

In the process of rising to a seemingly impossible PR challenge, the agency helped an indie band establish itself in a fiercely competitive market, invented a viable answer to a problem plaguing the music industry for decades, put physical discovery back on the table for music consumers starving for a more tangible relationship with their music, and used technology to solve a problem technology initially created.

There were no celebrity spokespeople. No exorbitant spends. Just an original idea and the effort to make it real.

The label of the beer began with the words "This beer is an experiment . . ."

The experiment worked.

This case is the recipient of 30 awards including PRWeek Creative Excellence and Media Campaign Awards, PRSA Society of America Silver Anvil Award, The Holmes Report Innovation & Insights SABRE Award, PR News Platinum PR Award, PR Daily Digital PR & Social Media Award, and the Bulldog Reporter Gold Award.

#LRNSMPR

Learn Social Media and Public Relations

Apply the principles learned in this chapter to the scenarios below.

- There are many social media monitoring and analytics tools on the market. Compare Cyfe, SocialBlade, Meltwater, and Hootsuite. What are their strengths and weaknesses?
- Explain what social media analytics is and how descriptive, predictive, and prescriptive analytics play a role in measuring social media's effectiveness as well as future planning.
- Take a moment to watch AMEC's Social Media Measurement Framework, United Kingdom's Chip My Dog campaign: http://bit.ly/ChipMyDog. In small groups discuss how the campaign was executed and then measured using AMEC's Social Media Measurement Framework.

Notes

1 H. Chen et al., "Business Intelligence and Analytics: From Big Data to Big Impact," *MIS Quarterly* 34, no. 4 (December 2012): 1165–88, http://citeseerx.ist.psu.edu/viewdoc/download?doi=10.1.1.362.1573&rep=rep1&type=pdf.

2 T. H. Davenport and J. G. Harris, *Competing on Analytics: The New Science of Winning* (Boston: Harvard Business Review Press, 2017).

3 G. F. Khan, *Seven Layers of Social Media Analytics: Mining Business Insights from Social Media* (Leipzig: Verlag Nicht Ermittelbar, 2015).

4 Khan, *Seven Layers of Social Media Analytics*.

5 I. Lustig et al., "The Analytics Journey," *Analytics Magazine*, May 10, 2017, accessed December 18, 2017, http://analytics-magazine.org/the-analytics-journey/.

6 K. Peterson, "Descriptive, Predictive, and Prescriptive Analytics Explained: The Two-Minute Guide to Understanding and Selecting the Right Descriptive, Predictive, and Prescriptive Analytics," halobi.com, accessed December 18, 2017, https://halobi.com/blog/descriptive-predictive-and-prescriptive-analytics-explained/.

7 B. Coleman, "The Real Social Media ROI Formula," *SEJ Search Engine Journal*, August 27, 2013, http://www.searchenginejournal.com/the-real-social-media-roi-formula/66047.

8 D. Bartholomew, "About," *MetricsMan*, http://metricsman.wordpress.com/about.

9 See the website of the International Association for Measurement and Evaluation of Communications (AMEC) at http://amecorg.com; Conclave, http://www.smmstandards.com/about/the-conclave-members.

10 AMEC.

11 J. Lovett et al., "Reach & Impressions," The Conclave on Social Media Measurement Standards, January 1, 2013, http://smmstandards.wixsite.com/smmstandards/reach-and-impressions.

12 AMEC.

13 AMEC.

14 N. Beam and E. Stevens, "Opinion & Advocacy," The Conclave on Social Media Measurement Standards, June 1, 2013, http://smmstandards.wixsite.com/smmstandards/opinion-and-advocacy.

15 P. Sheldrake et al., "Influence," The Conclave on Social Media Measurement Standards. June 1, 2013, http://smmstandards.wixsite.com/smmstandards/influence.

16 AMEC.

17 P. Sheldrake et al., "Impact & Value," The Conclave on Social Media Measurement Standards, June 1, 2013, http://smmstandards.wixsite.com/smmstandards/impact-and-value.

18 J. Marston, *The Nature of Public Relations* (New York: McGraw-Hill, 1963), 161–73.

19 W. Schramm, *Mass Media and National Development* (Stanford, CA: Stanford University Press, 1964).

20 D. Wilcox et al., *THINK Public Relations* (Upper Saddle River, NJ: Pearson Education, 2013).

21 D. Bartholomew, "The Digitization of Research and Measurement in Public Relations," *Social Media Explorer*, May 12, 2010, http://www.socialmediaexplorer.com/online-public-relations/the-digitization-of-research-and-measurement-in-public-relations.

22 D. Bartholomew, "A New Framework for Social Media Metrics and Measurement," *MetricsMan*, June 12, 2013, http://metricsman.wordpress.com/2013/06/12/a-new-framework-for-social-media-metrics-and-measurement.

23 D. Bartholomew and AMEC, *Unlocking Business Performance: Communications Research and Analytics in Action* (presentation delivered at the European Summit on Measurement, Madrid, Spain, June 2013), http://amecorg.com/wp-content/uploads/2013/06/Social-Media-Valid-Framework2013.pdf.

24 Bartholomew, "A New Framework for Social Media Metrics and Measurement."

25 Marston, *The Nature of Public Relations*, 161–73.

26 Bartholomew and AMEC, *Unlocking Business Performance*.

STRATEGIC MANAGEMENT: PUBLIC RELATIONS AND SOCIAL MEDIA

Social Media Ethics 11

Today's public relations (PR) professionals are faced with a variety of ethical dilemmas, many of which result from the introduction and use of social media. Due to their interactive nature beyond traditional media forms, social media possess unique characteristics that present unforeseen ethical dilemmas for working professionals.

KEY LEARNING OUTCOMES

1. Recognize how the PRSA code of ethics guides ethical social media practices.

2. Identify how to make ethical decisions on the social sphere.

3. Classify deceptive practices found on social media and acknowledge how to avoid making unethical decisions.

SOCIAL MEDIA EXPERT

LaSharah Bunting (@LaSharah)

LaSharah Bunting is the director of journalism for the Knight Foundation, an organization that fosters informed and engaged communities. Bunting was previously a senior editor at the *New York Times* for digital transition, where she developed and implemented cutting-edge strategies that advanced digital transformation across the newsroom.[1]

---

[1] Knight Foundation, "LaSharah Bunting," accessed December 18, 2017, https://knightfoundation.org/about/staff/lasharah-bunting.

Doing What's Right

The social sphere can be considered as an evolutionary entity, neither static in nature nor fixed. As in any developing system, there are a variety of challenges and moral opportunities that present themselves over time. If we consider the first generation of the web, while important in the advancement of technology for companies, it simply did not represent a major variation in how businesses and ethical situations were handled. In contrast, the most recent version of the web has in fact changed the way technology is used, and therefore it presents unique challenges to professionals.[1]

Ethics has been defined as "standards of conduct that indicate how one should behave based on moral duties and virtues."[2] These values provide the framework for determining the difference between behaviors that are considered correct and those

173

that are not. In principle, this may seem like a simple exercise; however, the line between conveying the truth, playing fair, telling a lie, and purposefully hurting others is oftentimes blurred. Each of us has our own litmus for what's right and wrong. A person's ethical beliefs and approach to decision making depend on a variety of factors, including culture, education, economics, and religion, among others.[3] It may be that one individual believes it is inappropriate to write a ghost blog on behalf of a client, while a colleague feels that it is just part of his or her job. The process of making ethics-based decisions can be murky at best.

As rapidly as business is conducted today, decisions are often made quickly, leaving much room for error. Many of the more severe, yet common, ethical dilemmas faced by practitioners include lying for a client, engaging in deceptive practices by gathering information about another practitioner's client, helping to conceal illegal acts, or presenting true but slightly misleading information in an interview.[4] Consider what you would do if a client asked you to tweet on his or her behalf, write a positive review on a forum, repin a post on Pinterest, or, better yet, friend the competition on Facebook. Would you judge these requests as unethical? The Public Relations Society of America (PRSA) has developed ethical standards for use in the profession to help answer such questions. Because social media have not yet adopted a set of standardized guidelines to use when faced with ethical situations, PR practitioners should refer to the PRSA code of ethics as their guide.

PR practitioners serve as advocates for the organizations that they assist, their clients, and various other stakeholders. Ethical situations are bound to arise with such a multitude of external factors. The PRSA standards help practitioners by providing guidance when making difficult decisions. The following six values provide the foundation for the PRSA member code of ethics and set the industry standard for the professional practice of PR[5]:

ADVOCACY: We serve the public interest by acting as responsible advocates for those we represent. We provide a voice in the marketplace of ideas, facts, and viewpoints to aid informed public debate.

HONESTY: We adhere to the highest standards of accuracy and truth in advancing the interests of those we represent and in communicating with the public.

EXPERTISE: We acquire and responsibly use specialized knowledge and experience. We advance the profession through continued expert-level development, research, and education. We build mutual understanding, credibility, and relationships among a wide array of institutions and audiences.

INDEPENDENCE: We provide objective counsel to those we represent. We are accountable for our actions.

LOYALTY: We are faithful to those we represent, while also honoring our obligation to serve the public interest.

FAIRNESS: We deal fairly with clients, employers, competitors, peers, vendors, the media, and the general public. We respect all opinions and support the right of free expression.

For PR professionals, ethical dilemmas arise when responsibilities and loyalties conflict and a resulting decision must be made regarding the appropriate ethical course of action. The following guide, which has been adapted to meet the specific needs of PR professionals, is offered as one approach for practitioners to reference when addressing ethical dilemmas[6]:

• Identify the specific ethical issue or conflict.
• Identify internal/external factors (e.g., legal, political, social, economic) that may influence the decision.

- Identify the key values associated with the PRSA code of ethics that may be under violation.
- Identify the parties who will be affected by the decision and understand the professional obligation to each that the practitioner possesses.
- Select the ethical principle to guide the PR practitioner through the decision-making process.
- Make a decision and justify it.

PRSA has been a leader in the effort to foster a strong sense of professionalism among its membership. The principles included in the PRSA code of ethics indicate that the practice of PR is built on trust, transparency, and the protection of the public interest by providing honest and accurate information. It is important that PR professionals who are responsible for managing social media outlets be well versed in workplace and business ethics.

Practicing Good Ethics within Social Media

The ability to make the appropriate ethical decisions can promote an increase in trust, loyalty, and friendship. As for poor ethical choices, well, we've seen where those lead far too often. There are several common ethical dilemmas that occur on social media which can result in challenging situations if not identified and dealt with appropriately.

CIPR Code of Ethics

According to the Chartered Institute of Public Relations (CIPR), "Reputation has a direct and major impact on the corporate well-being of every organization. That is why the professionalism of PR practitioners is so important. As the voice of the PR profession, we play a key role in setting and maintaining standards. We do this through a code of conduct which we encourage all our members to follow."

The CIPR provides a series of seven videos on its website that not only explain the code of ethics but also give real-world examples and provide solutions. Refer to http://www.cipr.co.uk/content/about-us/our-organisation/professionalism-and-ethics.

Source: CIPR, "Professionalism and Ethics," 2015, accessed November 20, 2015, http://www.cipr.co.uk/content/about-us/our-organisation/professionalism-and-ethics.

Spamming

Companies are continuously promoting their products and services; however, there is a big difference between reaching out, connecting, and engaging with consumers and spamming them by way of posting links and promotional messages. If you recall from earlier in the book, the Pareto principle comes into play here: 80 percent of the time you should be providing valuable information to consumers, with the remaining 20 percent devoted specifically to your company. Answer questions, give sneak peeks, and talk about what's happening in the industry. Share what's going on beyond the events that are occurring within your organization. Spam is never received well.

Public Feuds

With consumer relations at an all-time high because of social platforms, it can be easy to allow for an argument to go public on your social channels. Fans not only follow brands but are also loyal to the people who promote those brands. As practitioners, it is important to remember that you represent your company *all the time*, not just during work hours. Even when you are on the soccer field, at the grocery store, or enjoying that nice Sunday morning latte at the local café, you are still representing your company and your clients. Social media is about helping others, not about putting them down. Public feuds are far more likely to damage your personal or organizational reputation than help it.

Lying

As we have seen on multiple occasions throughout the book, transparency is a fundamental principle of social media. There is simply no place for lying within a transparent environment. The act of lying to your consumer base tarnishes the company's brand image and results in a substantial breach of trust.

Misrepresentation

This act should also be guided by the "be transparent" rule. While you may not necessarily be lying to your desired public by liking and sharing a new product that your client has launched, you are also being dishonest when you do not inform the social community of your association with that company. Be forthcoming.

As a rule, if you are being compensated by a client or organization to provide a product review or contribute to its digital footprint, the guidelines set forth by the U.S. Federal Trade Commission require that this information be officially recorded and disclosed. It is important to keep in mind that endorsements and reviews are intended to depict the views and feelings from actual consumers regarding a specific product or service. If you fail to reveal that you have been compensated for your review, one could consider this an act of wrongfully influencing a customer base.

> **"**Did you know that if employees tweet on behalf of their employer without disclosing their employee status, their employer can be fined up to $11,000 per incident? **"**
>
> *Eric Schwartzman, founder,*
> *Comply Socially*

Disclosing Sensitive Company or Client Information

Most PR practitioners typically have access to sensitive company information, including proprietary software; details about a planned product or service launch, event, or media release; or even a "secret ingredient." This information must always be protected.

As organizations become more sophisticated in their engagement with stakeholders, challenges surrounding ethical decisions and the subsequent legal implications of those actions are bound to frame some of the discussion. Social networking platforms are sometimes referred to by lawyers as the "Wild West" because social media still seem to operate outside normal laws and regulations.

Social Media and the Law

According to Eric Schwartzman, founder of Comply Socially, "Technology advances faster than government can adapt, so laws that were enacted before social media existed often determine its lawful use."[7] Unethical decisions often provide the potential for malpractice because they fail to conform to fundamental obligations of the professional communicator to foster informed decision making in a democratic society.[8] PRSA has identified three areas of concern.

Deceptive Online Practices

Defined under the PRSA code of ethics, the source of editorial material must be clearly identified. Any attempts to mislead or deceive an uninformed audience are considered malpractice. The PRSA code calls for truth and transparency and full disclosure of the causes and interests represented. The goal should be responsible advocacy on behalf of

Unethical behavior has heavy financial consequences.

clients, building and sustaining credibility with all audiences, and strengthening the public's trust in the information that it receives. Deceptive practices lead to unethical advocacy. Within the code, Professional Standards Advisory PS-8 specifically targets deceptive online practices by individuals or organizations using blogs, viral marketing, and anonymous Internet posting.[9]

Front Groups

Third-party groups, commonly referred to as "front groups," are established to foster misrepresentation and unethical advocacy by deceiving or misleading an audience about a particular position on a topic, as well as its source. In Professional Standards Advisory PS-7, the PRSA code of ethics details the unethical nature of engaging in or assisting such groups' deceptive descriptions of goals, causes, tactics, sponsors, intentions, or participants. The ethical communicator is obligated to reveal all information needed for informed decision making, thereby maintaining the public trust. Purposefully withholding or disingenuously concealing sources or sponsors of information, including their intentions or motivations, fails to satisfy the principles of truth in advancing the interest of clients and serving the public interest as responsible advocates.[10]

Pay for Play

Providing payment to generate or influence editorial coverage, regardless of the channel, is unethical and constitutes malpractice under the PRSA code. This should be obvious because such exchanges of value are hidden from the reader, viewer, or listener. The PRSA code defends the values of honesty, fairness, transparency, and objective counsel to clients. "Pay for play" directly contrasts with the code's warning to avoid any conflict of interest that impedes the trust of clients, employers, or the public. Under Professional Standards Advisory PS-9, professionals are told to disclose any exchange of compensation so that readers, viewers, or listeners have the opportunity to make up their own minds about the value, bias, accuracy, and usefulness of information provided by others.[11]

> **"**Tell the truth. Let the public know what's happening with honest and good intention; provide an ethically accurate picture of the enterprise's character, values, ideals and actions. **"**
>
> Arthur W. Page

Alternative Facts

The Trump administration's relationship with the press has been tumultuous. One of the first meetings between the White House and media included former press secretary Sean Spicer calling a news conference to reprimand reporters for their coverage of the president's inauguration ceremonies. Within the first few minutes of the press conference, Spicer told approximately five mistruths, among these that Trump's inauguration audience was the largest "ever," "period."[12] Counselor to the president Kellyanne Conway described Spicer's false claims as "alternative facts," in which she justified that there was nothing wrong with providing alternatives to the truth.

Jane Dvorak, former chair of the PRSA, immediately released the following statement on behalf of the organization:

> Truth is the foundation of all effective communications. By being truthful, we build and maintain trust with the media and our customers, clients and employees. As professional communicators, we take very seriously our responsibility to communicate with honesty and accuracy.
>
> The Public Relations Society of America, the nation's largest communications association, sets the standard of ethical behavior for our 22,000 members through our Code of Ethics. Encouraging and perpetuating the use of alternative facts by a high-profile spokesperson reflects poorly on all communications professionals.
>
> PRSA strongly objects to any effort to deliberately misrepresent information. Honest, ethical professionals never spin, mislead or alter facts. We applaud our colleagues and professional journalists who work hard to find and report the truth.[13]

According to a survey conducted by the USC Center for Public Relations at the Annenberg School for Communication and Journalism, 73.2 percent of PR industry professionals believe the Trump administration's White House communications team has negatively impacted public perceptions of the PR profession.[14] When asked about different aspects of the perceived performance of the overall White House communications team, the report noted that 80.2 percent of respondents agree that the White House "distorts the truth" and 63.5 percent agree that representatives from the White House "purposefully lie."[15] Fred Cook, director of USC Annenberg's Center for Public Relations, observed that professionals in the PR industry believe that the practices coming out of the White House do not reflect the values of the industry as a whole, and that the majority of PR practitioners observe open and honest communication. Richard Gray, from BBC Future Now, describes the world of "alternative facts" as a "bewildering maze of claim and counterclaim, where hoaxes spread with frightening speed on social media and spark angry backlashes from people who take what they read at face value."[16] PRSA is vehemently against any form of alternative facts. Offering anything but the truth is a violation of multiple aspects of the PRSA code of ethics. As practitioners, we hold ourselves to the highest standards.

Should Ethics Combine with Social Media Policies?

Both ethics and social media are undeniably essential and interrelated within the practice of PR. The question that arises is: What is the best way to manage these two aspects simultaneously?[17] Should they be treated as separate and distinct conversations? Should ethics be specifically addressed within a company's social media policy?

Ultimately, the conversations resulting from an employee's online presence are a direct reflection of the business. When creating a policy governing ethics and social media, it is imperative to address employee expectations and behavior. Expectations of a business online, and even offline, should be included to create an identity. Conversations on the social sphere are different from in-person conversations or even printed communication pieces. Be aware of the ways in which social media can be used: Which audiences are receiving your message, who is sharing messages, and what are they sharing? Take responsibility for any online behaviors—positive and negative—and understand the logic behind having an online presence. Whether a company chooses to incorporate ethics into its social media policy or deal with the two topics independently, setting expectations, conducting training, and enforcing accountable behavior is essential. The book delves more deeply into creating solid social media policies in a separate chapter.

Theory into Practice

It's a Match![1]

Avon and Somerset Police used Tinder to send an online safety message.

By utilizing a pop-up campaign on Tinder and Snapchat, the Avon and Somerset Police (UK) communications team educated hundreds of users about the safety of online dating.

Research/Diagnosis

Armed with statistics from the years 2011 to 2016, studies showed a 2,000 percent increase in the number of crimes related to online dating. Most crimes involved victims who had met the offender on dating apps Tinder and Grindr.

Initially a plan was set in place to reach the target audience by hanging posters in nightclub toilets (bathrooms). However, Avon and Somerset Police's communications team developed a campaign that would run directly on Tinder.

Objectives

Launched in November of 2016, the objective of the campaign was to change the behavior of eighteen-to-thirty-five-year-olds by understanding more closely how to safely date online. Using lighthearted content, the campaign had an overarching goal of reaching the intended audience on the platforms they were using—Tinder and Snapchat. Two

profiles were set up on Tinder and run by officers who were in the target audience themselves.

Strategies

The strategy was to connect directly with the target audience. According to Charlotte Lowe, digital communications officer at Avon and Somerset Police, the department "wanted to deliver the key messages straight to the target audience, cutting out the middle man. We didn't know if they read newspapers or used Facebook, but we did know that they used Tinder."[2]

Tactics

Using only the Tinder app, the team organically engaged users, as each dating "match" was sent a message featuring safe online dating tips. The officers shared tips such as Googling their date's full name, asking for multiple photos, telling others where and when the date was going to happen, and finally, that if a crime happened they should report it.

Implementation

The communications team expected the campaign to have a short life span. The profile was removed by Tinder after a week. In an interview in *PRWeek*,

Lowe said, "It was never meant to be a permanent campaign, but a temporary stunt that was all about talking to communities on the platforms they were using, in the language they were speaking."[3]

Reporting

According to Lowe, the profiles gained 250 Tinder "matches" in twenty-four hours, and this number rose to 1,000 over the duration of the campaign.

The day after the launch on Tinder, the communications team launched a similar campaign on Snapchat, creating a story asking followers whether they had "matched" with the force recently. The Snapchat story gained 124 extra followers in twenty-four hours, with a total 300 views of the story.

This case was not without its challenges. First, evaluation was not easy. Tinder required that all matches be counted manually, which presented challenges in and of itself. But more difficult was the fact that the team did not have a tangible way to connect the campaign back to either a drop or an upsurge in reports.

Since this launch, other police departments have adopted and carried out similar campaigns. For Lowe and her team, she sees this as an indicator of success.

1. M. Ibrahim, "Case Study: Tinder Stunt Gives Police Platform to Talk Dating Safety," *PRWeek*, December 6, 2017, accessed December 18, 2017, https://www.prweek.com/article/1451994/case-study-tinder-stunt-gives-police-platform-talk-dating-safety.
2. Ibrahim, "Case Study."
3. Ibrahim, "Case Study."

Learn Social Media and Public Relations

Apply the principles learned in this chapter to the scenarios below.

- The PRSA issued a statement that condemns instances of promotional tactics that are unethical in the field of PR. It reads, "PRSA states categorically that misrepresenting the nature of editorial content or intentionally failing to clearly reveal the source of message contents is unethical."[1] PRSA lists the following as examples of unethical practices:

  - A PR firm's engaging its interns to write positive product reviews for online message boards
  - Bloggers posting positive reviews of products and services while receiving products for free, as well as being paid by the sponsor for such positive reviews
  - A marketing firm's creating a program to match clients with influencers for positive mentions
  - A company's hiring a social media influencer to post images with products on various social media platforms without disclosing that the images are ads or that the influencer was paid

- While examples vary in method and execution, each scenario shares a common, unethical behavior. Discuss the unethical circumstances and consider your obligation as it relates to the PRSA code of ethics.

- Using the PRSA code of ethics as your guide, rationalize whether the following scenarios would be considered unethical, and then discuss how you would respond to your boss or client.

  Tweeting on Behalf of a Client[2]: You work at a PR agency, and your client is speaking at an international conference. The client is a well-known influencer in her field and one of the few C-suite executives who "get" social media. In fact, this individual has a loyal and active following on Twitter, posting regularly, often several times per day. Your client would prefer that her Twitter feed reflect her activity at the conference and highlight what else is happening. She's concerned that she will not be able to support everything with all her obligations to the conference. This client trusts your agency implicitly and asks you to "take over" her Twitter account during the conference. What do you do?

  Commenting to Consumers[3]: Your client is an absolute giant in the sports industry. It has deep pockets and an even bigger following on the social sphere but only one internal staff member responsible for managing its social media outlets. Admittedly, when one person must both monitor and engage directly with fans through multiple online channels, this can be overwhelming. This client has asked your agency to be its eyes and voice when engaging with its sports fans. It trusts you and feels that you know its audience just as much as an internal staff member. What do you do?

Posting Positive Reviews[4]: Your agency just took on a new client, a small restaurant serving burgers and craft beer. Eager to get good reviews on Yelp, it asks you to post positive reviews of the restaurant and the food. This is an obvious violation of the PRSA code of ethics, so you decline. However, a few days later you notice that

the restaurant has fifteen positive reviews and is not slated to open for another three weeks. You are an agency of record, with a reputation to protect. It is known within the community that your agency is working with this restaurant, conducting its PR efforts. What do you say to the client?

---

1 PRSA, "PRSA Condemns the Growing Use of Disingenuous Editorial Content, Deceptive Commentary on Blogs and Other Venues," August 27, 2009, http://media.prsa.org/article_print.cfm?article_id=1370.
2 T. Defren, "Real-World Ethical Dilemmas in Social Media," PRSquared Social Media Marketing and Public Relations RSS, January 25, 2010, accessed November 20, 2015, http://www.pr-squared.com/index.php/2010/01/real-world-ethical-dilemmas-in-social-media-upcoming-series.
3 Defren, "Real-World Ethical Dilemmas in Social Media."
4 Defren, "Real-World Ethical Dilemmas in Social Media."

Notes

1 D. Gunkel, "Social Media: Changing the Rules of Business Ethics," *NIU Newsroom*, March 15, 2015, accessed November 20, 2015, http://newsroom.niu.edu/2015/03/17/social-media-changing-the-rules-of-business-ethics.
2 M. Josephson, "Making Ethical Decisions: The Six Pillars of Character," Josephson Institute, accessed November 20, 2015, http://josephsoninstitute.org/med/med-2sixpillars.
3 F. P. Seitel, *The Practice of Public Relations*, 8th ed. (Upper Saddle River, NJ: Prentice Hall, 2014).
4 P. Swann, *Cases in Public Relations Management* (Boston: McGraw Hill, 2014).
5 PRSA, "Public Relations Society of America (PRSA) Member Code of Ethics," 2015, accessed November 20, 2015, https://www.prsa.org/aboutprsa/ethics/codeenglish/#.Vk8_enarS70.
6 K. Fitzpatrick, "Ethical Decision-Making Guide Helps Resolve Ethical Dilemmas," PRSA, accessed November 21, 2015, http://www.prsa.org/AboutPRSA/Ethics/documents/decisionguide.pdf.
7 E. Schwartzman, "How to Prevent a Social Media Crisis," *PR Newser*, June 25, 2015, accessed November 21, 2015, http://www.adweek.com/prnewser/how-to-prevent-a-social-media-crisis/115650.
8 PRSA, "PRSA Condemns the Growing Use of Disingenuous Editorial Content, Deceptive Commentary on Blogs and Other Venues," August 27, 2009, accessed November 20, 2015, http://media.prsa.org/article_print.cfm?article_id=1370.
9 PRSA, "PRSA Condemns the Growing Use of Disingenuous Editorial Content."
10 PRSA, "PRSA Condemns the Growing Use of Disingenuous Editorial Content."
11 PRSA, "PRSA Condemns the Growing Use of Disingenuous Editorial Content."
12 M. Conway et al., "Public Relations Association Rebukes Trump's White House on 'Alternative Facts,'" Politico, January 24, 2017, accessed December 18, 2017, https://www.politico.com/story/2017/01/trump-alternative-facts-234138.
13 J. Dvorak, "PRSA Statement on 'Alternative Facts,'" prsa.org, accessed December 18, 2017, https://www.prsa.org/prsa-statement-alternative-facts/.
14 F. Cook, "White House Communications Team Impacts the Perception of the Public Relations Profession, USC Annenberg Survey Reveals," USC Annenberg School for Communication and Journalism, June 20, 2017, accessed December 18, 2017, https://annenberg.usc.edu/news/faculty-research/white-house-communications-team-impacts-perception-public-relations-profession.
15 Cook, "White House Communications Team Impacts the Perception of the Public Relations Profession."
16 R. Gray, "Future—Lies, Propaganda and Fake News: A Challenge for Our Age," BBC, March 1, 2017, accessed December 29, 2017, http://www.bbc.com/future/story/20170301-lies-propaganda-and-fake-news-a-grand-challenge-of-our-age.
17 S. Lauby, "Ethics and Social Media: Where Should You Draw the Line?" Mashable, March 17, 2012, accessed November 20, 2015, http://mashable.com/2012/03/17/social-media-ethics/#C0O.TcSaZqqG.

Crisis Management on the Social Sphere

12

Social networks create significant opportunities for brands, but they also become platforms on which crises can develop and perpetuate at an unprecedented rate. In dealing with a rogue tweet, a product recall, an employee acting badly, a disparaging online review, or a spokesperson who has tarnished the brand, preparing for a crisis situation in a digital age requires a fresh perspective.

KEY LEARNING OUTCOMES

1. Prioritize levels of a crisis.
2. Apply crisis communication principles to social media outbreaks.
3. Synthesize crises and effectively select the best crisis management strategy.

SOCIAL MEDIA EXPERT
Chris Nelson (@CrisisAdviser)

Chris Nelson is FleishmanHillard's crisis management lead for the U.S. He helps corporate executives anticipate, prepare for, and manage crisis situations, high-profile litigation, and contentious public issues that could undermine business. During his twenty-five-year career, he has guided clients through high-stakes crises such as data breaches, product crises, class-action litigation, labor campaigns, and pressure campaigns by activists.[1]

---

[1] C. Nelson, "About the Author," fleishmanhillard.com, accessed December 19, 2017, http://fleishmanhillard.com/2015/04/true/companies-need-a-holistic-approach-to-cybersecurity-that-keeps-up-with-innovation/.

Millennial-Era Crises

In the age of social media, the potential for a crisis scenario to arise has increased exponentially. From lewd photos of a C-suite executive appearing on Facebook or Instagram to proprietary information being leaked and posted to Twitter and LinkedIn, crises happen in real time and only take minutes to spread to the masses.[1]

A recent survey revealed that more than 28 percent of reported crises spread internationally within an hour, and more than two thirds spread within the first twenty-four hours.[2] Despite having traditional crisis plans in place, organizations often find that they are not prepared to manage the crisis on the social sphere. In fact, 50 percent of communications professionals believe companies are not adequately prepared to handle such situations, and 94 percent think that the failure to effectively define how to handle online issues leaves an organization open to "trial by Twitter."[3]

These statistics illustrate the impact that social media has on crisis management for the public relations (PR) profession. Governments, educational institutions, non-profit organizations, corporations, and even private citizens are not immune. The following examples highlight this exact point.

Governments: During the Arab Spring movement, social media–savvy activists across the Middle East and North Africa contributed to the downfall of two dictators, causing widespread disruption. "We use Facebook to schedule the protests, Twitter to coordinate, and YouTube to tell the world," an Arab Spring activist told a reporter during the riots.[4] These types of demonstrations force countries and governments to move into a crisis-response mode.

Civic Engagement: In the weeks leading up to the Women's March held on January 21, 2017, in Washington, D.C., women from around the world used social media—Twitter, Instagram, Facebook—to rise up and provide a platform for the masses to amplify their voices and, in turn, work together to mobilize activists. Some political representatives viewed these marches as a crisis, while others viewed them as collective action.

Educational Institutions: Penn State University and Michigan State University remained silent amid allegations of sexual abuse, years of cover-ups, and acts of misuse and exploitation, while the larger community took to Twitter, Facebook, and hundreds of other online news and media sites to voice their opinions.

Nonprofit Organizations: After admitting to doping and using performance-enhancing drugs to win seven Tour de France titles, Lance Armstrong stepped down as chairman of the Livestrong Foundation. The public lambasted Armstrong on several social sites, tarnishing the reputation of both his charity and his personal image. In the aftermath of this crisis, the Livestrong Foundation amped up efforts to detach itself from the cyclist.

Corporations: United Airlines suffered one of the worst crisis situations in social media history when a video emerged of law enforcement officers forcibly dragging a passenger, Dr. David Dao, off Flight 341.[5] Due to such a forceful removal, Dao suffered a concussion, broken nose, injury to the sinuses, and the loss of two front teeth.

Private Individuals: The social sphere acted swiftly, harshly, and without mercy when the Harvey Weinstein scandal broke. The film producer was accused of sexually harassing young women. Among the many accusations are that "he forced women to massage him and watch him naked. He also promised to help advance their careers in return for sexual favors."[6]

These six examples represent instances of events that unfolded in real time across social media. The reputation of a brand can easily be tarnished in mere moments because an active public can now take a stance, make a statement, and judge that brand based on how the company chooses to address (or not address) the crisis at hand.

Social media is immediate, pervasive, and widely available, and it appeals to hundreds of millions of people. However, for many of those same reasons, social media can also be dangerous for brands, especially during a time of crisis, requiring the addition of entirely new components in crisis communication. The days of "textbook" crisis situations (think of the Johnson & Johnson Tylenol and *Exxon Valdez* oil spill cases) are long gone. Today, PR practitioners employ an amalgam of tactics, strategies, and responses during a time of crisis via the social web. A fresh perspective is necessary to effectively respond to today's crisis situations.

Five Stages of Crisis Management in the Digital Age

Konrad Palubicki (@konradpalubicki), from Edelman Digital in Seattle, Washington, developed what he considers the five most important stages of crisis management in the digital age[7]:

> Prepare in advance.
> Isolate the origin.
> Evaluate the impact.
> Mitigate the crisis.
> Learn from the crisis.

Prepare in Advance

We all love watching viral videos just as much as the next person. Laughing Chewbacca mom Candace (http://bit.ly/ChewbaccaMomCandace), the couple who pretend that the ground is hot lava (http://bit.ly/HotLavaFloor), and Amanda Bell's Kohl's Cash (http://bit.ly/AmandaBell) are all funny, shareable, and lighthearted videos. But when a viral video is about your company, brand, or products, it may not be as funny.[8] It is unrealistic to believe that brands can prepare for every potential crisis, but pre-crisis planning is essential. Author and crisis communication professional Kathleen Fearn-Banks suggests creating a crisis communication plan.[9] The plan should list the individuals on the crisis-management team; generate a crisis audit; and develop key messages, objectives, procedures, and specific guidelines. Some companies take the added step of developing a "dark" website that only goes live in the event of an emergency.[10] Prewritten messaging and critical information can be created ahead of the crisis, uploaded to the site, and launched if a crisis ever breaks.

Preparing in advance also means that companies must pay attention to the conversations occurring on their social channels. The task of perusing the company Twitter feed or browsing the company Facebook posts should not be considered truly listening. Organizations need to use specific social media–monitoring software such as Meltwater Buzz, Crimson Hexagon, Sysomos, Lithium, Viralheat, and Social Mention to understand the messages that pertain to their company or brand. These software systems help companies monitor who is participating in conversations and what is being said across multiple social media platforms, blogs, and website comments. Monitoring also aids in identifying where a crisis originated.

CRISIS ON THE SOCIAL SPHERE

1 Prepare in Advance
- Create a plan
- Set up monitoring tools

2 Isolate the Origin
- Identify where the crisis originated and on which social channels
- Don't fight back - with journalists or consumers

3 Evaluate the Impact
- Take inventory of the situation
- Establish a clear chain of command

4 Mitigate the Crisis
- Respond quickly and with empathy
- Take appropriate action

5 Learn from the Crisis
- When it's over go back and review

Organizations are vulnerable to crisis. Creating a crisis communication plan can help guide brands through tough times and save reputations.

Isolate the Origin

Being able to identify where a crisis initiates and on what social channels the conversations fueling the crisis are happening is paramount in controlling the crisis situation.[11] When brands understand the cause of the crisis, they can better assess how to respond. Proper identification helps a company determine whether a full social media crisis is present and is also invaluable in helping a company decide the next steps in formulating a proper response.

Evaluate the Impact

Take inventory of the situation. Create a log to determine which stakeholders require attention first—and fast. There are two primary audiences during a crisis: those directly affected and those whose attitudes about the company could be influenced.[12] Determine whether one group is being impacted more than another and evaluate the immediate impacts of the situation, which could include the following[13]:

Uptick in calls to the customer service hotline
Rise in media inquiries
Flurry of comments on social channels
Interest from government regulators
Inquiries from the board of directors
Disaffection toward brands or products
Drop in sales
Potential lawsuits
Vulnerability to personal, societal, and economic conditions

If a company waits too long to acknowledge and respond while a crisis breaks, it can quickly lose credibility. Social media crises will not disappear after a few days. On the contrary, without proper management, a crisis will continue to build momentum and accelerate to a tipping point. Twenty-four hours on the social web is too long to wait to acknowledge and respond. Heck—four hours could be too long!

Mitigate the Crisis

The more rapid the response time, the better a company's chance of limiting the total duration of the crisis. The first rule in crisis management is "Stop the bleeding." Acting fast and responding to the situation is paramount. Once the crisis team establishes an initial response, focus should then shift toward ensuring a continuity of messages across all traditional and social channels.

It is important to sustain real-time updates by including details that are honest and straightforward. Remember the "dark" website suggestion from earlier in the

Social Media Crisis or Not?

Would you know if your company was in the midst of a social media crisis? These three characteristics can help determine whether a company is in a true social media crisis mode:

1. *Definite Change from the Norm:* Companies should watch for sudden changes in tone and sentiment in discussion and comments on social media sites.

2. *Information Separation:* The company is not aware of the situation any more than the public.

3. *Widespread Impact throughout the Company:* The scope and scale are so large and incomprehensible during the initial stage when the crisis breaks that it has ramifications at every level.

Source: J. Baer, *Youtility* (New York: Penguin, 2013).

chapter? Bring that to life. A website dedicated to the crisis serves two purposes. First, the website can minimize the conversations happening on social sites. Second, the website illustrates that the company is proactive in resolving the issue at hand. A website of this nature can provide companies with a platform for providing regular updates, contact information, video or photo updates, current actions related to the crisis, and plans to ensure the incident will not happen again.

Continue listening using the monitoring tools set in place prior to the crisis. Establish an in-house crisis command center so that the crisis team can collaborate in real time.[14] Companies can track the crisis using all traditional media channels and social platforms simultaneously. Companies can use Twitter and Facebook to proactively post statements such as "We are aware of the issue. Live updates are here: [provide URL]." The URLs will drive traffic back to the company-dedicated website that contains the most relevant information.

Learn from the Crisis

All crises are learning opportunities. Crises may not necessarily be the type of lessons we love, but they are opportunities to gain valuable insights. Companies should conduct a post-crisis meeting to determine how the organization performed during the crisis. An analysis of emails sent, offline media coverage garnered, company statements, and all social mentions, including tweets, snaps, blog comments, pins, videos, Facebook updates, and any other online media mentions, should be conducted. The process of analysis is evaluative and designed to bring about change that helps prevent similar future crises.[15]

Smart Companies, Unfortunate Crises

Some organizations are better equipped to handle a crisis than others. Regardless of how prepared a company believes it is to handle a crisis, there is always something to learn from the experience. Companies can learn how to strengthen their own social media crisis-management strategies by examining how other organizations, like media company Shea Moisturizer, Oreo, Pepsi, and KitchenAid, handled their own crises on the social sphere.

Not So Smooth

In an effort to be more inclusive, Shea Moisturizer attempted to expand its reach in a series of television commercials. However, the majority of women featured were white. Considering that women of color have been Shea Moisturizer's core audience from the inception of the company, the backlash was ferocious.[16] In a candid apology through the company's Instagram account, Shea Moisturizer admitted to its mistake and vowed to do better:

> Wow, okay—so guys, listen, we really f-ed this one up. Please know that our intention was not—and would never be—to disrespect our community, and as such, we are pulling this piece immediately because it does not represent what we intended to communicate. You guys know that we have always stood for inclusion in beauty and have always fought for our community and given them credit for not just building our business but for shifting the beauty landscape. So, the feedback we are seeing here brings to light a very important point. While this campaign included several different videos showing different ethnicities and hair types to demonstrate the breadth and depth of each individual's hair journey, we must absolutely ensure moving forward that our community is well-represented

in each one so that the women who have led this movement never feel that their hair journey is minimized in any way. We are keenly aware of the journey that WOC face—and our work will continue to serve as the inspiration for work like the Perception Institute's Good Hair Study/Implicit Association Test that suggests that a majority of people, regardless of race and gender, hold some bias towards women of color based on their textured or natural hair. So, you're right. We are different—and we should know better. Thank you all, as always, for the honest and candid feedback. We hear you. We're listening. We appreciate you. We count on you. And we're always here for you. Thank you, #SheaFam, for being there for us, even when we make mistakes. Here's to growing and building together . . ."[17]

Colorful Cookie

Kraft Foods, the brand behind Oreo cookies, found itself in some trouble after it posted a rainbow-stuffed cookie with the caption "Proudly support love!" in honor of Gay Pride Month.[18] The backlash to this initiative came from some consumers who felt that the brand should not support gay rights. Consumers voiced their opinions on both Twitter and the Oreo Facebook page. Kraft Foods was facing a possible boycott from the public over this initiative. Basil Maglaris, a spokeswoman for Kraft Foods, responded by saying, "We are excited to illustrate what is making history today in a fun and playful way. As a company, Kraft Foods has a proud history of celebrating diversity and inclusiveness. We feel the OREO ad is a fun reflection of our values."[19]

On the flip side, there were also numerous fans who supported the campaign. Loyal Oreo cookie supporters from across the globe defended the issue on the company's Facebook page and Twitter feed. Talk about devotion! Fans who are willing to help in a time of crisis are just the kind of fans a brand wants to attract. This example illustrates how much trust consumers have in Oreo and the type of genuine relationship that Oreo has built with its customer base. The tone and consistency with which Kraft Foods responded to the public contributed greatly to the success of its response. From email to social media, Kraft Foods consistently stood by its company values and stopped the crisis from igniting into a maelstrom of negativity.

Chaos for Pepsi

Set against a backdrop of protest against police brutality, Pepsi missed the mark completely when it created its new campaign based on peace and understanding. Immediately social media users called for an all-out boycott against Pepsi and accused the company of undermining the Black Lives Matter movement, as well as exploiting the movement to sell products.[20] Pepsi apologized and quickly removed the ad.

Messy Mix-Up

What happens when an employee tweets from the company account rather than his or her own personal Twitter account? KitchenAid knows all too well the ramifications of a crisis like this. So, when KitchenAid found itself in a messy situation, it took full responsibility. A member of the KitchenAid social media team posted an insensitive tweet about President Barack Obama's grandmother during Obama's first presidential campaign.[21] Rather than using a personal Twitter account, the employee posted the message to the KitchenAid Twitter account. The outrageous tweet read, "Obamas gma even knew it was going 2 b bad! She died 3 days b4 he became president." The tweet was deleted from the KitchenAid account within fifteen minutes of its original post, but countless people had already seen it, shared it, and commented

Amy Neumann on Crisis Communication

Amy Neumann (@CharityIdeas), a digital media and technology expert, recommends incorporating the following actions during a crisis:

- Stay on top of conversations about your company with simple tools.
- Watch for sudden changes in tone and sentiment from positive or neutral to negative.
- Set up and monitor keywords related to your business.
- Monitor who is talking to you across all social media platforms and website comments.
- Respond, both individually and more broadly.
- Provide updates on the same platforms users talk on and invite them to email you if deeper interaction is needed.
- Acknowledge there is a situation.

- Keep real-time updates flowing.
- Be honest and straightforward with details.
- Make sure customers feel heard by replying, directing them to resources for updates.
- Answer questions directly.
- Thank them for their feedback, and do not delete negative comments.
- Update social media platforms with outcomes; update websites.
- Notify the media for additional outreach.
- Outline the resolution, what was learned, and how similar situations will be prevented in the future.

Source: Amy Neumann, "5 Steps for Crisis Management Using Social Media," *Huffington Post*, August 20, 2012, accessed October 16, 2013, http://www.huffingtonpost.com/amy-neumann/5-steps-for-crisis-manage_b_1791673.html.

on it. It only took fifteen minutes to damage the KitchenAid brand. Cynthia Soledad, the head of the KitchenAid brand, immediately apologized to both President Obama and the public. In a series of 140-character tweets and a full apology on the company website, Soledad issued the following apology: "During the debate tonight, a member of our Twitter team mistakenly posted an offensive tweet from the KitchenAid handle instead of a personal handle. The tasteless joke in no way represents our values at KitchenAid, and that person won't be tweeting for us anymore. That said, I lead the KitchenAid brand, and I take responsibility for the whole team. I am deeply sorry to President Obama, his family, and the Twitter community for this careless error. Thanks for hearing me out."[22]

Several actions on the part of the brand manager deserve applause in this time of crisis. Soledad's response was quick and sincere; she confronted the situation head-on, showing empathy, compassion, and transparency; and she humanized the brand through her words. She also stated what the company was going to do to address the situation so that it did not happen in the future. There are many takeaways from this social crisis, but stressing the importance of keeping personal and company accounts separate is an imperative lesson for businesses and employees alike. Many social strategists use tools like HootSuite to manage their personal and client accounts, but this social media crisis keenly illustrates the ramifications of not paying attention. If a mistake like this does occur, it should be addressed immediately. What saved KitchenAid was Soledad's candid, authentic explanation and personal tone of regret. By regaining control quickly, the company ensured that the apology was well received, minimizing any long-term damage to the brand's reputation.

Shea Moisturizer, Oreo, Pepsi, and KitchenAid are all examples of what should be done during a social media crisis. Not all brands understand the power and magnitude of consumers on the Internet. Just as a quick and well-timed reaction or sincere apology can prevent a potential crisis from forming, the opposite response can have an equally rapid, disastrous consequence for a brand. With that in mind, let us examine what happened when Senator Ted Cruz, Juicero Press, Volkswagen, TalkTalk, Applebee's, Paula Deen, and British Airways faced their own social media crises.

I Didn't Do It: Blaming the "ScapeTern"

As ideally as KitchenAid handled its rogue tweet, Senator Ted Cruz's attempt had the reverse outcome. In September of 2017, Cruz blamed a junior staff member for a pornographic video being "liked" by his Twitter account. Rather than take responsibility, Cruz said, "It was a staffing issue and it was inadvertent, it was a mistake, it was not a deliberate action. We're dealing with it internally but it was a mistake, it was not malicious conduct."[23]

Juicy Mess

Juicero Press, a company that once produced Wi-Fi-enabled devices for juicing fruits and vegetables, came crashing to a halt when a Bloomberg video revealed that the $700 product wasn't even needed to squeeze the company's single-serving packets of chopped fruits and vegetables.[24] The mockery and backlash were relentless. Juicero did not survive this crisis. After just sixteen months in business, the company closed its doors. Juicero offered customers a full refund during a set ninety-day period. In a brief statement posted on the company website, it said: "In a short period of time, you've validated that there is national demand for easier access to fresh produce and hassle-free cold-press juicing—thank you again for coming on this journey with us."[25]

Under a Haze of Smog

It took some time, but Volkswagen finally admitted that it had falsified the results of vehicle emission tests for years in order to pass requirements set by the U.S. Environmental Protection Agency (EPA). The company said that more than 11 million diesel engine vehicles had software installed that manipulated the emissions test results to make sure that emissions levels met EPA standards.[26] The company issued several statements admitting that Volkswagen had "totally screwed up," apologized for what had happened, and noted that it was working to find a solution to the problem. Chief Executive Martin Winterkorn and other senior-level executives issued apologies using both statements and videos, but the corporate response was lackluster at best. The company's initial statement confirmed that it had received notice of an EPA investigation and that the company "takes the matter very seriously and is cooperating with the investigation."[27] This comment radiated a lack of any personal, human response. Ira Kalb, assistant professor of clinical marketing at the University of Southern California's Marshall School of Business, noted that the vilest part of this crisis was that "Volkswagen evaded regulators and deceived the public regarding the emissions of its diesel vehicles by employing a 'defeat device.'" Because this was a deliberate deception that endangered public health and violated Volkswagen's "clean diesel" branding, the company seriously compromised its integrity. Even worse, the company did not disclose the deception.[28] Volkswagen will need to put forth a great deal of effort to change public opinion and win back customers. It remains to be determined if Volkswagen will survive this crisis.

Trouble for TalkTalk

The UK-based telecom giant faced fierce criticism after a delay in communicating that the company was the victim of a "significant and sustained" cyberattack that led to the theft of credit card and bank details for up to four million customers.[29]

In recent years global customers have seen an increase in hackers' accessing of private information from numerous organizations. It should not be a surprise that TalkTalk customers were outraged to learn that the company had not tightened security, especially since the most recent incident was the third cyberattack to directly affect TalkTalk. In August 2015 hackers breached the personal data of customers on its mobile site. This security lapse occurred less than six months after scammers accessed thousands of account numbers and names from the company's computers.[30] The thefts were only discovered when TalkTalk began to look into a spike in complaints from customers about scam calls between October and December 2014.[31]

Rather than being open and honest with its customers, TalkTalk responded with panic and shared very little information with its customers. In its initial response to the crisis, the company waited approximately thirty-six hours before notifying customers of the most recent breach, arguing that it would have been difficult to communicate any earlier. TalkTalk also completely shut down its website and did not inform customers about what they should be doing to protect their information.[32]

According to Jacques de Cock, a faculty member at the London School of Marketing, "TalkTalk needs to invest much more in its client communication and social media management if it is to succeed in the modern hyperlinked and interactive world. It has a long way to go."[33]

What's Good for the Goose Isn't Always Good for the Gander

This crisis has become has become the archetype for what *not* to do in a crisis.

A seemingly innocent note incited fury on the social web and set in motion a series of bad events for the Applebee's restaurant chain.[34] Pastor Alois Bell had eaten at an Applebee's restaurant and, upon paying her bill, crossed out the automatic 18 percent tip charged for parties of more than eight people and left the following message on the receipt above her signature: "I give God 10% why do you get 18?" The waitress, Chelsea Welch, was so upset that she took a photo of the receipt and posted it on the social news and entertainment website Reddit. Subsequently the waitress was fired for "violating customer privacy." Actions related to violating this policy would have been completely understandable if Applebee's had not posted a similar receipt that was *complimenting* the company only two weeks prior. As news of this incident spread and enraged people across virtually every social media platform, Applebee's responded with this short post defending its actions on its Facebook page: "We wish this situation hadn't happened. Our Guests' personal information—including their meal check—is private, and neither Applebee's nor its franchisees have a right to share this information publicly. We value our Guests' trust above all else. Our franchisee has apologized to the Guest and has taken disciplinary action with the Team Member for violating their Guest's right to privacy."[35] Almost instantaneously, the Applebee's statement precipitated more than 10,000 comments—most of which were negative in nature. At this point Applebee's was knee-deep in a social media crisis that it did not appear prepared to manage. Applebee's began posting the same message in its response to comments on multiple social media platforms. The repetitive response only garnered additional negative feedback. Applebee's then deleted all negative messages and started to block fans. The downward spiral of contempt continued as Applebee's persisted in defending its actions and arguing with—even criticizing—its fans during the crisis. Another questionable move by Applebee's involved a decision to hide the original post. Not surprisingly, this action spawned even more public fury and annoyance.

In retrospect, it may be easy to see that Applebee's broke many rules regarding crisis communication. Companies must remember that it is not about winning an argument; rather, it is about responding with empathy, honesty, patience, authenticity, and transparency. During a period in which a crisis exists, people are angry. In some instances, anger is at such an elevated level that any company response may incite added rage. Make sure that employees know not to go "tit for tat" with upset consumers. Applebee's also failed to observe the "rule of three": never, ever, send a third reply.[36] A third reply is an argument and no longer an answer. If a company feels that it must explain its actions a third time, then it is time to take the conversation offline. In this case, Applebee's was well past having a conversation; instead, it was engaged in a full-blown argument with fans. The defensive and confrontational approach amplified the disastrous crisis situation. Intentionally hiding comments or criticisms should never be a consideration, because these actions can only make the crisis worse. Simply put, arguing with Facebook fans is always wrong and never appropriate. This crisis, including the Applebee's response in handling it, may be remembered as one of the most ill-thought-out social media crisis communication strategies to date.

Now in Session: The Court of Public Opinion

June 2013 was a very bad month for Paula Deen, the "Queen of Butter" and a celebrity personality on the Food Network.[37] After allegations surfaced that Deen had testified under oath to using the N-word, mistreating and harassing employees, and demonstrating a dubious level of awareness as to what it means to have racist tendencies and intolerance, she found herself watching her career careen out of control. Deen failed to obey the golden rule of crisis management: acknowledge, say sorry, and truly mean it. A company, brand, or (in this case) individual has only one opportunity to apologize. After posting three insincere video apologies *days after the crisis broke*, and following an in-person appearance on the *Today Show* in which she displayed a defensive attitude, the Food Network, Walmart, Sears, Kmart, JCPenney, Walgreens, and a laundry list of other high-profile sponsors all ended their long-term relationships with Deen. And sponsors were not the only ones who'd had enough. Many of Deen's loyal followers had also thrown in the towel. The Paula Deen Facebook page and Twitter feed were littered with comments from outraged fans. Deen had very quickly lost control of the crisis, and the court of public opinion had taken over.

The challenge here is that Deen had never fully recovered from her first crisis when a second crisis occurred shortly thereafter. An image posted on her social media accounts showed Deen and her son Bobby dressed as Lucy and Ricky Ricardo from the classic 1950s TV comedy show *I Love Lucy*. Many on social media were quick to call out Bobby's look as "brownface." In a statement issued by a spokeswoman, Deen apologized "to all who were offended" and blamed a social media manager for posting the image from a Halloween episode of *Paula's Best Dishes* that had aired in 2011.[38] "As such, Paula Deen Ventures has terminated their relationship with this Social Media Manager," noted the statement.[39]

Flying the Not-So-Friendly Skies

Promoted tweets are all the rage for celebrities and businesses alike, but when an angry customer buys a promoted tweet, you can imagine that a social media crisis is quick to ensue. In September 2013 an unhappy customer of British Airways purchased a promoted tweet to complain about the lack of customer service provided by the airline. In response to a lack of information regarding his missing luggage, British Airways passenger Hasan Syed had this to say: "Don't fly @BritishAirways. Their customer service is horrendous."[40] After what could be deemed a lifetime on social media—ten hours!—British Airways finally responded with an apathetic tweet of its own: "Sorry for the delay in responding, our twitter feed is open 09:00–17:00 GMT. Please DM your baggage ref and we'll look into this."[41] Today's consumers are more empowered than ever before. Social networks give people immediate platforms from which they can broadcast their messages. As in the case of Syed's lost luggage, consumers are now even taking the added step of buying their messages in an effort to communicate with companies. On a business level, there is really no excuse for not providing a real-time response to any type of social media issue. If a company is going to have a presence on social networking sites, it must also have a well-thought-out, online, strategic customer service policy in place. This plan should instruct employees in how to respond to disgruntled customers, provide examples of messaging, and include an action plan for escalated incidents deemed potential crises for the company or brand. The takeaway here is that with any crisis situation, it is vital to respond with humility. The response from British Airways lacked any degree of understanding, empathy, or compassion. Social customer service teams should be empowered to engage in a timely, personalized manner that illustrates to customers that the brand is listening and cares about what the customer is saying.

Today's Reality

PR practitioners should expect that within the first seconds or minutes after a crisis arises targeting a company, brand, or organization, conversations related to the crisis will be mentioned, shared, and talked about online. In the highly interconnected environment in which we conduct business today, the chance that a crisis can go viral has become extremely high. Knowing how to communicate with fans on the correct social networking platforms is critical to being able to properly manage a social media crisis.

Theory into Practice

Berkshire Museum Banking on a Quick Buck

Contributed by John Boudreau

In 2017 the Berkshire Museum in Pittsfield, Massachusetts, announced its New Vision plan, which was meant to re-envision the museum's role in the community and put the organization back on firm financial footing after years of million-dollar operating deficits. As is typical with small museums, the Berkshire Museum hired two outside communications consultants to help with communications initiatives surrounding the New Vision plan.

To help generate the estimated $60 million that the New Vision plan required, the museum decided to auction off forty works of art from its collection, including two pieces by Norman Rockwell, a beloved American artist who spent much of his career working in the Berkshires. The controversial decision to put the paintings up for auction sharply polarized community response. According to *New York Times* reporter Colin Moynihan, the debate was also closely watched within the art world. It drew protesters to the steps of the museum.[1]

Research/Diagnosis

The New Vision planning process lasted for two years and involved consulting with both internal and external stakeholders, including museum employees, local schoolchildren, business owners, and both seasonal and full-time residents of the region. In all, the museum estimates that it consulted with around 400 people during the planning process, at multiple points in the development of the strategic plan.

Objectives

The museum had hoped to help community members and museum members understand the reasoning behind the decision to put the artwork up for auction. More broadly, they wanted to reunite the community and the board of trustees around a similar vision for the museum. Selling the artwork meant that the museum could update its facilities and educational experiences as well as establish an endowment and strengthen the financial viability of the museum for years to come.

Strategies

The situation was dire. Without the infusion of money from the sale of the artwork the museum would eventually be forced to close its doors. This was arguably a no-win situation. Going ahead with the sale meant they would forever damage their reputation. Changing their course of action based on public sentiment was not an option either. There was no clear path forward. The fate of the museum hung in the balance. Elizabeth McGraw, president of the museum's board, said the sale would mean a promise of a long future for the museum.[2]

Tactics

Since the public outcry about the museum's decision to auction off part of its collection, the institution limited itself to mostly official statements, press releases, and top-down communications that have largely been posted on the museum's website and occasionally pushed out to some social media outlets, particularly Facebook. It temporarily provided opportunities for community members to schedule one-on-one meetings with museum board members and/or staff, but only after the crisis had reached its height. In examining their use of the PESO model, the museum largely leaned on earned, shared, and owned media.

Earned: Much of the communication both for and against the museum's decision played out in the pages of the local newspaper, *The Berkshire Eagle.* The issue has proven to be such a draw that a permanent link to coverage of the story was placed on the homepage of the paper's website. The case also drew national and international media attention, with coverage in the *New York Times, Boston Globe, CBS Evening News,* and the *Telegraph* (UK).

Shared: Posts surrounding the New Vision on the museum's Facebook page see significantly higher rates of organic interaction than any other type of post—dozens of comments and shares and hundreds of reactions are not uncommon. Not all of these interactions, however, are in support of the museum's actions, and the majority of commenters use these posts as an opportunity to voice their continuing opposition to the sale. It's interesting to note that as negative as the comments are, commenters restrain themselves to posts specifically about the New Vision. Posts on any other facet of the museum do not spark such negative—or such high—levels of interaction. Arguably this was one of the most contentious chapters in the history of the museum.

Owned: The museum has leveraged its owned media well during the crisis. An FAQ and several pages devoted to the New Vision plan have a dedicated home on the museum's website, alongside a dedicated page for press releases. The institution has been using its social media pages to push out mostly event-related content that circumvents the issue of the New Vision, but it does occasionally use its Facebook page to share official communications about the New Vision plan's progress. It also uses the Facebook page to share op-eds and other media coverage of the New Vision that paint the museum in a positive light. Its Twitter and Instagram accounts don't generally address the New Vision, and as a result don't see nearly as many negative comments or interactions in general.

Reporting

The museum's media efforts have not significantly altered the attitudes of many of its affected public, nor have they diminished coverage of the crisis in legacy media. As the legal battle began, the museum spoke less about the New Vision plan and the associated auction. The affected publics did not forget about the issues. Members of the dissatisfied public started Facebook groups against the sale and staged several protests outside of the museum. These actions, in turn, spurred wider and wider media coverage—the *CBS Evening News* covered the story in November 2017, a full four months after the New Vision plan was unveiled.

On April 5, 2018, almost half a year after the announcement, the Massachusetts Supreme Court ruled that the museum could sell some of their works of art. As many as 40 pieces of artwork could be sold, including pieces by the beloved Norman Rockwell, Alexander Calder, Albert Bierstadt, and Francis Picabia.

For more information, see http://bit.ly/John BoudreaBerkshireMuseum.

1 Moynihan, Colin. "Massachusetts Agrees to Allow Berkshire Museum to Sell Its Art." *New York Times.* February 10, 2018. https://www.nytimes.com/2018/02/09/arts/massachusetts-agrees-to-allow-berkshire-museum-to-sell-its-art.html.

2 Moynihan, Colin. "Massachusetts Agrees to Allow Berkshire Museum to Sell Its Art."

#LRNSMPR
Learn Social Media and Public Relations

Apply the principles learned in this chapter to the scenarios below.

- Choose an organization you are familiar with. This could be a place where you have interned, worked, or hope to work one day. Identify three possible crises it could face, and then outline a set of recommendations to handle the issue. Consider what you've learned in the chapter to develop your responses.

- Crises happen almost daily on the social sphere. Search for one and report back on how the company used social media to handle the crisis. Consider the following questions: What could the company have done to prevent the crisis? How shareable was the story? Was the brand hurt? Was the company's response

sufficient? Would you have handled this social media crisis differently?

- In 2015, Miss Puerto Rico, Destiny Velez, was suspended from the pageant indefinitely after launching into a lengthy anti-Muslim Twitter rant. Responding to Michael Moore's #WeAreAllMuslim campaign, she wrote the following tweets: "All what Muslims have done is provided oil & terrorize this country & many others!!!! There's NO comparison between Jews, Christians & Muslims. Jews nor Christians have terrorizing agendas in their sacred books. If we are all the same then Muslims need to take off their napkins off of their heads cuz I feel offended by it." If you were the PR director for Miss Puerto Rico Organization, what response would you offer?

Notes

[1] PR Council, "Crisis Management in the Social Media Age," 2014, accessed November 16, 2015, http://prcouncil.net/wp-content/uploads/2011/03/Affect_Social_Media_Crisis_Management_White_Paper.pdf.

[2] Freshfields, "Half of Businesses Unprepared to Handle 'Digital Age' Crises," Freshfields Bruckhaus Deringer, November 13, 2013, http://www.freshfields.com/en/news/Half_of_businesses_unprepared_to_handle_%E2%80%98digital_age%E2%80%99_crises.

[3] Freshfields, "Half of Businesses Unprepared to Handle 'Digital Age' Crises."

[4] P. Howard, "The Arab Spring's Cascading Effects," *Pacific Standard*, February 11, 2011, accessed November 13, 2013, http://www.psmag.com/politics/the-cascading-effects- of-the-arab-spring-28575.

[5] S. Czarnecki, "Timeline of a Crisis: United Airlines," *PRWeek*, June 6, 2017, accessed December 19, 2017, https://www.prweek.com/article/1435619/timeline-crisis-united-airlines.

[6] BBC News, "Harvey Weinstein Timeline: How the Scandal Unfolded," accessed December 19, 2017, http://www.bbc.com/news/entertainment-arts-41594672.

[7] K. Palubicki, "Friday Five: Crisis Management in a Digital Age," Edelman Digital, June 14, 2013, http://www.edelmandigital.com/2013/06/14/friday-five-crisis-management-in-a-digital-age.

[8] A. Neumann, "5 Steps for Crisis Management Using Social Media," *Huffington Post*, August 20, 2012, accessed October 16, 2013, http://www.huffingtonpost.com/amy-neumann/5-steps-for-crisis-manage_b_1791673.html.

[9] K. Fearn-Banks, *Crisis Communication: A Casebook Approach*, 4th ed. (New York: Routledge, 2011).

[10] Palubicki, "Friday Five: Crisis Management in a Digital Age."

[11] Palubicki, "Friday Five: Crisis Management in a Digital Age."

[12] Fearn-Banks, *Crisis Communication*.

[13] Palubicki, "Friday Five: Crisis Management in a Digital Age."

[14] Palubicki, "Friday Five: Crisis Management in a Digital Age."

[15] Neumann, "5 Steps for Crisis Management Using Social Media."

[16] M. Le, "PR Crisis Comms in Action: Top 7 Social Media Fires of 2017 (So Far)," Meltwater, August 12, 2017, accessed December 19, 2017, https://www.meltwater.com/blog/pr-crisis-comms-in-action-top-7-social-media-fires-of-2017-so-far/.

[17] Sheamoisture, Real Talk, April 24, 2017, https://www.instagram.com/p/BTSF_rBgop4/.

[18] L. Poston, "Shining Examples of Excellent Social Media Crisis Management," Salesforce Marketing Cloud, September 21, 2012, http://www.salesforcemarketingcloud.com/blog/2012/09/shining-examples-of-excellent-social-media-crisis-management.

19 A. Bingham, "Oreo Pride: Rainbow-Stuffed Cookie Sparks Threats of Boycott," ABC News, June 26, 2012, accessed October 19, 2013, http://abcnews.go.com/blogs/politics/2012/06/oreo-pride-rainbow-stuffed-cookie-sparks-boycott.

20 C. Norton, "The Top 11 Social Media Crises of 2017," Influence, July 28, 2017, accessed December 19, 2017, https://influence.cipr.co.uk/2017/07/26/top-11-social-media-crises-2017/.

21 K. Lee, "What a Twit! KitchenAid Takes a Beating over Tasteless Rogue Tweet about Obama's Dead Grandmother," *Huffington Post*, October 4, 2012, accessed October 19, 2013, http://www.huffingtonpost.com/2013/02/18/burger-king-twitter-hacked_n_2711661.html.

22 B. A. Hernandez, "KitchenAid Tweets Joke about Obama's Dead Grandma [Updated]," Mashable, October 3, 2012, http://mashable.com/2012/10/03/kitchen-aid-obama-dead-grandma.

23 S. Tatum, "Cruz: 'It Was Not Me' on Tweet Porn Video Like," CNN, September 13, 2017, accessed December 19, 2017, http://www.cnn.com/2017/09/13/politics/ted-cruz-porn-interview/index.html.

24 Le, "PR Crisis Comms in Action."

25 H. Shaban, "Say Goodbye to Juicero, the Maker of the $400 Juicer," *Chicago Tribune*, September 1, 2017, accessed December 19, 2017, http://www.chicagotribune.com/business/ct-juicero-folds-20170901-story.html.

26 B. Dipierto, "Crisis of the Week: Volkswagen Scandal Pollutes Carmaker's Reputation," Risk Compliance (blog), *Wall Street Journal*, September 28, 2015, accessed November 16, 2015, http://blogs.wsj.com/riskandcompliance/2015/09/28/crisis-of-the-week-volkswagen-scandal-pollutes- carmakers-reputation.

27 Dipierto, "Crisis of the Week."

28 Dipierto, "Crisis of the Week."

29 N. Khomami, "TalkTalk Hacking Crisis Deepens as More Details Emerge," *Guardian*, October 23, 2015, accessed November 16, 2015, http://www.theguardian.com/business/2015/oct/23/talktalk-hacking-crisis- deepens-as-more-details-emerge.

30 Khomami, "TalkTalk Hacking Crisis Deepens as More Details Emerge."

31 J. de Cock, "TalkTalk's Crisis PR: Its Hack Response Is 'Mirroring the Incredulity and Panic of the Public,'" The Drum, October 23, 2015, accessed November 16, 2015, http://www.thedrum.com/opinion/2015/10/23/talktalks-crisis-pr-its-hack-response-mirroring-incredulity-and-panic-public.

32 de Cock, "TalkTalk's Crisis PR."

33 de Cock, "TalkTalk's Crisis PR."

34 R. L. Stollar, "Applebee's Overnight Social Media Meltdown: A Photo Essay," Overturning Tables, February 2, 2013, http://rlstollar.wordpress.com/2013/02/02/applebees-overnight-social-media- meltdown-a-photo-essay.

35 D. Spencer, "Social Media Storm Hits Applebee's Hard," American Citizens Daily, February 8, 2013, http://tacdnews.com/2013/02/08/social-media-storm-hits-applebees-hard.

36 J. Baer, *Youtility* (New York: Penguin, 2013).

37 M. Agnes, "Lessons to Learn from Paula Deen's Three Crappy Apologies," Melissa Agnes Crisis Management, June 24, 2013, http://www.melissaagnescrisismanagement.com/lessons-to-learn-from-paula-deens-three-crappy-apologies.

38 E. Grinberg, "Paula Deen under Fire for Photo of Son in Brownface," CNN, July 7, 2015, accessed November 16, 2015, http://www.cnn.com/2015/07/07/living/paula-deen-brownface-feat.

39 Grinberg, "Paula Deen under Fire for Photo of Son in Brownface."

40 T. Wasserman, "Man Buys Promoted Tweet to Complain about British Airways," Mashable, September 2, 2013, http://mashable.com/2013/09/02/man-promoted-tweet-british-airways.

41 K. Ryan Schamberger, "British Airways Sponsored Tweet: Customer Service Is Critical," Business 2 Community, September 9, 2013, http://www.business2community.com/customer-experience/british-airways-sponsored-tweet-customer-service-critical-0609554.

Rules of Engagement

13

> Organizations that conduct business in today's
> on-demand media environment should possess a
> social media policy; yet, surprisingly, very few do.
> Social media policies provide a framework for car-
> rying out social strategies and implementing tactics.

KEY LEARNING OUTCOMES

1. Summarize the importance of social
media policies.

2. Recommend the best route to roll out
social media policies.

3. Construct a set of social media
guidelines.

SOCIAL MEDIA EXPERT

Victoria Coker (@AddVic_e)

Victoria Coker is the founder of CLRED Media, Inc. and ColoredContent, an online platform
that amplifies the voices of Black media makers by sharing narratives from a diverse range
of genres, including comedy, romance, and action.[1] Coker runs the company's marketing,
project management, design, and business development. The mission of CLRED Media is
to promote diversity in media. In 2017 she launched the Black Web Fest, a festival dedicated to celebrating Black media makers.[2]

---

[1] V. Coker, "About Us." ColoredContent, accessed December 19, 2017, http://coloredcontent.com/about/.

[2] V. Coker, "Victoria Coker https://www.linkedin.com/in/victoria-coker-2149611b/," ColoredContent.com, accessed December 19, 2017.

Losing Control and Going #Rogue

As we have learned throughout the book, social media is an integral component
when developing strategic campaigns. As quickly as social media can build a
global brand, it can tear one down. Recently there has been an increase in the proliferation of "rogue" social accounts across the social sphere.[1] Attacks like these are not
new. In 2013 hackers accessed both the Associated Press's and FIFA World Cup's
Twitter accounts. A single tweet from the AP Twitter handle stating that an explosion at the White House had injured former President Barack Obama resulted in a
$136.5 billion drop in the S&P 500 index's value in minutes.[2]

A year later Burger King's Twitter account was made to look like McDonald's,
while Jeep's account was hacked, noting that the company was sold to Cadillac. Now,

well-known agencies like the Environmental Protection Agency (EPA), National Park Service (NPS), and National Aeronautics and Space Administration (NASA) have all fallen victim to "rogue" takeovers.[3] Rand Research suggests that stolen Twitter accounts are now worth more than stolen credit cards.[4] Rogue accounts attract followers by the thousands, which should be a warning signal for brands across the globe. Imagine losing control of your company's online messaging or branding.

When hackers took over the Associated Press Twitter account and sent out a tweet claiming that Former President Barack Obama had been injured in explosions at the White House, havoc ensued.

Like traditional public relations (PR) and social media planning, social media policies are part of a larger, more encompassing strategy. To stave off problems such as those just described, companies must initiate and communicate the organization's social media policies.

Establishing the Groundwork

As a company establishes the groundwork for its PR and social media efforts, instituting clear objectives and a strategy to achieve them is paramount. Development of such a strategy fosters cross-departmental coordination and encourages synergistic cooperation throughout the organization. It also requires strategic input from the individuals tasked with drafting the document and those intending to engage in social media communications on behalf of the organization. The most successful strategies result from the combined opinions and recommendations of many individuals, and regardless of job title or level, all contribute to the larger cause.

Companies face various forms and levels of risk when engaging in social media strategies. However, the necessary steps to mitigate risks tend to all be fairly similar. Often referred to as social media policies or social media guidelines, these parameters provide a framework for when employees interact online. Some companies may choose to implement rigid policies that spell out exactly what is permissible on company-sponsored social media channels, while others may develop policies that serve as a reference point for staff but allow them flexibility in making decisions on their own.

According to the UK-based Chartered Institute of Public Relations (CIPR), European businesses are also debating the boundaries companies should set for their

The 4 P's of Social Governance

According to Ed Terpening from the Altimeter Group, an integrated system of people, policies, processes, and practices defines organizational structure and decision-making process to ensure effective management of social business[1]:

1. *People:* Clear accountability for roles and structures that support social media.
2. *Policy:* Agreements are outlined, and policies are solidified.

3. *Process:* Procedures are defined, roles identified, and execution is consistent.
4. *Practice:* Training, tools, and resources are provided that offer support.

---

[1] E. Terpening, "A Framework to Execute Social Business Strategy," Prophet, May 18, 2017, https://www.prophet.com/thinking/2014/11/social-business-governance-a-framework-to-execute-social-business-strategy/.

employees' use of social media. While there is no definitive answer, the CIPR advises that both the employer and employee take responsibility for understanding and adhering to social media best practices. The CIPR suggests that employers should support their employees and ensure that employees know what defines good practice and clear company policies.[5]

All companies are unique; as a result, their social media policies are also unique. Social media policies tend to reflect the personality of the company. While a single template or set of standards applicable to all businesses or organizations has yet to be developed, most social media policies share the following characteristics[6]:

Trust and Respect: Good policies stem from mutual trust. The policy should foster a positive atmosphere in which employees are free to share personal opinions while respecting the opinions of others without living in fear of retribution. Effective policies outline acceptable online employee behavior rather than listing the actions that are forbidden.

Values: Companies should reflect upon their core values and overarching company culture when drafting their social media policies.[7] This will provide the correct foundation to build a policy that is central to the work that the company does. These values might include integrity, respect, humility, teamwork, and accountability. Respect is a core value often found within many organizations. It might then make sense to include a point within the social media policy related to respecting others' opinions and valuing all contributions. A policy addressing respect may read as follows: "It's OK to be yourself and say what is on your mind, but do so respectfully. We want you to connect with colleagues and engage with the larger community. We just ask that when you do, you provide value, share content, ask questions, and participate in meaningful conversations politely, considerately, and without malice toward others."

Fluidity: Companies should be open to adjusting and incorporating changes into their policies over time. Just as social media sites change over time, policies should be fluid enough to accommodate future modifications. If policies and guidelines are narrowly focused, they may become outdated rather quickly.[8] Successful social media policies tend to capture the big picture, are not overly complicated, and are easy to understand.

Avoidance of Zero Tolerance: Stay away from using words such as "always," "must," "shall," and "never."[9] A "zero-tolerance policy" can be extremely tough to implement and problematic to enforce. The legal restrictions within this area are currently evolving at an unprecedented rate. Consider it a best practice to consult the legal and human resources departments for guidance during severe or ongoing circumstances.[10]

Lack of Jargon: Eliminate highly technical language or legalese. Develop a policy that can be understood across departments. This will encourage participation and become more meaningful to employees.

Sensibleness: The policy should not be so complicated that employees need a reference book to understand what to do when they need to interact on social media channels. Provide practical examples and easy-to-understand points. Encourage employees to reference the policy when they are faced with a new or unfamiliar situation.

Friendliness: Policies should be written in such a way that encourages participation. This should include all acceptable actions and employee empowerments.

Consistency: The best policy is one that is consistent with regard to participation and enforcement throughout the organization. Consistency helps organizations keep their social media efforts on course while also avoiding accusations of favoritism or discrimination.[11]

Social Media Policy

52%

52% of online adults use multiple social media sites

Setting the right expectations at work is paramount

Policies

- Provide clear expectations
- Protect the reputation clients & the business

Qualities every policy should include:

- Trust & Respect
- Values Driven
- Fluid
- Jargon Free
- No Zero Tolerance
- Sensible
- Friendly
- Consistent
- Clear Consequences

Quality

80%

80% of employers have official social media policies

70% have disciplined an employee for social media misuse

Less than one-third offer training on how to use social media responsibly

Sources:

Cision, "Developing Social Media Policies," last modified 2009, accessed November 8, 2013.

"Social Media Update 2014." Pew Research Center Internet Science Tech RSS. January 9, 2015. Accessed November 21, 2015. http://www.pewinternet.org/2015/01/09/social-media-update-2014/.

Schwartzman, Eric. "How to Prevent a Social Media Crisis." PRNewser. June 25, 2015. Accessed November 21, 2015. http://www.adweek.com/prnewser/how-to-prevent-a-social-media-crisis/115650.

It is essential to develop a comprehensive social media policy, inclusive of best practices, guidelines, and tips for employees.

Clear Consequences: Employees should know what actions the company will take if they violate any part of the social media policy. Should the company need to take action, make certain that the employees are afforded due process and are allowed to present their side of the story.[12] If the transgression requires serious disciplinary consequences, including termination, due process will become even more important.

Social media policies are "living" documents. This means that once the policy is created, it should not simply be put away and forgotten. Organizations should review and modify their policies on a recurring basis—perhaps quarterly or biannually. A company might consider some of the following questions when revising its social media policy or guidelines:

* Is the policy still relevant?
* Have any social media sites changed? If so, do the changes impact our policy?
* Has the online environment changed? If so, what should we consider revising?
* Are there legal updates that need to be addressed?
* Does anything new need to be added? If so, what?
* Are there any gaps?
* Does a guideline require any clarification? Are examples necessary?

As these policies are revised, seek employee feedback. Keeping the line of communication open and free will maintain continued interest among staff.

Rolling Out the Policy

Once the social media policy is finalized and ready for implementation, take the time to communicate to employees the importance of every aspect of the policy. An organization's human resources, legal, and PR departments can serve as hosts for various events to roll out the new social media policy. As with any other company initiative, create a buzz and drive excitement. Make a big deal out of the new policy.

"80% of employers have official social media policies. Less than one-third offer training on how to use social media responsibly in the workplace."

Going #Rogue: Losing Control of Your Social Media

Consider starting with a number of informal "brown bag lunch" sessions. Invite staff to attend several planned luncheons at which the policy is presented and explained and employees have the opportunity to ask questions. For smaller businesses, one session may be sufficient, but in larger organizations with numerous sites, it may be necessary to schedule multiple sessions. Employees are more likely to participate if they are given flexibility regarding attendance at an informational meeting.

Once the in-person, educational sessions are completed, companies can create and post a video outlining the guidelines, allowing employees to access the information at will. This material can be posted to the company website or Intranet. A series of blog posts can also be written to illustrate examples, best practices, and case studies.[13] Employees tend to respond with the same enthusiasm that is exhibited by the company. If a company shows a low level of interest regarding the social media policy, it should expect that employees will mimic that same behavior.

Key Sections

Social media policies have three main sections: an introduction, the main policy points, and a conclusion. The following list highlights five examples of corporate

ESPN and Jemele Hill

In October of 2017 ESPN host Jemele Hill was suspended for what the company said was a second violation of the network's social media guidelines. The first violation occurred from a series of tweets she wrote that President Donald Trump was a "white supremacist" and a "bigot."[1] Hill's second offense ensued when she tweeted "This play always work. Change happens when advertisers are impacted. If you feel strongly about JJ's statement, boycott his advertisers."[2] This was a result of her speaking out about the owner of the Dallas Cowboys NFL franchise, Jerry Jones, who threatened to bench any of his players who took a knee during the playing of the national anthem.[3]

In a company statement ESPN wrote: "Jemele Hill has been suspended for two weeks for a second violation of our social media guidelines. She previously acknowledged letting her colleagues and company down with an impulsive tweet. In the aftermath, all employees were reminded of how individual tweets may reflect negatively on ESPN and that such actions would have consequences. Hence this decision."[4]

---

[1] J. Delk, "ESPN Host Calls Trump a 'White Supremacist,'" The Hill, September 13, 2017, http://thehill.com/blogs/in-the-know/350308-espn-host-calls-trump-a-white-supremacist.
[2] B. Carter, "ESPN Suspends Jemele Hill for Violation of Social Media Policy," The Hill, October 9, 2017, http://thehill.com/homenews/media/354588-espn-suspends-jemele-hill-for-violation-of-social-media-policy.
[3] Carter, "ESPN Suspends Jemele Hill for Violation of Social Media Policy."
[4] ESPN PR, "ESPN's Statement on Jemele Hill," Twitter, October 9, 2017, https://twitter.com/ESPNPR/status/917469637033512960/photo/1.

---

social media policies that you can review, analyze, and consider as you draft your own set of guidelines. Make note of the key sections as you read these policies.

Best Buy: Under the premise of "Be smart. Be respectful. Be human," Best Buy clearly presents its dos and don'ts for all company employees engaging in social media activities (http://bit.ly/HJee3k).

Oracle: Oracle provides a stricter approach to its social media policy. This set of guidelines includes a higher degree of specificity and also provides pertinent examples (http://bit.ly/HNDs0y).

Walmart: Walmart's social media policies speak to almost every area of online engagement, from intellectual property to disgruntled employees and social media engagement (http://bit.ly/18mihJn).

IBM: This clear-cut social media policy is specific enough to avoid mistakes created by a lack of common sense demonstrated by employees (http://ibm.co/1gDnS6i).

Shippensburg University (Shippensburg, Pennsylvania): This set of social media guidelines is specific to official university social media accounts. What is great about these guidelines is that they provide employees with numerous outside links that assist with everything from privacy to graphics standards (http://bit.ly/1iZyv0i).

Ubiquitous Sphere

A social media policy is one of the most important sets of guidelines that an organization can develop and execute. A well-thought-out policy will encourage employee participation and interaction with customers, build relationships, foster transparency, and minimize risks. It is unrealistic to think that any company can foresee or protect against what may happen on social media platforms used by employees. A proactive and thoughtful approach to creating social media policies can help avoid many of the pitfalls before they are realized. As long as a company has the appropriate team in place, asks the right questions, revisits the guidelines every now and again, and acknowledges that the culture within the social sphere values transparency, trust, empowerment, and creativity, it is well on its way to creating a policy that fits its needs.

Theory into Practice

National Labor Relations Board

As the presence of social media expands within business, the court systems throughout the United States are experiencing an influx of employee lawsuits against their employers.[1] Numerous court cases regarding social media within business arenas that focus on labor relations issues and related violations by employers continue to appear. For this reason, in May 2012 the National Labor Relations Board (NLRB) created a sample of a lawful social media policy for employers to use as a guideline. Take a moment to read the policy from the NLRB and then choose a social media policy presented within the chapter or one found on the Social Media Governance website (http://bit.ly/18cWVOl). Compare the two.

What are the differences?
Are the guidelines too broad?
Are there any guidelines that might be considered open to interpretation?
How might you need to amend these guidelines in order to apply them to your organization?
Are there any guidelines that are not clear or that could be misinterpreted by an employee?

A Sample Social Media Policy from the NLRB[2]

At [Employer], we understand that social media can be a fun and rewarding way to share your experiences and opinions with family, friends, and coworkers around the world. However, the use of social media also presents certain risks and carries with it certain responsibilities. To assist you in making responsible decisions about your use of social media, we have established these guidelines for appropriate use of social media.

This policy applies to all associates who work for [Employer], or one of its subsidiary companies in the United States. Managers and supervisors should use the supplemental Social Media Management Guidelines for additional guidance in administering the policy.

Guidelines

In the rapidly expanding world of electronic communication, social media can mean many things. Social media includes all means of communicating or posting information or content of any sort on the Internet, including to your own or someone else's web log or blog, journal or diary, personal website, social networking or affinity website, web bulletin board or chat room, whether or not associated or affiliated with [Employer], as well as any other form of electronic communication.

The same principles and guidelines found in [Employer] policies and three basic beliefs apply to your activities online. Ultimately, you are solely responsible for what you post online. Before creating online content, consider some of the risks and rewards that are involved. Keep in mind that any aspect of your conduct that adversely affects your job performance, the performance of fellow associates, or otherwise adversely affects members, customers, suppliers, people who work on behalf of [Employer] or [Employer's] legitimate business interests may result in disciplinary action up to and including termination.

Know and Follow the Rules

Carefully read these guidelines, the [Employer] Statement of Ethics Policy, the [Employer] Information Policy, and the Discrimination and Harassment Prevention Policy, and ensure your postings are consistent with these policies. Inappropriate postings that may include discriminatory remarks, harassment, and threats of violence or similar inappropriate or unlawful conduct will not be tolerated and may subject you to disciplinary action up to and including termination.

Be Respectful

Always be fair and courteous to fellow associates, customers, members, suppliers, or people who work on behalf of [Employer]. Also, keep in mind that you are more likely to resolve work-related complaints by speaking directly with your coworkers or by utilizing our Open Door Policy than by posting complaints to a social media outlet. Nevertheless, if you decide to post complaints or criticism, avoid using statements, photographs, video, or audio that reasonably could be viewed as malicious, obscene, threatening, or intimidating; that disparage customers, members, associates, or suppliers; or that might constitute harassment or bullying. Examples of such conduct might include offensive posts meant to intentionally harm someone's reputation or posts that could contribute to a hostile work environment on the basis of race, sex, disability, religion, or any other status protected by law or company policy.

Be Honest and Accurate

Make sure you are always honest and accurate when posting information or news, and if you make a mistake, correct it quickly. Be open about any previous posts you have altered. Remember that the Internet archives almost everything; therefore, even deleted postings can be searched. Never post any information or rumors that you know to be false about [Employer], fellow associates, members, customers, suppliers, people working on behalf of [Employer], or competitors.

Post Only Appropriate and Respectful Content

Maintain the confidentiality of [Employer] trade secrets and private or confidential information. Trade secrets may include information regarding the development of systems, processes, products, know-how, and technology. Do not post internal reports, policies, procedures, or other internal business-related confidential communications.

Respect financial disclosure laws. It is illegal to communicate or give a "tip" on inside information to others so that they may buy or sell stocks or securities. Such online conduct may also violate the Insider Trading Policy.

Do not create a link from your blog, website, or other social networking site to a [Employer] website without identifying yourself as a [Employer] associate.

Express only your personal opinions. Never represent yourself as a spokesperson for [Employer].

If [Employer] is a subject of the content you are creating, be clear and open about the fact that you are an associate and make it clear that your views do not represent those of [Employer], fellow associates, members, customers, suppliers, or people working on behalf of [Employer]. If you do publish a blog or post online related to the work you do or subjects associated with [Employer], make it clear that you are not speaking on behalf of [Employer]. It is best to include a disclaimer, such as "The postings on this site are my own and do not necessarily reflect the views of [Employer]."

Using Social Media at Work

Refrain from using social media while on work time or on equipment we provide, unless it is work related as authorized by your manager or consistent with the Company Equipment Policy.

Do not use [Employer] email addresses to register on social networks, blogs, or other online tools utilized for personal use.

Retaliation Is Prohibited

[Employer] prohibits taking negative action against any associate for reporting a possible deviation from this policy or for cooperating in an investigation. Any associate who retaliates against another associate for reporting a possible deviation from this policy or for cooperating in an investigation will be subject to disciplinary action, up to and including termination.

Media Contacts

Associates should not speak to the media on [Employer's] behalf without contacting the Corporate Affairs Department. All media inquiries should be directed to them.

For More Information

If you have questions or need further guidance, please contact your human resources representative.

1 S. Gardner, "Two Great Social Media Law Cases Involving Facebook and Linked-In," The 2morrowknight, September 28, 2013, http://www.2morrowknight.com/two-great-social-media-law-cases-involving-facebook-and-linkedin.

2 National Labor Relations Board, "The NLRB and Social Media," http://www.nlrb.gov/news-outreach/fact-sheets/nlrb-and-social-media.

#LRNSMPR

Learn Social Media and Public Relations

Apply the principles learned in this chapter to the scenarios below.

- Consider, analyze, and discuss how crisis situations and social media policies are connected.

- Write your own set of social media policies for your personal blog or other social media platforms.

- Think about an organization that has recently faced a crisis. Determine whether they have a set of social media policies. If they do, how could they strengthen them? If they don't, what could they include?

Notes

1. R. Luttrell et al., "Going #Rogue: Losing Control of Your Social Media," PRSA International Conference, Boston, October 2017.
2. P. Foster, "'Bogus' AP Tweet about Explosion at the White House Wipes Billions off US Markets," *The Telegraph*, April 23, 2013, http://www.telegraph.co.uk/finance/markets/10013768/Bogus-AP-tweet-about-explosion-at-the-White-House-wipes-billions-off-US-markets.html.
3. Luttrell et al., "Going #Rogue: Losing Control of Your Social Media."
4. C. Barakat, "Stolen Twitter Accounts," *Adweek*, March 27, 2014, http://www.adweek.com/digital/stolen-twitter-accounts-valuable-credit-cards-hackonmics/.
5. "Public Relations Social Media Panel" (lecture, Chartered Institute of Public Relations, December 1, 2013).
6. Cision, "Developing Social Media Policies," last modified 2009, accessed November 8, 2013.
7. A. Berry and B. Stuart, "Create a Social Media Policy for Your Nonprofit Elines to Cover All of Your Social Media Bases," Socialbrite, February 5, 2013, http://www.socialbrite.org/2013/02/05/create-a-social-media-policy-for-your-nonprofit.
8. Berry and Stuart, "Create a Social Media Policy."
9. Berry and Stuart, "Create a Social Media Policy."
10. A. Asghar Dotson, "NLRB Outlines Employers' Social Media Policy Dos and Don'ts," Spilman Thomas & Battle, April 29, 2013, http://www.spilmanlaw.com/Resources/Attorney-Authored-Articles/Labor---Employment/NLRB-Outlines-Employers--Social-Media-Policy-Dos-a.
11. L. Dwyear et al., "Social Media, Risk, and Policies," SocialFish, last modified 2009, accessed November 18, 2013, http://www.socialfish.org/wp-content/downloads/socialfish-policies-whitepaper.pdf.
12. Dwyear et al., "Social Media, Risk, and Policies."
13. S. Gardner, "Two Great Social Media Law Cases Involving Facebook and Linked-In," The 2morrowknight, September 28, 2013, http://www.2morrowknight.com/two-great-social-media-law-cases-involving-facebook-and-linkedin.

The Future of PR and Social Media 14

This last chapter provides a glimpse into important trends facing the public relations (PR) and social media industry, ways in which PR and social media professionals can cross-promote their efforts for maximum results, and one final case study.

The Burgeoning Horizon: A Look Forward

And so, we have arrived at the end of our journey. You have been introduced to the first instances of people using social media as well as how it has evolved and is practiced today. We've covered much ground, exploring the good, the bad, and the ugly, as well as many of the finer points of social media and PR. However, I have yet to answer the question of where the profession is headed. I'm sure you are wondering what's next, so let's peek into the future!

Over the past several years, social media has experienced explosive growth. PR practitioners are now able to create and implement viable social strategies, explore new integrated marketing communication approaches, and evaluate a variety of platforms to make content public.

What does all this mean? It's all good news for PR professionals and social media strategists. Fantastic news, in fact. And before we part ways, I'll share with you a few of my final thoughts and predictions for the future of social media. But remember, I'm always eager to continue our conversations. Let's chat and connect using Twitter (@ginaluttrell) and through my website (www.ginaluttrellphd.com), where you will find tidbits, video footage, case studies, new research, and articles that didn't make it into the book. It is my hope that our relationship will grow and mature in the years to come.

On to the good stuff now!

Artificial Intelligence and Data-Driven Results

The use of artificial intelligence (AI) and machine learning within PR will explode over the next few years. We've already begun to see brands such as Yves Saint Laurent using AI in their promotional efforts. The research firm Markets and Markets estimates that AI, as well as machine learning, will grow from $1.41 billion in 2017 to $8.81 billion by 2022.[1] Sixty percent of PR and marketing professionals will use AI to create dynamic landing pages, full websites, advertising campaigns, and media buys. AI's impact on social media listening and analytics will become a powerful tool in social media. In fact, according to Saif Ajani, CEO of Keyhole, a hashtag analytics company, "Google and Amazon have put up AI clouds dedicated to machine learning just in the past 12 to 24 months. Keyhole can now plug its huge data set for social into the AI cloud and get results for clients quickly and affordably. Our data is 80 to 90 percent accurate in predicting what is going to happen after 30 days. Within 3 days we can predict how big the trend is going to be after 30 days."[2] Christopher Penn, from SHIFT Communications, notes that because of open source software offered by Microsoft, Amazon, Facebook, Google, and IBM, PR professionals will have access to some of the most revolutionary predictive, AI algorithms.[3]

Rediscovering Credibility

With the introduction and proliferation of "alternative facts," pressure is rising for journalists to prove their credibility. Kevin Kelly, technology author and cofounder of *Wired* magazine, said, "The major new challenge in reporting news is the new shape of truth. Truth is no longer dictated by authorities, but is networked by peers. For every fact there is a counter-fact. All those counter-facts and facts look identical online, which is confusing to most people."[4] Respect for once-revered national media outlets is in question and steadily decreasing. According to the British Labour Force Survey, over the past year the number of journalists fell by 11,000 while the number of PR specialists rose by 5,000.[5] In the United States the U.S. Bureau of Labor Statistics reported that the number of journalist positions is at a record low, falling by 60 percent.[6] This presents an opportunity for PR professionals to establish ourselves as credible and reliable sources using owned channels to convey truth, honesty, and accuracy in the dissemination of organizational messages.

Privacy, Trust, and Accountability

With another year of high-profile security breaches such as Facebook/Cambridge Analytica, Equifax, Russian meddling in the U.S. presidential elections, and the proliferation of bots, privacy, trust, and accountability will continue to be important to consumers. Facebook, Google, and Twitter executives appeared on Capitol Hill to answer tough questions surrounding many aspects of these concerns. It is not unrealistic to consider that the most relevant and widely used social platforms should be the ones that provide users with a high level of privacy and security.

Once Upon a Time . . .

Fans love their stories on both Instagram and Snapchat. To respond to this need, brands will need to up the ante and develop content that fans can embrace. What's great about Instagram stories is that they are fun, discoverable (meaning that even people who do not follow the brand can see the posts), and add personality. Snapchat stories offer brands a way to connect with fans in a brief and interesting way. Regardless of the platform, one thing is for sure, brands need a "Stories" strategy.

Live-Stream and Go

All the major social media platforms are moving toward full adoption of video to capture more real-time content that drives so much global conversation. Social media is already moment to moment by nature, but live streaming allows for more "in the now" than ever before. The obsession with live streaming and live social events will ramp up, particularly as Snapchat adds new features and Facebook, Twitter, and Instagram hone their live-streaming game. Social apps will aim to put the user at an event—virtually—as much as possible. Instagram and Snapchat already support on-the-go, in-the-moment updates as opposed to after-event retrospectives and could collectively usher in a new era of immediacy in social media. As virtual reality technology becomes more mainstream, practitioners may have to forget about scheduling the company's social media posts in advance.

Click and Buy

Leading the trend of enabling mobile consumers to purchase products with a single click, Facebook and Pinterest both introduced the "Buy" feature on their platforms. This allows users of these social medial channels the option of purchasing a product without ever leaving the app. One can imagine that Instagram and other social platforms will not be far behind in incorporating some form of "Buy" button as part of their social campaigns.

Read and Stay

When Facebook rolls out innovative initiatives, you can bet that other social platforms will follow suit. In 2015 the company introduced "Instant Articles" as a new form of publishing, allowing users to locate referenced articles and play videos instantly when scrolling. Think of this feature as an in-post search engine. Similarly, other platforms such as Twitter and Instagram are trying to expand their platforms, allowing users to access additional resources without ever leaving the app. This "never leave our app" trend is expected to increase over time, providing social strategists more opportunities to engage with their audiences on one platform—their own.

$upport

Commitments from C-suite executives will continue to increase in support of social media efforts. These executives not only understand the importance of social media but are also responding with bigger budgets and dedicated resources for social strategies. Reports indicate that social networking spending will reach $119 billion over the next few years, representing 16 percent of all digital spending globally.[7] The United States and Canada are focused on social media and will increase budget spend by 31 percent, passing $10 billion for the first time in history. Decision makers clearly understand the value that social media adds to their companies and are willing to support smart initiatives.

The future of public relations and social media is exciting. When I look at where our profession has come and where it's headed, I am filled with anticipation. PR practitioners have always been at the epicenter of building relationships with consumers, and social media has only enhanced what we already knew. Companies are searching for professionals who can combine social media understanding with tried-and-true PR strategies. It's a good time to be in PR—truly it is! Before I bid you farewell, I wanted to share with you how to tie everything you have learned together with the ways in which PR and social media fuels success on the social sphere.

Eight Ways Public Relations Can Fuel Successful Content Marketing

Paul Roetzer, founder and CEO of PR 20/20, shares eight ideas that PR and social media professionals can implement to cross-promote their strategic planning efforts.[8]

After months of planning, research, writing, and design, your new business-to-business (B2B) research report is set to launch. Personas have been defined. Databases have been segmented. Website traffic, lead generation, and sales conversion goals are all set. And your project management system has been stacked with all the standard elements of a successful content marketing campaign, such as

- *An Ebook:* All of the brilliant (and statistically valid) research and insights you've gathered have been neatly packaged into a downloadable ebook.
- *An Infographic:* The design team has taken the most tweet-worthy stats and created a tantalizing infographic to accompany the ebook and drive social shares.
- *The Landing Page:* Your dedicated landing page is live, complete with a contact form that's been integrated with your customer relationship management (CRM) system. There's even an A/B test setup to monitor conversion rates using varying headlines and images.
- *A Blog Post:* Your team has written an engaging blog post, featuring key takeaways and a call to action (CTA) to download your ebook.
- *SlideShare:* The infographic and an ebook teaser have both been uploaded to SlideShare to maximize reach and sharing potential.
- *Social Media:* Social updates have been scheduled from your company's accounts on LinkedIn, Facebook, and Twitter.
- *Website CTAs:* Banner and tile CTAs have been added to popular pages throughout your company website to convert visitors to leads.
- *Lead Scoring:* Marketing has collaborated with Sales to determine criteria that define sales qualified leads (SQLs), and lead scoring has been set up in your marketing automation system.
- *Lead-Nurturing Emails:* An automated email workflow has been created and scheduled to nurture contacts that download the ebook.
- *An Associated Webinar:* A webinar featuring insights from the research has been planned for the purpose of capturing the leads that are further along in their buyers' journeys. The CTA to register for the webinar has been featured in your series of lead-nurturing emails.
- *Webinar Emails:* Another lead-nurturing email workflow has been configured to follow up with those who have already downloaded your eBook *and* attended your webinar.
- *Internal Team Alignment:* An email has been sent to your sales team members detailing the content marketing campaign and offering tips on how they can integrate the new content asset into their sales activities.
- *Campaign Tracking:* All URLs that will be shared have been tagged using Google's URL builder tool, in order to monitor traffic and conversion sources.

Seems pretty thorough. Right? But there's more you can do to help your content marketing plan surpass your expectations for success. Let's explore how public relations can add fuel to this content fire.

Understanding the Role of PR

PR encompasses any activity, online or offline, designed to improve communications and build relationships with audiences that matter to your business. This includes, but is not limited to:

- analyst relations
- blogger relations
- community relations
- crisis communications
- employee relations
- media relations
- public speaking

Unfortunately, PR has gotten a bad rap at times because professionals have historically relied on "soft" metrics such as placements, impressions, and ad equivalency to create the perception of value. They have failed to connect actions to outcomes, and clearly demonstrate how PR activities impact key performance indicators (KPIs) that are relevant to the C-suite.

But times are changing, and modern PR pros are becoming adept at building strategies that have an undeniable impact on expanding reach, driving website traffic, generating leads, increasing sales conversions, and enhancing customer loyalty.

Amplify the Content

Here are eight ways an integrated PR strategy can accelerate your content marketing success:

1. *Build a Media Database:* Start with a media database that includes business publications, blogs, and trade publications in relevant vertical markets. At minimum, the information you track should include outlet name, organization, phone, email, social profile links, areas of interest/beat, and notes. Ideally these contacts will be uploaded and managed in your marketing team's CRM system.

    Tip: Journalists and bloggers are in the business of telling stories that matter to their readers. If your content isn't relevant to their audiences, don't waste their time (or yours) blasting out pitches and press releases to them.
2. *Pull Editorial Calendar Information:* Traditional print publications often publish editorial calendars that show the topics they plan to cover throughout the year. Research the calendars of your target media outlets and look for topics that align with the content in your campaigns.
3. *Pitch Story Ideas to Relevant Media Contacts:* Once your media database and editorial calendar list are complete, seek opportunities for customized pitches. For example, if you knew a targeted trade publication planned to write about content marketing in an upcoming issue, you might consider pitching your ebook, *A Guide to Cognitive Content Marketing,* to its editors.
4. *Identify Bylined Article and Guest Post Opportunities:* Publications and blogs often accept contributions from outside writers. Bylined articles and guest blog posts from your executives and marketers are a great way to expand reach, build quality inbound links, and drive referring visits to your website.
5. *Conduct Influencer Outreach:* Does your ebook feature insight from industry influencers? Is the content highly relevant to influential bloggers? If so, take a strategic approach to get the information in front of them—and (hopefully) their audiences.
6. *Consider Partnerships:* Evaluate the associations and organizations in your network that have expansive reach. Consider ways to collaborate and distribute your content through their events, emails, and websites.
7. *Pursue Speaking Engagements:* Identify opportunities for your company's leaders to speak at industry events. This will give you a platform to discuss relevant topics and concepts from your content marketing with members of your target audience, as well as a way to use your content to showcase your company's credibility, thought leadership, and expertise.
8. *Submit Your Content for Industry Awards:* Look for programs, such as the Content Marketing Awards, that recognize excellence in marketing. Award programs are a great way to extend the life of a content marketing program and extend your reach to new audiences.

Pink Power: The Pussyhat Project

The idea was straightforward: create a sea of pink at the Women's March in Washington, D.C., on January 21, 2017. With this in mind, Jayna Zweiman and Krista Suh, both avid knitters, created a symbol of solidarity when they launched the Pussyhat Project.

Research/Diagnosis

According to an article by the Houston Center for Contemporary Craft, "the project connected people fighting for women's rights around the world by providing knitting templates and videos to teach people how to crochet and knit. On the day of the Women's March, the sweeping ribbon of pink hats worn by protesters visually united the over 5 million people who marched for women's rights, LGBTQ rights, racial equality, immigration reform, healthcare reform, and a number of other issues following the inauguration of President Donald J. Trump."[1] Today, the Pussyhat has become a symbol of unity for women's rights around the globe.

Objective

For one day in unison, the Pussyhat Project focused on presenting a powerful visual statement at the Women's March. According to the creators, the project was driven by these three tenets:

1. "Creating a concrete, accessible, thoughtful way for those who cannot attend activism events in person to be heard and represented,
2. Developing meaningful, respectful connections among people who care about women's rights, and
3. Creating a framework for community and personal agency from the local to the national level."[2]

The color pink was deliberately chosen because it is often associated with femininity, but more than that, the color represents kindheartedness and love. Zwieman and Suh write on their website: "Wearing pink together is a powerful statement that we are unapologetically feminine, and we unapologetically stand for women's rights!"[3]

Strategy

Through craftivism (craft + activism = craftivism), which is the practice of engaged creativity surrounding political or social causes,[4] the creators developed an iconic symbol that united women across the globe. Craftivism dates to the early twentieth century when activists including the suffragists embroidered flags that supported the movement for women's right to vote in the United States and the United Kingdom.[5] There are countless examples throughout history of people using crafting skills to promote symbiotic relationships while advocating for causes. The Pussyhat is a modern example.

Tactics

Leveraging social media and the website https://www.pussyhatproject.com/, the creators reached millions of women. Crafters from around the globe would not only make hats for themselves, but those who could not physically attend could also send hats to marchers as a way to represent themselves by gifting Pussyhats.

> *Shared:* The Pussyhat Project maintains a Twitter, Instagram, and Facebook presence. Here, the creators and community come together to share images, updates, and stories of inspiration. Hashtags including #pussyhat, #pussyhatproject, #whyipussyhat, and #pussyhat global are used to unify conversations happening on the social sphere.
>
> *Owned:* Website and blog: On the website visitors can download Pussyhat patterns (https://www.pussyhatproject.com/the-pdf/); check out local allies; find knitting gatherings; and download printable items that help make giving, wearing, and sharing a Pussyhat easy. The blog provides readers with updates and insights surrounding women's issues. More recently the blog was used as a place to support the #metoo movement.

Implementation

The Pussyhat and subsequent Pussyhat Project were direct by-products of the Women's March. In the eleven weeks leading up to the March, women from around the world knitted and sewed thousands of hats to wear and share.

Reporting/Evaluation

The original goal was to provide 1.17 million hats because the National Mall could hold that many people.[6] While the exact number of Pussyhats worn at the March is not known, Zweiman and Suh estimated that at least 60,000 hats were made prior to the event.[7] This estimate could be quite low. So many hats were made that the project led to a "shortage of pink yarn across the country, with more and more yarn being dyed to feed the growing demand for the pussy hats."[8] Knitters and sewers of all ages made pink hats for themselves and to share with others.

Leading up to and on the day of the March, celebrity influencers including Madonna, Krysten Ritter, Julianne Moore, Amy Schumer, Nick Offerman, Patti Smith, Roseanne Cash, and Texas State Senator Wendy Davis all donned pink Pussyhats, fueling momentum for the cause.[9]

The organization's social media channels have seen much success. On Twitter, @PussyhatProject has more than 8,000 followers, while 35,000 people follow the group's Facebook page. Instagram (@p_ssyhatproject) boasts 26,400 fans who are keen on sharing and interacting. Zwieman and Suh regularly connect with their followers. There is a steady exchange of dialogue on all social media platforms.

It's been quite a year for the now iconic pink, cat-eared hats. The impact of the Pussyhat Project was covered on just about every mainstream media outlet. From the *New York Times* and *Elle* to the covers of *Time* and *The New Yorker*, the significance of the Women's Movement and the now famous Pussyhat is a bold symbol of resistance, resilience, and unity. The Pussyhat Project was announced as first ever "Brand of the Year" by SVA Masters in Branding chair Debbie Millman,[10] and was nominated for the prestigious Beazley Designs of the Year 2017.[11]

Today, many of the Pussyhats have been collected and are on display in museums across the world. They serve as a lasting reminder of a cultural phenomenon, earning their rightful place in the archives of political symbolism.

One mother and her young daughters made hats to send to others and included the following message: "Every Pussyhat has a story and here is yours. Sewn by tiny hands; guided by mature hands; with a hope for the future and a resolve to never give up. Wear your hat with pride!"

1 Houston Center for Contemporary Craft, "Case Study: Pussyhat," March 17, 2017, https://www.crafthouston.org/2017/03/case-study-pussyhat/.

2 J. Zweiman and K. Suh, "Pussyhat Project™ Global Outreach," Pussyhat Project™, February 18, 2017, https://www.pussyhatproject.com/blog/2017/2/17/yziene25963eoqq26n0sv7ihp82fps.

3 J. Zweiman and K. Suh, "FAQ," Pussyhat Project™, https://www.pussyhatproject.com/faq/.

4 B. Greer, "Craftivism Defintion," Craftism, http://craftivism.com/definition/.

5 Houston Center for Contemporary Craft, "Case Study: Pussyhat."

6 J. Zweiman and K. Suh, "Why 1.17 Million Hats?" Pussyhat Project™, November 23, 2016. https://www.pussyhatproject.com/blog/2016/11/23/why-17-million-hats.

7 D. Pearl, "'Pussyhats' Galore: Inside the Pink Toppers Thousands Will Wear to the Women's March on Washington," *People*, January 21, 2017, http://people.com/politics/pussyhats-galore-inside-the-pink-toppers-thousands-will-wear-to-the-womens-march-on-washington/.

8 Pearl, "'Pussyhats' Galore."

9 Pearl, "'Pussyhats' Galore:"

10 School of Visual Arts, "Democratizing Branding with the Pink Pussyhat: Chair of SVA Masters in Branding Program Debbie Millman Announces Inaugural 'Brand of the Year,'" November 14, 2017, https://www.prnewswire.com/news-releases/democratizing-branding-with-the-pink-pussyhat-chair-of-sva-masters-in-branding-program-debbie-millman-announces-inaugural-brand-of-the-year-300556295.html.

11 O. Wainwright, "Beazley Design Awards Feature Brexit, Refugees and Political Activism," *The Guardian*, August 16, 2017, https://www.theguardian.com/artanddesign/2017/aug/16/political-protest-equality-humanitarian-aid-inspire-best-designs-year.

#LRNSMPR
Learn Social Media and Public Relations

Apply the principles learned in this chapter to the scenarios below.

- Taking into consideration what is on the horizon for the industry, discuss the pros and cons of each projection. Are there any trends you see coming that were not mentioned?
- Long-term strategic thinking and planning is essential for brands. Visit your favorite brand and examine its PR and social media strategy. What makes the strategy strong? Is a content strategy evident? How active is the brand's social community? Can you develop an outline of its social media campaign? Try using the Public Relations and Social Media Planning Template found in Appendix A of the textbook.

- How do the eight suggestions provided by Paul Roetzer endorse a cross-promotional strategy? Choose one of the many case studies provided in the book and identify the components of the campaign. Is a defining symbol, logo, or brand representation evident? Does the campaign provide an ebook? If an infographic has been developed, is it effective? Are there CTAs or trackable URLs utilized? What distinguishing tactics are used to promote the message across multiple channels?

Notes

[1] T. Callinan and J. Vargas, "How AI, Machine Learning and Automation Will Impact Business in 2018 and Beyond," Tenfold, accessed December 20, 2017, https://www.tenfold.com/artificial-intelligence/ai-machine-learning-automation-will-impact-business-2018-beyond.

[2] A. Cohen, "AI Will Turn PR People into Superheroes within One Year," VentureBeat, September 12, 2017, https://venturebeat.com/2017/09/12/ai-will-turn-pr-people-into-superheroes-within-one-year/.

[3] C. Penn, "{PR}edict: Predictive Analytics and the Future of PR, Part 1," Shift Communications, http://www.shiftcomm.com/blog/predict-predictive-analytics-future-pr-part-1/.

[4] R. Gray, "Future—Lies, Propaganda and Fake News: A Challenge for Our Age," BBC, March 1, 2017, accessed December 29, 2017, http://www.bbc.com/future/story/20170301-lies-propaganda-and-fake-news-a-grand-challenge-of-our-age.

[5] R. Brownes, "Breaking News: Media Relations Is Dead," *PRWeek*, December 14, 2017, https://www.prweek.com/article/1452838/breaking-news-media-relations-dead?bulletin=uk%2Fprweekweekly&utm_medium=EMAIL&utm_campaign=eNews Bulletin&utm_source=20171217&utm_content=PRWeek UK Weekly Bulletin %2832%29%3A%3A&email_hash=18D1A129722A460D199D39F002D5CE88.

[6] R. Greenslade, "Almost 60% of US Newspaper Jobs Vanish in 26 Years," *The Guardian*, June 6, 2016, https://www.theguardian.com/media/greenslade/2016/jun/06/almost-60-of-us-newspaper-jobs-vanish-in-26-years.

[7] E. LePage, "All the Social Media Advertising Stats You Need to Know," Hootsuite Social Media Management, September 20, 2017, https://blog.hootsuite.com/social-media-advertising-stats/.

[8] Written by Paul Roetzer, this article was originally published by the Content Marketing Institute and has been edited for comprehensiveness. Permission to reprint has been provided.

Appendix A: Public Relations and Social Media Planning Template

A downloadable version of this template can be found at www.ginaluttrellphd.com.

Pre-Planning: The Circular Model of SoMe for Social Communication

Share	Optimize
Consider where you might publish information or trends within the industry that can be capitalized upon.	Think about who could be subject matter experts. Consider various converged media approaches.

Manage	Engage
Compare social media monitoring tools, research communities to converse with, or identify influencers.	Contemplate when to enter the conversation and how quickly responses to the target audience will be met.

ROSTIR Public Relations Planning Guide Template

Step 1: Research & Diagnosis

In this first phase gather information, analyze what you've found, and begin to build a plan for execution. Strengths and weaknesses are often deemed internal to the organization, while opportunities and threats most commonly relate to external factors.

Strengths	Weaknesses
Chronicle what your organization does well or the advantages it has over the competition.	Reflect on what others see as a weakness or an area your organization could improve.

Opportunities	Threats
Consider areas of growth or events that the organization could attend.	List obstacles, financial issues, or threats to the organization.

Identify and define a target audience. Some campaigns have multiple audiences with varying personas. Develop a consumer profile.

Target Audience/Consumer Profile:	
	Consider: **What do you know about your intended audience? Buying patterns, habits, demographics, psychographics, and income should be considered. What persona do they have? Give your target audience a name.**
Audience	

Step 2: Objectives

Brainstorm and write S.M.A.R.T objectives, then prioritize. Include how each objective will be accomplished and measured.

> *Weak:* Increase social media sentiment on Instagram.
> *Stronger:* Improve positive sentiment on fifteen Instagram posts by 15 percent within three months by focusing on customer-centric content using customized URLs for data collection.

Objectives		Prioritize by Importance
Objective 1		
Objective 2		
Objective 3		

Step 3: Strategy

Describe how and why various campaign components will accomplish the overall objectives.

Strategy	
Component 1	
Component 2	
Component 3	

Step 4: Tactics

These are the tangible aspects of the campaign: social media posts, videos, infographics, and other assets. Tactics include activities from the PESO model. For every tactic use one outline as provided below.

Tactic 1:		
Key Audience/Customer Profile:		
Message:		
Channel	**Activity**	**Time Spent**
Paid		
Earned		
Shared		
Owned		

Step 5: Implementation

Consider how to carry out the plan. Identify the tactic and the task associated with the activity, the person responsible (the owners) for carrying out that task, the beginning and end date, and the cost or budget associated with the tactic.

Tactic & Task	Owner	Start Date	End Date	Cost/Budget
Sample: Tactic 1: Content Creation/Blog Category: Owned/Shared Media Measurement: Engagement				
Tactic 2: Category: Measurement:				
Tactic 3: Category: Measurement:				

Step 6: Reporting/Evaluation

Measuring results validates that the efforts put forth were either effective or not and provides data to refine for future planning. Evaluation should happen throughout a campaign, not merely at the end. For every tactic, use one outline provided below to evaluate the outcomes.

Tactic 1:	
Evaluation for Measurement: **Depending on the activity, choose one method for measurement as outlined by AMEC:** **Exposure, Engagement, Influence, Impact, Advocacy**	
Channel	**Reporting/Measurement**
Paid	
Earned	
Shared	
Owned	

Appendix B: Social Media Audit

This simple social media audit can help organizations understand, evaluate, and optimize their social media profiles in an effort to both understand how they are performing on their social media channels as well as develop a comprehensive strategy. Social media audits assist in sound decision making and help businesses stay on top of their social media presence. Avery Wagner from Hoot Design Company suggests thinking about consistency, branding, company descriptions, and owned media channels.[1] To conduct a social media audit, Wagner suggests first opening all social media profiles and then answering these four questions[2]:

1. *Do your profiles exude consistency?* Is your @handle the same across all of your social media accounts? If not, it should be. The company @handle is part of your brand, brand persona, and profile.
2. *Is the company logo and name prominent?* Ensure the company logo and name is on all sites. You want your company to be recognizable across all platforms.
3. *Does each platform have a company description?* If not, write a short "About us" that can be used across platforms.
4. *Is the company website link or blog URL provided?* Include the company website or blog link whenever you can. Driving customers to owned media channels is important.

For each platform ensure there is consistency regarding tone, imagery, color palette, and voice. Use the 80/20 rule and balance the content between promotional posts, behind-the-scenes posts, campaign-specific posts, and aesthetic posts. Conduct a social media audit on yourself. Are you consistent across your social media platforms? Are you showcasing your most "professional self"? In what ways can you improve? Are there platforms you should be on that you are not?

Notes

[1] A. E. Wagner, "How to Conduct Your Own Social Media Audit," Hoot Design Co., April 1, 2016, https://www.hootdesignco.com/blog/how-to-conduct-your-own-social-media-audit.
[2] Wagner, "How to Conduct Your Own Social Media Audit."

Appendix C: Resources in Public Relations and Social Media

Public Relations
- Public Relations Society of America: www.prsa.org
- Arthur W. Page Society: https://awpagesociety.com/
- Chartered Institute of PR: https://www.cipr.co.uk/
- IABC: https://www.iabc.com/
- WOMMA: http://womma.org/
- Women in Communication: http://www.womcom.org/
- PRSA Tactics: http://apps.prsa.org/Intelligence/Tactics/Issues
- AEJMC: http://www.aejmc.org/
- National Communication Association: https://www.natcom.org/

Social Media
- AMEC: https://amecorg.com/social-media-measurement/
- Social Media Association: http://socialmediaassoc.com/
- Hootsuite Resource Library: https://hootsuite.com/resources
- Meltwater: https://www.meltwater.com/
- Google Analytics: www.google.com/analytics
- Google Trends: www.google.com/trends
- Zignal Labs: http://zignallabs.com/
- Cyfe: https://www.cyfe.com/
- Hootsuite: www.hootsuite.com
- Sprout Social: www.sproutsocial.com
- SXSW: https://www.sxsw.com/
- Answer the Public: https://answerthepublic.com/
- Google's URL Builder: https://ga-dev-tools.appspot.com/campaign-url-builder/
- MentionMapp: http://mentionmapp.com/

Blogs
- Edelman: https://www.edelman.com/insights/
- Ketchum: https://www.ketchum.com/insights
- PRSay: http://prsay.prsa.org/
- *Ragan's PR Daily:* http://www.prdaily.com/
- *Adweek:* http://www.adweek.com/category/social-pro-daily/
- Holmes Report: https://www.holmesreport.com/
- Social Media Examiner: https://www.socialmediaexaminer.com/
- Spin Sucks: https://spinsucks.com/

- Mashable: www.Mashable.com_
- Influence & Co: https://blog.influenceandco.com/
- Cision: https://www.cision.com/us/blog/
- StraTECHery: https://stratechery.com/
- Brian Solis: www.briansolis.com
- Solo PR Pro: http://soloprpro.com/
- *Social Media Today:* https://www.socialmediatoday.com/

Podcasts

- For Immediate Release: https://firpodcastnetwork.com/for-immediate-release/
- Content Inc.: http://contentmarketinginstitute.com/content-inc-podcast/
- Marketing over Coffee: http://www.marketingovercoffee.com/
- Inside PR: https://www.insidepr.ca/
- PRWeek: http://www.prweek.com/us/podcasts
- Social Media Marketing: https://www.socialmediaexaminer.com/podcasts/
- The #AskGaryVee Show by Gary Vaynerchuk: https://www.youtube.com/user/garyvaynerchuk
- Hashtagged: http://hashtaggedpodcast.com/
- Mainly Pinterest Tips: http://manlypinteresttips.com/podcast/
- #TwitterSmarter by Madalyn Sklar: http://www.madalynsklar.com/

Content Curation

- Paper.li: https://paper.li/
- Scoop.it: https://www.scoop.it/
- Pocket: https://getpocket.com/
- Curata: http://www.curata.com/
- Trap.it: http://trap.it/
- List.ly: https://list.ly/
- Feedly: https://feedly.com/i/welcome

Graphics

- Adobe Spark, which includes Spark Post, Spark Video, Spark Page: https://spark.adobe.com/
- PicsArt: downloadable in the app store
- Picmonkey: https://www.picmonkey.com/
- Piktochart: https://piktochart.com/
- Canva: https://www.canva.com/
- 1001 Free Fonts: https://www.1001freefonts.com/
- Visme: https://www.visme.co/
- Google Charts: https://developers.google.com/chart/
- Infogram: https://infogram.com/
- Easel.ly: https://www.easel.ly/

Video Development

- Animoto: https://animoto.com/
- Camtasia & Snagit from Techsmith: https://www.techsmith.com/
- Magisto: https://www.magisto.com/

- Flipagram: https://flipagram.com/
- Diptic: http://www.dipticapp.com/
- iMovie: https://www.apple.com/imovie/
- Movie Maker: https://www.moviemaker.com/

Videos and Articles

- "How Data Is Changing PR": https://www.youtube.com/watch?v=ZCOChTJe1v4&t=5s
- "How Visual Communication Drives Shares in Content Marketing": https://www.youtube.com/watch?v=bYn0-MjtjFQ&t=7s
- "Crisis Communications and Social Media": https://www.youtube.com/watch?v=2HrLM3GvtaI
- "Handling a Social Media Crisis: Domino's": https://www.youtube.com/watch?v=llnZn7vLV20
- "Social Media Ethics": https://www.udemy.com/social-media-ethics/
- "Social Media: Sacrificing Privacy for Sake of Success": https://www.youtube.com/watch?v=0g6o9MAIi0Q
- "The Story of Content: Rise of the New Marketing": https://www.youtube.com/watch?v=dBnpr3pkFlk
- "The PESO Model: An Organizing Framework for Digital Content Marketing": https://www.linkedin.com/pulse/peso-model-organizing-framework-digital-content-michael-estevez/
- "How PESO Makes Sense in Influencer Marketing": https://www.prweek.com/article/1350303/peso-makes-sense-influencer-marketing
- "2016 Nielsen Social Media Report": http://www.nielsen.com/us/en/insights/reports/2017/2016-nielsen-social-media-report.html
- "How to Learn Social Media Marketing: 30 Resources for Beginners": https://blog.hubspot.com/marketing/social-media-marketing-resources

Glossary

Advertising: Paid communication; information placed in a communication delivery vehicle by an identified sponsor that pays for time or space. Advertising is a controlled method of delivering messages and gaining media placement.

Audience: The immediate listeners/ viewers or targets of a particular campaign or message. Audiences are distinct from publics in that they are created or made distinct by the organization rather than being self-selecting.

Authenticity: When interacting online, the ability to convey feeling trustworthy and genuine.

Authority: A person who is an expert on a particular subject.

bit.ly: A free URL-shortening service that provides statistics for the links that users share online. Bit.ly condenses long URLs, making them easier to share on social networks such as Twitter.

Blog: Created from two words: "web" and "log." Blogs are maintained by individuals or businesses with regular entries of commentary, descriptions of events, and other material such as graphics and videos.

Blogger: A person who writes for and/ or maintains a blog.

Blogroll: Typically found on blogs, a list of links to other blogs or websites that the blogger commonly references or is affiliated with. Blogrolls help bloggers establish and build their blogging communities.

Bookmarking: Saving content that users find important.

Brainstorming: When a group of people come together to generate ideas about a specific topic for a set period of time.

Brand persona: Human characteristics given to a brand.

Branding: Part of a corporation's identity. Branding can be applied to an individual, a product, or a service.

Budget: An estimate of income and expenditure for a set period of time.

Channel: The medium through which messages are sent, such as the elements within the PESO model. These could include paid print advertising, earned media placements, company social media channels, or a website.

Circular Model of SoMe for Social Communication: *S*hare, *o*ptimize, *M*anage, *e*ngage. This is the first step considered when planning a full social media campaign.

Citizen journalism: Any type of news gathering and reporting (including writing and publishing articles, posting photographs, and creating videos about newsworthy topics) that is done by members of the larger general public rather than the mainstream media.

C-level executive: "C-suite" is a term used to collectively refer to a corporation's senior executives, such as the chief executive officer, chief operating officer, and chief marketing officer.

Click-through rate (CRT): A method for measuring the success of online campaigns by the number of clicks on a specific link.

Cloud: A network of servers that exist in data centers across the world that allow people to conduct simple activities like checking email, logging into social networking sites, and accessing applications.

Comment: A response that provides an answer or reaction to a blog post or message on a social network. Comments are a primary form of two-way communication on the social sphere.

Community relations: An area of public relations that is responsible for building relationships with constituent publics such as schools, charities, clubs, and activist interests of the neighborhoods or metropolitan area(s) where an organization operates.

Content analysis: The process of analyzing data including articles, social media posts, or website content.

Content creation: The generation of a variety of different written and visual communication on behalf of an organization.

Content curation: Searching for and filtering through content across the social sphere and sharing that information on your social channels.

Converged media: Within the PESO model, media that overlaps several categories, such as boosted through social media that maintain qualities of both paid and shared content.

Corporate social responsibility: Also referred to as CSR, an organizational philosophy that emphasizes an organization's obligation to be a good corporate citizen through programs that improve society.

Creative Commons: Licenses that help creators retain copyright while allowing others to copy, distribute, and make some uses of their work.

Creativity: The process of attempting to discover new ideas.

Crisis communication: Protecting and defending an individual, company, or organization facing a public challenge to its reputation. These challenges can involve legal, ethical, or financial standing.

Crowdfunding: The practice of funding a project or venture by raising many small amounts of money from a large number of people, typically via the Internet.

Crowdsourcing: The practice of obtaining needed services, ideas, or content by soliciting contributions from a large group of people, especially from an online community, rather than from traditional avenues. Wikipedia is the most prominent example of crowdsourcing.

Cyfe: A platform to manage social media, analytics, marketing, sales, support, and overall social media infrastructure.

Dashboard: A user interface that organizes and streamlines online activity so that a person can publish content, respond, monitor, update, and listen from one central place. Hootsuite and Cyfe are two examples of dashboards.

Data: The content analyzed through research.

Demographic: A particular sector of a population.

Descriptive analytics: Gathering and describing social media data in the form of reports and visualizations. Likes, views, and Tweets are examples of this type of analytics.

Diagnosis: Part of the initial stage of campaign planning whereby the organization identifies the problem or opportunity. Research and diagnosis happen together.

Diversity: Differences among people within a group, stemming from variations in factors such as age, gender, ethnicity, religion, sexual preference, education, etc.

Earned media: The published coverage of an enterprise, cause, or person's message by a credible third party, such as a journalist, blogger, trade analyst, or industry influencer.

Ebook: An electronic version of a printed book.

Engagement: Participation in the online community via direct conversations.

Ethical codes: Formalized, written standards of behavior used as procedures for decision making.

Ethics: A set of moral principles that govern a person's behavior or the conducting of an activity.

Facebook: A social networking site that connects people with friends, brands, colleagues, family, and other people across the globe.

Favorite: A means to bookmark information or to illustrate to the online community that you like what you are reading.

Feed: Frequently updated content published by a website. Feeds are usually used for news and blog websites, as well as for distributing a variety of digital content, including pictures, audio, and video. Feeds can additionally be used to deliver audio content. They are commonly referred to as RSS feeds, XML feeds, syndicated content, Twitter feeds, or web feeds.

Formal research: A systematic collection of information that can be replicated and subject to an analysis of its reliability and validity.

Friends: Individuals you consider close enough to see your social media profile and engage with you.

Goal: The desired outcome that solves a problem, meets a challenge, or advances an opportunity.

Government relations: An aspect of relationship building between an organization and government at local, state, and/or national levels, especially involving flow of information to and from legislative and regulatory bodies. The goal often is to influence public policy decisions compatible with the organization's interests. Government relations involves dealing and communicating with legislatures and government agencies on behalf of an organization.

Hashtag: A word or phrase prefixed with the hash, or pound, symbol ("#"), such as #LRNSMPR or #PRStudChat. Hashtags link conversations among people with similar interests.

Hootsuite: A social media management system that allows brands to streamline social media efforts and campaigns across social networks that include Twitter, Facebook, LinkedIn, WordPress, and Google+ Pages. Social strategists collaboratively monitor, engage with, and measure the results of social campaigns from one secure, web-based dashboard.

Implementation: The point in the campaign process where the campaign plan is put into operation.

Influencer: An expert in a specific category that has the most loyal and engaged following.

Infographic: Also known as an information graphic. A graphically represented image with information in a format designed to make data easily understandable at a glance.

Informal research: The ability to gather information through conversations and a general assessment of important issues and trends. Informal research does not enjoy a high degree of reliability and validity, often because of its use of nonprobability sampling.

Instagram: A photo-sharing application that lets users take photos, apply filters to their images, and share the photos instantly on the Instagram network and other social networks, including Facebook, Flickr, Twitter, Pinterest, and Foursquare.

Integrated marketing communications: A combination of activities including public relations, communications, advertising, marketing, and social media designed to sell a product, service, or idea. Activities are designed to maintain consistent brand messaging across all communication channels.

Internet: A worldwide system of computer networks conceived by the Advanced Research Projects Agency (ARPA) of the U.S. government in 1969 and first known as the ARPANET. The original aim was to allow users of a research computer at one university to "talk to" research computers at other universities.

Key performance indicator (KPI): A form of measurement connected to a campaign or social media objective to quantify success.

Keywords: Specific words used to describe content that ultimately boost visibility and rankings on the web.

Like: An action that can be taken by users on various social media platforms to illustrate appreciation of content shared by others.

Link-back: A notification to authors, such as bloggers, when other authors link to one of their online publications. This enables authors to keep track of who is linking, or referring, to their articles, blogs, and other online publications.

LinkedIn: A business-oriented social networking site.

Listening: Monitoring conversations and activity occurring on the web.

Live streaming: Streaming of video or audio so that users can experience an event together live via the web.

Marketing: Marketing is the activity, set of institutions, and processes for creating, communicating, delivering, and exchanging offerings that have value for customers, clients, partners, and society at large.

Mash-up: The combination, visualization, and aggregation of webpages and applications that use and combine data from two or more sources.

Media relations: Mutually beneficial associations between publicists or public relations professionals and journalists as a condition for reaching audiences with messages of news or features of interest (publicity). The function includes both seeking publicity for an organization and responding to queries from journalists about the organization. Maintaining up-to-date lists of media contacts and a knowledge of media audience interests are critical to media relations.

Meltwater: A social media dashboard that allows companies to conduct media monitoring and business intelligence through their software.

Meme: An image with text above and below it (although it can also come in video and link form). A meme on the Internet is used to describe a thought, idea, joke, or concept shared online.

Microblogging: The short posts, often including links, images, and video, that characterize social media content on platforms such as Facebook, LinkedIn, and Twitter.

Newsworthiness: The qualities that make a particular story appealing for journalists to cover, including timeliness, uniqueness, breadth of impact, and relevance to the media outlet's audience.

Objectives: Specific, measurable statement of what needs to be achieved as part of reaching the goal.

Online media center: A webpage or group of pages that provide reporters and other outside entities with materials necessary for research on the organization. Press releases, fact sheets, executive bios, backgrounders, and high-resolution images, videos, informational links, and prior media coverage are usually included on the pages.

Owned media: Communication channels, media, and tools that are owned by an organization. Websites and blogs are examples of owned media.

Paid media: The channels in which money is paid to place the message and control its distribution.

Participation: Engagement in online activity while contributing content.

Periscope: A video streaming/broadcasting service from Twitter.

Permalink: An address, or URL, for a particular post within a blog or website.

PESO: An acronym for paid, earned, shared, and owned. In the PESO model each channel delivers unique importance.

PESO model: A public relations planning model.

Pin: Individual visual bookmarks that users post to boards on Pinterest.

Pinboard: Pages found on Pinterest where users save pins organized by topic or theme.

Pinterest: A visual bookmarking tool that helps you discover and save creative ideas.

Podcast: An audio file that can be found on the Internet whereby users can download and listen to content.

Predictive analytics: Analyzing large amounts of data to predict a future event.

Prescriptive analytics: Applying mathematical and computational sciences to suggest decision options to take advantage of the results of descriptive and predictive analytics. Anticipates what will happen and when it will happen, but also why.

Public relations: Public relations is a strategic communication process that builds mutually beneficial relationships between organizations and their publics.

Publicity: In media relations, the process of sharing information with journalists with the aim of publishing it for a wider audience.

Qualitative research: A research method that uses flexible and open-ended questioning, often with a small number of participants/respondents, and that cannot be extrapolated to large populations. Examples include in-depth interviews, case studies, and focus groups.

Quantitative research: A research method that uses standardized and closed-ended questions, often with many participants/respondents, and that generally can be extrapolated to large populations. Examples include surveys, content analysis, and experiments.

R-A-C-E: A type of four-step communication planning model. R-A-C-E: *r*esearch, *a*ction, *c*ommunication, and *e*valuation.

Real-time search: The method of indexing content being published online into search engine results with virtually no delay.

Reporting: The analysis of completed or ongoing activities that determine or support a public relations campaign. Also known as evaluation.

Research: The methodical collection and explanation of information used to increase understanding of needs.

Retweet (RT): To share another person's tweet. This is a great way to spread links exponentially. A best practice is to credit the tweet that you are retweeting. Clicking the "Retweet" button on the newsfeed page of your Twitter account will make this happen automatically.

R-O-P-E: A type of four-step communication planning model. R-O-P-E: *r*esearch, create *o*bjectives, *p*lan, and *e*valuate the outcomes.

ROSTIR: A public relations planning model that uses research/diagnosis, objectives, strategies, tactics, implementation, and reporting/evaluation. Tactics utilize paid, earned, shared, and owned media.

RSS feed: RSS (really simple syndication) is a group of web-feed formats used to publish frequently updated content such as blogs and videos in a standardized format. Content publishers can syndicate a feed, which allows users to subscribe to the content and read it when they have time, from a location other than the original website or blog, such as a reader or mobile device.

Search engine optimization (SEO): The process of improving the volume or quality of traffic to a website from search engines via unpaid or organic search traffic such as Google.

Sentiment: The attitude of user comments related to a brand online.

Shared media: The pass-along sharing and commenting upon your message by the community through social channels.

Skype: A free program that allows for text, audio, and video chats between users.

SlideShare: An online social network for sharing presentations and documents.

SMART objectives: Objectives that are written as follows: *s*pecific, *m*easurable, *a*ttainable, *r*ealistic, and *t*imely.

Snapchat: A mobile messaging application used to share photos, videos, text, and drawings.

Social listening: The process of monitoring digital conversations to understand what customers are saying about a brand and industry online.

Social media: Forms of electronic communication through which users create online communities to share information, ideas, personal messages, and other content.

Social media analytics (SMA): Refers to the approach of collecting data from social media sites and blogs and evaluating that data to make business decisions.

Social media monitoring: Active monitoring of social media channels for information about a company or organization.

Social sphere: The intertwining of online social spheres constituted by the online social networking ecosystem.

Sponsored content: Online content that is paid for by a company.

Strategies: Public-specific approaches specifying the channel to send the message to achieve objectives.

SWOT analysis: A process to help organizations define their strengths, weaknesses, opportunities, and threats.

Tactics: Strategy-specific communication products that carry the message to the key publics. Tactics are tangible items such as a press release, social media post, or website.

Tag: A keyword used to describe content on a blog or in social networks.

Tag cloud: A visual collection of the most frequent tags produced by a user, blog, profile, page, or descriptions on webpages.

Transparency: Honest, open, authentic participation in social media.

Tweet: An update shared on Twitter.

Twitterchat or Tweet-Up: An organized event on Twitter that uses a hashtag to unify the conversation.

Two-way symmetrical model of public relations: Uses communication to confer with publics, resolve conflict, and promote mutual understanding and respect between the organization and its public(s).

Uncontrolled media: Messages that are not owned or controlled by an organization.

Views: Number of times content (including text, photos, and videos) is viewed by people.

Vlogs: Video blogs that are largely YouTube based.

Webinar: Online conference or one-hour session whereby participants can see and hear a presentation.

Wiki: Web app that allows users to add, modify, or delete content in collaboration with others. Wikipedia is the best-known wiki.

Index

Prior to entering the educational field, **Regina (Gina) Luttrell** spent the first portion of her career in corporate public relations and marketing. Her extensive background includes strategic development and implementation of public relations and social media, advertising, marketing, and corporate communications. She has led multiple rebranding campaigns, designed numerous websites, managed high-level crisis situations, and garnered media coverage that included hits with the *New York Times*, the *CBS Evening News*, and the Associated Press.

Gina is currently an assistant professor of public relations and social media at the S.I. Newhouse School of Public Communications at Syracuse University. A contributor to *PR Tactics*, *PR News*, book chapters, as well as peer-reviewed journals within the public relations arena, Luttrell is a noted speaker, frequently presenting at national and international conferences and business events on topics related to the current social media revolution, the ongoing public relations evolution, and Millennials within the classroom and workplace. She is the (co)author of the following books: *Social Media: How to Engage, Share, and Connect*; *The Millennial Mindset: Unraveling Fact from Fiction*; *Brew Your Business: The Ultimate Craft Beer Playbook*; *Public Relations Campaigns: An Integrated Approach*; *The PR Agency Handbook*; *A Practical Guide to Ethics in Public Relations*; and *Trump Tweets: The World Reacts*.